IN SEARCH OF A MOTHER'S LOVE

A Daughter's Journey of Love, Forgiveness and
Redemption of a Mother She Never Knew

MICHELLE B. WILSON

Library of Congress Control Number: 2025921209
ISBN: 979-8-9868766-8-9
Printed in the United States of America

Cover design by Michelle B. Wilson

DEDICATIONS

To God, my Heavenly Father, Jesus my Savior, and the Holy Spirit, my constant companion, my best friend, my guide:

This book is foremost for You, Lord—the One who walked with me through every valley and mountaintop. Even as a little girl, when I didn't fully know You, Your Spirit was guiding and protecting me. Without Your grace and love, I would not be who I am today.

Thank You, Jesus, for redeeming me with Your blood. When I had nothing but brokenness, You gave me access to the Father and a life of purpose. You are the cornerstone of my faith.

Precious Holy Spirit, thank You for giving me a heart that trusts and surrenders. My journey is a testament to the goodness of the Trinity, and I give You all the glory for choosing me to help lead my mother to repentance and salvation. To God be all the glory!

To My Future Husband and Children:

You are the reward of my obedience, the fruit of years sown in faith, tears, and sacrifice.

I laid down my desire for early companionship and motherhood to partner with God in a deeper way—trusting Him to redeem time, rewrite legacy, and birth a righteous generation through me.

Every wound healed, every battle won, every generational chain broken in this story was for your sake.

May you walk in the fullness of the blessing, the wholeness I fought for, and the love I prayed into existence.

To My Three Older Brothers:

Though our journeys diverged, we walked through the same storms in our humble beginnings. This memoir reflects part of that shared journey. My prayer is that God continues to shape His beautiful plan in your lives. I see resilience in each of you—men of valor molded by God's grace. Carry forward the lessons of our mother's life with courage.

While you may appreciate the value of this book, it is equally important to share your story. You each carry a testimony worth telling—your voice matters.

God has plans to prosper you, to give you hope and a future. Step into the fullness of all God has for you. His light will shine through you in ways that will exceed your expectations.

To My Precious Nieces and Nephews:

God has chosen you to break chains, to rise above the patterns of the past, and to create a new legacy – one rooted in faith, hope, and healing for generations to come. No matter your past, God's purpose for your life remains great. He sees you, loves you, and has equipped you to walk boldly into your purpose. God is faithful to heal every broken place, to fill the empty spaces, and lead you into a life that overflows with His goodness and grace. Forgive quickly, love deeply, and walk boldly in the truth of who God says you are.

You are more than conquerors—God's workmanship, created for good works. This is your time. Step into your calling with confidence, grace, and unwavering faith. The journey will be worth it.

To Those Still Bleeding From the Wounds of Childhood:

My prayer is that God anoints these pages to speak to your heart, bringing healing where suffering runs deep, peace where chaos and questions reside, and freedom from the weight of lingering wounds. May the reoccurring tape of the memories of past abuses be erased, making room for new thoughts rooted in the abundant life God longs to pour into you.

May God give you the grace to release the pain caused by your mother, father, guardian and others into His hands. Not because they deserve it, but because you have been forgiven of much. Forgiveness breaks chains. It doesn't excuse the past; it frees you from it. If the Almighty calls you on the sacred assignment to care for those who didn't properly care for you, trust His plan. Obedience brings generational rewards.

Your identity comes from God's declaration of who you are, not from your past. Discover the beauty of God's redemption and the depth of His love as you boldly walk into the purpose for which He created you.

To Parents Carrying the Weight of Regret:

It's not too late.

God specializes in restoration. Redemption is always within reach, no matter how broken the pieces may seem. I've lived it—He healed what seemed irreparable between my mother and me.

Let this book—and this moment—remind you:

God's mercy covers every mistake. His love heals every wound. Let Him rewrite your story. Trust that His grace can carry you forward into a future filled with the sweetness of reconciliation and the beauty of redemption.

He can restore what was lost.

God is not far from you. Repent, and ask Him for forgiveness—He is ready to restore. He's also waiting for you to release the burden you've carried too long. You cannot go back and change the past, but you can let grace change you.

God is waiting—not just on your surrender, but on one of the most important steps you'll ever take: forgiving yourself.

When you forgive yourself, your heart will no longer need distractions to numb the pain.

You will be free to walk in the newness of life—fully present, fully loved, and finally at peace. Ready to receive the love of your children and most importantly the love of God.

This is the beginning of a new chapter.

Only God can write it.

And it begins with your yes.

ACKNOWLEDGMENTS

I give all glory to God and acknowledge the Holy Spirit, who led me through every stage of this journey. Without His wisdom, strength, and support, this book would not exist. He inspired the words and carried me through every moment of writing, rewriting, and surrendering. This book is His.

The journey began years ago with a divine command—God literally shook me in my bed and said, "Write your story." I obeyed, not knowing how long or how sacred the road would be. The first half, recounting my early life, unfolded slowly over time. The second half was written beside my mother's hospital bed, just three months before she entered Heaven's glory on December 17, 2023.

To every intercessor, friend, and supporter who covered me in prayer—thank you. Please know, your prayers made all the difference. There were moments when only grace held me together, and I believe it was your faith that helped carry mine.

Special thanks to my editors, Elijah Ayoola and Teresa Kephart, for their valuable contributions during the early stages of this manuscript. Your insights helped shape the foundation that the Holy Spirit later refined. I'm grateful for the space you created for the message to emerge with clarity and power.

I also want to honor the memory of my late father, James D. Wilson, whose artistic eye captured the photo of my mother that now graces the book cover. Taken on the day they met—at a wedding—she wore a black spaghetti-strap dress she designed. She was radiant, elegant, and full of quiet strength. That image, preserved through my father's lens, now carries forth a legacy. Thank you, Daddy, for capturing a moment that is now being used to tell the story of a lifetime.

FOREWORD

How is it that life can be such a beautiful, possibility-filled gift, and at the same time so filled with hurt, disappointment, and loss? None is exempt from the difficulties and challenges – no one!

Michelle's story is a validation of the significance of a mother's love. As the mother of several adopted children, I have seen firsthand the deep loss the absence of a biological mother, or father, can have on a child's heart. In my work with Orphan's Promise and vulnerable children around the world, it is called "having an orphan spirit." God has a spiritual order for things and when it is out of order, we suffer. Sometimes the loss of a parent is an abandonment issue, sometimes divorce, sometimes death, sometimes adoption. In every situation, the child feels left behind. When a parent is living and does not appear to care, the heart wound is especially deep. So it was, in Michelle's story.

An "orphan spirit" cannot simply be "loved" away, though good people who truly care may do all they can to fill the wounded heart. It must be healed. As Michelle's story clearly shares – God specializes in healing hearts. It is a process, and it requires vulnerability. Not for the faint of heart!

The real heart of this book is not how Michelle's story began, but how she was healed and set free. She made two critical decisions at important moments in her journey – she was obedient to an unusual request from God, she <u>chose</u> to forgive. Neither choice would be simple, but both led to her freedom. None of us get to choose the families we are born into or the circumstances of our lives, but we all get to choose how we will respond. Michelle shares a path to freedom and healing, and the love of a Creator who designs us to love and be loved. *"I knew you before <u>I formed you</u> in your mother's womb."* Jeremiah 1:5. God has <u>always</u> had a plan for your life. It is for good! Don't settle for less. Our choices matter.

Terry Meeuwsen,
Co-host, *The 700 Club,* Founder, Orphan's Promise

INTRODUCTION

Dear reader,
You are holding a story not born of perfection but shaped by perseverance—a journey marked by sorrow, resilience, and the unrelenting grace of God. Like many, my path began in the shadows of pain and longing. Yet even in the darkest moments, one truth remained: God never forsakes His children.

Long before I ever took my first breath, the choices of my parents—and those before them—cast shadows that shaped my earliest days. Still, God was present, weaving purpose through every broken piece to make me a living testimony of His unfailing love.

My mother's decisions, like all of ours, carried consequences that touched many lives. However, this is not a story of shame or blame—it is a testimony of forgiveness and redemption. In her brokenness, she did the best she could with what she had. Though she wrestled with the weight of her past, God's grace strengthened her to hope for a brighter future. In the end, she surrendered fully—a beautiful witness of God's redeeming love.

Three scriptures have anchored me through every season:

"But the God of all grace… after that ye have suffered a while, make you perfect, stablish, strengthen, settle you." (1 Peter 5:10, KJV)

"The Spirit of the Lord God is upon Me, Because the Lord had anointed me to preach the good tidings to the poor; He has sent Me to heal the brokenhearted, To proclaim liberty to the captives, And the opening of the prison to those who are bound." (Isaiah 61:1, NKJV)

"Being confident of this very thing, that He which hath begun a good work in you will perform it until the day of Jesus Christ." (Philippians 1:6, KJV)

These verses remind me that trials do not destroy us; they act as God's refining fire, preparing us for a destiny that only He can create.

For years, I sensed God calling me to write this book, but I hesitated. Which story should I tell? Our lives are layered with sacred and painful moments, and I longed to protect the privacy of others. Yet the whisper remained: Write anyway.

And so, I share, this is not a blame-filled exposé. It is a redemptive testimony—one my mother gave me permission to reveal. I do not write as a hero. Jesus is the only hero in this story. I write as a witness to the power of His restoring love.

If you're reading these pages hoping to confirm a suspicion or satisfy curiosity, I invite you to look deeper. This is not a story of scandal—it's one of the greatest love stories I've ever lived. I watched God pursue my mother with unwavering love, even when she rejected Him. And in the end, He used me as His vessel – to love her, reach her, and walk with her into healing. This is our story. More than that, it's God's story He commanded me to write.

Though our paths and experiences may differ, one truth remains: we all carry battles we rarely speak of—some so sacred we wouldn't dare to write about, even if God asked us to.

So, before you draw conclusions, pause. Ask God to open your heart. Honor the courage it takes to write your story – not for the approval of man, but in obedience to God, and for someone else's healing.

May the transparency in these pages stir compassion in your heart, awaken courage in your soul, and lead you to deeper healing on your own path.

For years, I searched for worth through accomplishments and the approval of others. Over time, I realized that only by fully surrendering to God can one discover their true identity. God alone defines who we are.

The human heart is fragile yet miraculous—layered, complex, and known fully only by its Creator. We often want to understand or judge someone's journey…only God sees the whole story. What He asks of us is love.

Jesus said the greatest commandment is to love God - and the second is like it: to love others, (Matthew 22:36–40). This kind of love transforms. It heals. It redefines purpose. Romans 2:4 reminds us of it's not judgment, but God's goodness, that leads us to repentance. It was His relentless love that met my mother and me, carried us, and ultimately called me to write.

This is more than a memoir—it's a love story. A divine pursuit. A testament to how God's unwavering love finds us, heals us, and rewrites the narrative. My prayer is that as you read, you'll find His fingerprints all over your own story and find the healing you need.

At one time, I was like a rosebud—longing to bloom, yet afraid of what it would cost. Once I surrendered to God's plan, I began to blossom. The beauty you'll find here isn't the absence of pain—it's the transformation of it.

I once asked God, "Why didn't others warn me of the traps ahead?" Their silence pushed me to break the cycle. I couldn't bear the thought of others stumbling because I stayed quiet. This book is my response: to testify, to teach, to love boldly.

As I share my story, I remember the broken pieces of my early life—shards that needed truth and restoration. I had to stop seeking man's approval and embrace God's. I know I'm not alone.

Many have reached out, longing to be seen, understood, and healed. I listened to their cries–to find a safe place to share their pain. They asked, can you hear my story? Can you see beyond my struggles and truly see me for who I really am? Can you guide me toward true freedom and peace in Jesus? And to them—and now to you—I say: Yes, I hear you. I see you. And more importantly, God does, too. He has an appointed time for your healing. And perhaps - this book is the beginning – or will aid in some way in that healing journey.

Please know, this story is for anyone who feels unseen, misunderstood, or silenced by shame and rejection. The same God who walked with my mother and me will walk with you. He is still writing everyone's story. He finishes what He starts.

Saying yes to sharing your testimony may lead to misunderstanding, even from those who have traveled similar paths. It's easier for some to remain silent than face their own shame. Yet, silence becomes complicity. And I don't want anyone's blood on my hands. Testifying is one of the purest forms of love—it allows others to leap over what once trapped us.

Your testimony carries power. Revelation 12:11 says, "They overcame him by the blood of the Lamb and by the word of their testimony…" Sharing our story opens doors for someone else's breakthrough.

Eventually, we must choose between pleasing man or pleasing God. Freedom begins when we live for an audience of One. And God promises to never leave nor forsake you.

Through the tears, the fasting, the prayers, and the fire, I came to know God not just as my Savior—He became the Parent I had always longed for. "When my father and my mother forsake me, then the Lord will take me up." (Psalm 27:10). He did. And He will for you too.

Let me also introduce my closest companion—the Holy Spirit. He has guided me through darkness, reminded me of truth, and anchored me in peace. As Jesus promised, "When the Spirit of truth comes, He will guide you into all truth." (John 16:13). He has guided me—and He will guide you.

I've made a choice: I will not let anything, or anyone stop me from fulfilling God's call. My prayer is that this story will ignite a fire in you—to rise above fear and walk boldly in your assignment.

You may feel unqualified, weary, or uncertain. I'm here to remind you: God chooses the yielded, not the perfect. And if He can use me—He can use anyone.

To move forward in freedom, you must confront the past—not to dwell on it. Seek God's truth as you face what you'd rather forget. He heals what we surrender.

Will you join me in lifting your voice to declare His goodness? Together, we can be vessels of healing and hope.

I urge you to consider the words of Paul, written to the church in Corinth:

"Praise be to the God and Father of our Lord Jesus Christ, the Father of compassion and the God of all comfort, who comforts us in all our troubles so that we can comfort those in any trouble with the comfort we ourselves receive from God" (2 Corinthians 1:3-4, *NIV*)

I pray that as you read this book, you'll see a reflection of your own story—and discover the freedom, identity, and beauty God desires to bring forth in you. Years ago, God asked me during prayer a simple yet profound question: Will you do it for Me? Will you step out of the comfort of your life, surrender your fears, and allow me to use your pain, your victories, and your journey to help others? Without hesitation, I said "Yes."

Now, I ask that same question of you. Will you allow your life to be used for something greater - a purpose that extends beyond yourself? Will you let God's healing and transformative power flow through you to touch the lives of others?

Take a moment, listen to the whisper of His voice, and ask yourself if He is prompting you to step forward. Your story, no matter how messy or unfinished it feels, could be the very spark that ignites healing and hope in another's heart and brings about blessings for many generations to come. The choice is yours - are you ready to answer the call?

Will you trust God with your story?

PROPHETIC DECLARATION

To everyone who reads this book, I decree and declare - by the authority of the Lord Jesus Christ - that every yoke of bondage in your life will be destroyed by the power of God's anointing. May the Spirit of the Living God breathe healing into every wound, restore every broken place, and bring freedom to your heart and soul.

As you read these pages and align yourself with God's truth, I prophesy that generational curses—trauma, bitterness, unforgiveness, and strongholds passed through your bloodline—are broken in Jesus' name. Let the glory of God invade your life in undeniable ways. I declare that every part of you comes into agreement with the victory of Jesus Christ.

I speak a release of generational blessings—like a mighty outpouring— over your life, your children, and your children's children. May God's love heal families, restore relationships, and renew every fractured bond. I call forth reconciliation between mothers and daughters, fathers and sons, siblings, and generations. May unity, grace, and truth reign in your home.

Let the words of this book carry an anointing so heavy that testimonies of deliverance rise from every reader. I declare God will use it as a global instrument of healing—touching hearts, breaking chains, and igniting revival. I decree that this book, born out of obedience to God's call, will spark transformation not only in your life but also in the lives of countless others who encounter it, impacting even a thousand generations.

May His unfailing love, abundant grace, and limitless power fill every corner of your being, transforming you from the inside out. May God's Word saturate your heart and mind, and may He fulfill His purpose for your life as you walk boldly in His freedom and perfect plan.

In the mighty name of Jesus Christ. Amen and Amen.

DISCLAIMER

This book is a memoir, chronicling my personal journey through trauma, healing, and faith. While it is my hope my story will inspire and encourage, it is important to remember that every individual's path to healing is unique. This book is not a substitute for professional medical, psychological, or psychiatric care. If you are navigating similar challenges, I encourage you to seek guidance from trusted medical professionals, mental health experts, and, above all, the wisdom and guidance of God as you pursue your wholeness.

This memoir is a work of non-fiction based on the life of the author and her biological mother. While certain names and events have been changed or fictionalized to protect the privacy of individuals, other names and places remain true to the author's lived experience. The events are true to the best of my recollection and are not intended to harm or defame any individual. Any resemblance to persons not explicitly identified by the author, living or deceased, is purely coincidental.

TABLE OF CONTENTS

CHAPTER 1:

UNINVITED GUESTS CHANGE EVERYTHING

"There is a time for everything, and a season for every activity under the heavens: a time to be born and a time to die, a time to plant and a time to uproot a time to kill, and a time to heal ...."
(Ecclesiastes 3:1-3, NIV)

Boom, Boom, Boom!
"Police! Open up!"

The deafening sound ricocheted throughout our tiny two-bedroom home, silencing the chaos of toys strewn across the floor, laundry scattered in heaps and the busyness of children at play. The air grew thick with fear as the normalcy of my dysfunctional world quickly faded. What did they want? Why were they here?

Frozen in place, my youngest brother and I watched in dread as our two older brothers cautiously approached the door. Our mother had given us strict instructions to never let strangers in, and the thought of disobeying her filled me with a gnawing anxiety. With every creek of the floorboards, my pulse quickened. The hollow sound of my brother's footsteps echoed through the stillness, heavy – as if announcing our doom. As the door opened, revealing the stern faces of police officers and social workers, the fragile walls of our world began to crumble.

Familiarity often veils dysfunction, numbing our senses and closing our eyes to the harsh realities we'd rather not face. However, an intrusion has the power to pierce that illusion, exposing what we are now forced to no longer ignore. I stood there, a six-year-old girl in an oversized, dirty t-shirt that barely covered my bottom, exposed and disgraced. Shame burned through me as strangers with badges stepped inside, their presence ripping apart the fragile façade of normalcy we had clung to for so long. Tugging on my tattered shirt, I tried to cover myself, yet nothing could protect me from the raw humiliation of that moment.

It's interesting how the smallest, seemingly inconsequential moments become etched into your mind during the most traumatic times. The toy bunny rabbit, the dirty floors, the lazy day, the stagnant tub of water, and the knock on the door remain vivid like photographs slowly developing in the darkroom of my memory. Like fragments of a fragile reality, each detail had settled into sharp focus, refusing to fade with time. A quiet sense of dread crept over me, a feeling that life as I knew it was about to change forever. What made it more unsettling was that this house, once a place of stability and comfort, now felt exposed for what it truly was: deteriorating. Yet, it was still my home because the most important person was there with me – My mother.

Our mother had built delicate walls of denial to keep our world hidden. Whether someone had reported us—maybe a neighbor, relative, or teacher noticing our dirty clothes and empty lunchboxes—or it was just the system conducting a welfare check, the barriers she constructed had collapsed.

Now, as officers restrained our mother, a social worker handed me a pair of pants to cover my nakedness - a small comfort in the moment that defied comprehension. My three older brothers and I were being torn away from the only parent who had always been there, no matter how broken and unstable our world had become.

UNVEILING THE SHADOWS

Even in the chaos and instability of our world, moments from the past began to surface – moments where I now recognize glimpses of God's protection woven into our story. When I was five years old, Saber, our Siberian Husky-German Shepherd mix, lunged at me for teasing him after touching his food bowl.

"He's going to kill me!" The thought screamed in my head as his teeth bared and a low, guttural growl rumbled through the kitchen. My heart raced as Saber's wrath unleashed, and I scrambled backward, the food bowl skidding across the floor.

'Why did I do that?" I thought, panic rising like a wave I couldn't escape. "Mother's not here to stop him. Nobody's here to help me."

In that split second, I froze, certain that the next thing I'd feel would be his razor-sharp teeth sinking into my legs, tearing through my skin. "This is it. This is how it ends." Then, something extraordinary happened.

It was as if the invisible hands of angels grabbed me, lifting me off the ground from danger and placing me gently on the kitchen countertop, just out of the reach of Saber's fury. I clung to the edge, staring down at him as he barked and snarled, frustration blazing in his eyes. I couldn't move, breathe, or understand what had just happened. "How did I get up here? I didn't climb."

To this day, I can only describe it as divine intervention. Angels protecting me in a moment that defied explanation.

THE ILLUSION OF PLENTY

Mother was fiercely determined to give her children the best life possible. Education was her passionate mission, and she ensured that we attended the finest Catholic schools, even if it meant stretching the monthly payments we received from her two ex-husbands to their limits. With alimony from her first husband and financial assistance from my father, she gladly became a stay-at-home mom.

Yet we still lacked the basic necessities at times. Despite the steady flow of money, the question lingered: *Where did all the money go?* It was a puzzle none of us could complete, an invisible weight that grew heavier with time.

Our moments at school were a brief reprieve from the secrets and struggles waiting at home. "Tell them Mother isn't home," we were instructed when bill collectors came knocking. My brothers became experts at weaving tales, voices steady even as anxiety took over.

In the classroom, however, it was a different story. Amidst a lack of resources at home, God gave me a supernatural ability to understand the subjects I studied, especially math. One day, a nun whose kind eyes seemed to see beyond the surface – pulled my mother aside during a visit to the school. "Your daughter is like a rosebud waiting to bloom," she said, her voice brimming with hope.

Those words were a quiet prophecy, a subtle hint at the great plan God had in store for me. Even amid the illusion of plenty, with our home lacking stability and provision, God was planting seeds of promise in my life. The path ahead was unclear, yet it was as though he was already showing me glimpses of His hand at work.

SURVIVING SCARCITY

I believed the turmoil surrounding me was simply how life was supposed to be. When the water stopped running, I didn't question it. "Maybe it simply dried up," I thought, picturing the pipes emptying like a leaky faucet. It wasn't strange to me – just another piece of our world.

"Boy, go get me some water from the back of the tank of the toilet," Mom called from the kitchen. My oldest brother walked toward the bathroom without hesitation, a bowl in hand. I sat quietly, watching as he returned with the water. "Why the toilet? Why not the sink?" I wondered but kept my mouth shut. Mom poured the water into the pot, her hands moving quickly as she prepared something for us to eat - Hamburger Helper. The thought of where the water came from tugged at my stomach, but I didn't say anything. It wasn't my place to question. "At least we'll have food," I told myself.

Hunger and survival became the rhythm of our lives. The scarcity of basic needs—food, water, clean clothes—entwined itself into our daily existence. It was a weight we all carried, too young to understand, too powerless to escape.

I remember one day when the hunger pains became overwhelming. I can't recall how many hours or days we had gone without food, but one thing was for certain: we were hungry. I followed one of my older brothers to the refrigerator. As he opened the door, the emptiness of its shelves was like a nightmare—a single onion and an almost-empty bottle of mustard. These scraps would have to be split between the four of us.

At that moment, our mother was nowhere to be found. She may have been out on a date while we were alone at home. We all lay on the living room floor together, stomachs growling, pondering when we would eat again.

In retrospect, I realized how often the Lord must have intervened, shielding us from harm in ways we couldn't comprehend. I think of when our electricity was unexpectedly turned back on after days of being in darkness or how food appeared on the doorstep just at the right time. Amidst the neglect and uncertainty of that season, God's divine mercy ran through it all, creating small and undeniable miracles in our story. Survival itself was a testament to God's unseen hand, and I can't help but feel an overwhelming sense of thankfulness.

BEFORE THE STORM

Yet it wasn't always like this. Before those days of scarcity, I remember the warmth of our mother's love shining through simple joys. She would make us Rice Krispies Treats, our favorite snack, pouring the sticky, gooey marshmallow mixture into a pan and spreading it out. We'd crowd around, eager to devour the sweet treat.

I also remember sitting on the floor, glued to the TV, watching my favorite cartoons, like *Winnie the Pooh*, or one of my favorite movies, *Willy Wonka and the Chocolate Factory*. As I watched the Willy Wonka movie, I felt a special connection to Charlie, the poor boy who grew up in scarcity, just like our lives had become. Maybe that's why I loved the movie—it mirrored our lives.

What I loved most was the ending, when Charlie inherited the entire Chocolate Factory, a symbol of limitless abundance and the end of his struggles for himself and his family. Perhaps, in the back of my mind, I dreamed of our circumstances changing, just like Charlie's. I longed for a rescue - a world where all my wildest dreams could come true, and we'd never have to worry about food or lack again.

Yet even in those moments of uncertainty, my love for my mother never wavered. She was a source of comfort and security; a presence I clung to like a shield against the world. Her flaws didn't diminish her light in my eyes; instead, they made her human—complex and resilient.

Before our world began to unravel, before the hardships weighed us down, as a little girl, I saw my mother as the epitome of perfection.

CHAPTER 2:

AN EARLY PORTRAIT
OF MOTHER

"For You created my inmost being, you knit me together in my mother's
womb...All the days ordained for me were written in your book before
one of them came to be."
(Psalm 139: 13-16, *NIV*)

My mother was bad – the fine Angela Davis, Afro-wearing, Foxy Brown-swaggering, fist-pumping, strut-through-the-room-like-a-movie-star kind of bad – radiating that unshakable 1960s "I'm Black and I'm proud" energy. I called her "Mother," a title that carried both elegance and reverence to me. Her presence was magnetic, and everything seemed to pause when she entered a room, as if time itself bowed.

She commanded attention without uttering a word, her head held high and her soul humming with a quiet assurance: "You are more than enough. God made you special. Walk like the Queen you are and let your light shine bright." It wasn't just her confidence that drew people in; her beauty and aura made others want to stay close, as if being near her might unlock some secret treasure.

She needed no one's approval – she knew who she was. She marched with the authority of someone who didn't follow the crowd because she was the standard. Extraordinary by design, she carried herself as though she was set apart, a woman who understood her worth. Whether it was her sharp mind, striking beauty, or magnetic pull, she had a presence that made others instinctively want to follow her. Yet, in her private moments, that attention was sometimes more of a burden than a compliment. Still, she walked with the belief she was destined for greatness, owning every room she stepped into as if the world itself belonged to her.

To me, she was the most beautiful woman I'd ever seen. God had broken the mold when He made her, blessing her with heaven's finest attributes. Her rich, chocolate-brown complexion glowed with timeless radiance. She exuded sophistication and grace as if she'd stepped off the pages of a high-fashion magazine. At 5-foot-1 with a size 5 figure and a tiny waist, she glided through life like a runway model, turning heads and leaving whispers in her wake. People often marveled at how she maintained her graceful form after giving birth to four children, but to me, it was just another part of her allure.

Her crowning glory was her hair —long, thick, and jet-black. Whether styled into the perfect afro, cascading curls, or the iconic beehive of the 1960s, it was always a masterpiece. "I'm tender-headed," she'd say with a laugh, yet no matter the style, her hair radiated the same effortless beauty as everything else about her.

THE VOICE THAT STIRRED SOULS

Her tone was rich, layered with a depth that seemed to shift and fluctuate like rolling waves. At times, it carried a deep resonance, almost like the rhythmic beat of distant drummers, steady and full of life. It wasn't just melodic—it held a vibrato; an energy that made every word linger as if it carried a story of its own. There was an earthy warmth to her voice that could soothe even the most troubled heart yet also an unmistakable strength, like the echo of a striking cadence that demanded attention. Her full, brown lips, slightly darkened perhaps from her love of Newport cigarettes, which she began smoking after her first husband asked her to light them for him, added to the mystique of her voice. Her sound felt as if it had been shaped by life and God Himself, making it unmistakably her own.

Yet, her voice could turn firm and authoritative, especially when addressing her oldest boys. "Didn't I tell you not to do that?" she'd say, her words steady and unwavering, carrying an undertone of urgency, as if to remind them: discipline at home was better than consequences from the police later.

The other side of Mother was very loving and tender and soft-spoken, never seeming to run out of hugs that comforted and enveloped her children in warmth, "Come here, baby, give Mama a hug, darling," she'd often say, opening her arms wide, her harmonic tone wrapping around you like a soft blanket. You felt safe and cherished in those moments as if no trouble in the world could touch you while she held you close.

As most little girls tend to admire their moms, I often found myself trying to mimic the essence of who my mother was – whether by trying on her clothes, playing in her make-up, or wobbling around in her heels. One time, I looked at her and said, "Mother, I want 'big hair' like you." My curly shoulder-length hair seemed small in comparison to hers. She smiled and replied, "Darling, you will have big hair like me one day." I beamed, already imagining how glorious that day would be.

Through the eyes of a six-year-old, I knew there was something truly special about my mother. She wasn't just stunning; she was captivating. I felt privileged to be a part of her sphere and honored to be her only daughter, as though I held a front-row seat to someone who was a superstar in my small world.

A RENAISSANCE WOMAN: MULTI-TALENTED

Mother was a Renaissance woman full of creativity and talent. As a self-made businesswoman, she took immense pride in her dressmaking craft, transforming yards of fabric into works of art that flattered each contour. Her clients trusted her hands to bring their visions to life, and she never disappointed. Mother's style was a 1960s and 1970s elegant masterpiece, blending timeless sophistication with her creative flair. She sashayed in striking A-line shift dresses she expertly tailored, cinching the waists to perfection. Her signature touch – a lace scarf wrapped delicately around her hair or tied in a dramatic bow at the collar, set her ensemble apart. On cooler days, she wore a long wool coat with a luxurious fur trim wrapping seamlessly from top to bottom or a flowing cape adorned with lace and fringes. She dazzled in breezy, collared dresses that danced with the wind for summer days. Every outfit was completed with stockings, chic kitten heels, a perfectly paired purse, oversized shades, and jewelry that sparkled as bright as her confidence. Mother's elegance wasn't just in her clothing – it reflected in her strength and individual traits that extended into her personal life.

From the very beginning, my mother's life was marked by strength, determination, and a sense of purpose that seemed destined for greatness. She was born in Mississippi, to a strong mother who shaped her character and resilience. Beyond the boldness, the beauty, and the swagger, there was a story God had already written long before I ever understood the complexities of her life.

As the eldest of four siblings on her mother's side, Odessa Westmoreland, and with seven additional half-siblings from her father's second marriage, James Gray, my mother was a natural-born leader. Raised in Bruce, Mississippi, her exceptional intellect and undeniable potential were evident from a young age. Recognizing these gifts, her mother sent her to Detroit, Michigan, to live with her aunt, and her aunt's husband. This move was made to provide her with greater educational and life opportunities.

Her mother must have said something like this before sending her to live in Detroit: "Baby, I love you more than anything, but I have to let you go. Bobbie Jean, you're smart and God has given you a gift. I want you to have the kind of life I can't give you here – a life with opportunities and a good education, and a chance to shine. Your Aunt Bessie and Uncle Charlie will take good care of you, and no matter how far you go, my love is always with you, and you can always come home."

NEW BEGINNINGS IN DETROIT: THRIVING ACADEMICALLY

My mother arrived in Detroit with a single suitcase in hand, eyes wide with both wonder and determination. Stepping into the bustling city alive with promise, she knew her life would never be the same. Known as the 'Motor City,' its factories hummed with activity, and neighborhoods buzzed with the families building their dreams. On Detroit's west side, she settled on Alden Avenue with her aunt and uncle, surrounded by tree-lined streets, modest homes and the sounds of children playing in nearby parks.

The city must have seemed to have endless possibilities to a girl from Bruce, Mississippi. Nonetheless, my mother didn't let the bright lights or new surroundings overwhelm her. She was determined to embrace the opportunities her mother's sacrifice had afforded her.

Aunt Bessie wasted no time enrolling her in the neighborhood schools—Higginbotham Elementary and Middle School, and later Samuel C. Mumford High School—ensuring she began her journey toward an exceptional education.

My mother thrived, excelling both academically and athletically. She captained her school's basketball and field hockey teams and became the president of the French, glee, and fashion clubs. Her vibrant personality and natural leadership skills stood out in every circle she entered. Her love for literature, sewing, and sports formed a foundation for the creative and industrious life she would later lead.

At the same time, she was fiercely protective of her cousins, Mary – affectionately called Tita and Paris, the children of Aunt Bessie and Uncle Charlie. She had no tolerance for anyone picking on them. If someone dared to mess with Mary at school, my mother didn't hesitate to step in and defend her. As she often said, "I was always kicking somebody's butt. I was mean, and people feared me, and they knew not to mess with me." My mother's toughness earned her a reputation - one that warned others, "Don't mess with Bobbie Jean!" Yet it also reflected her deep loyalty to those she loved. The duality in her character was a force to be reckoned with, shaping the dynamic woman she would one day become.

A RISING STAR: THE EARLY CAREER

My mother graduated with honors and after high school, her ambition led her through various careers, from commercial modeling to managing departments at Sears and Stillman's Company. Tapping into her entrepreneurial spirit and drawing on the sewing skills her mother and Aunt Bessie had lovingly taught her, she founded "Miss Bobbie Jean's Sewing and Things," recognizing the world's need for the unique talents and creativity she could provide. Her custom design business showcased her remarkable skill as a seamstress and dressmaker and caught the attention of Motown legends, for whom she created one-of-kind colorful show stopping garments. Ever the trailblazer, she designed her stylish wardrobe, always completing her looks with gloves and heels.

HER FIRST MARRIAGE TO AN OFFICER

When Bobbie turned 21, she married her first husband, Gene LaMaster, a handsome, dashing Navy officer. Mother often told me how it all began, reflecting on those early days with a mix of humor and honesty. Gene had heard about her through a friend who knew the family. She had never dated before and, at the time, was still a virgin, unaccustomed to the attention of a suitor. Gene, however, was persistent. He would come to Aunt Bessie's door, confidently knock, and wait patiently.

'What do you want?' she would snap through the slightly opened door, her tone as sharp as her gaze.

Gene, unshaken, would flash a charming smile. 'Are you Miss Bobbie Jean? The beautiful Miss Bobbie Jean?'

She'd pause, reluctant to engage. 'Yes, I am. What do you want?'

'I'd like to take you out on a date,' he would reply, ever undeterred.

At first, she dismissed him, turning down his advances and slamming the door with no intention of entertaining him. Undeterred, Gene kept coming back, day after day, wearing down her resistance. Finally, she agreed to one date.

It wasn't long after that date that Gene asked for her hand in marriage. With her frankness, she later admitted to me, 'I just married the first man who came along so I could get out of Aunt Bessie's house and see more of the world.'

Her honesty about that decision spoke to the intricacy of her choices. While it wasn't a grand romantic gesture, it was a bold step toward the independence and life experiences she deeply desired. That first marriage marked a new chapter that would lead her into a life of transformation and discovery.

Soon, they began building a life together, welcoming two sons, as they traveled on naval assignments throughout the U.S. Though their marriage ended in divorce after the birth of their second son, it marked the beginning of her journey as a single mother. This path brought joy and challenges and reflected the nuanced layers of her life. The season shaped her unexpectedly, even as she embraced a different path.

A SNAPSHOT OF INFATUATION: MEETING THE CHARMER

Despite life's pressures and routines, God has a way of surprising us – introducing people, places, or moments that breathe new life into weary wings or add an ingredient of hope. For my mother, she thought that moment came at the wedding of her cousin Mary, who was marrying the dashing Palmer. Amid the celebration and joy, she met the man who would come to play a significant role in her life: the photographer and college professor James Wilson.

The celebration was in full swing, with laughter and music filling the air. Bobbie's black spaghetti-strapped dress shimmered under the soft lights, and the scoop neckline and delicate fabric were a testament to her skill as a seamstress. Her hair was styled in perfectly set curls, and she wore double pearl earrings and a gold necklace that complemented the elegance of her sheer stockings and heels. Despite the lively atmosphere, she sat alone on a bench, her thoughts drifting.

That's when Wilson, the wedding photographer, noticed her. His gaze lingered for a moment, captivated by the poised and stunning woman sitting apart from the crowd. He hesitated briefly before approaching her, camera slung over his shoulder and a mixture of curiosity and confidence in his stride.

'I see you sitting here alone,' he said, his voice smooth and warm. 'I couldn't help but approach you. You look… beautiful. If I may, could I take a photograph of you? I'd love to capture this moment.'

Bobbie, taken aback by his boldness, was ready to default to her usual defenses and refuse his request. Yet, something about him—his charm, genuine smile, wavy jet-black hair, and smooth chocolate skin —completely disarmed her. Against her instincts, she found herself nodding. 'Yes,' she said softly, surprising even herself.

James smiled, his endearing eyes lighting up. He lifted his camera, but before clicking, he leaned slightly closer. 'Just relax,' he said gently. 'Place one hand over the other, like this.' He motioned for her to cross her feet delicately. 'Perfect. Now, give me that smile that's been hiding.'

Bobbie couldn't help but beam, her heart beating fast as the camera clicked. She thought to herself, *There's something different about this man.*

Throughout the wedding, James moved seamlessly from one group to the next, capturing the joy of the occasion. His lens seemed to find her again and again. When the event ended, he returned to her, holding a small card.

'I'm going to have these pictures ready in about a week,' he said, his tone easy but hopeful. 'Can we keep in touch?'

Still caught off guard by the attention and how quickly she had let her walls down, Bobbie found herself nodding again. 'Yes, we can.'

Following his promise, James visited Bobbie at her home seven days later and showed her the beautiful photographs he had developed in his makeshift darkroom. As he shared each image, Bobbie was captivated by his talent and how he had captured her beauty in a light she had never seen before. One photograph stood out in particular – the first one he had taken of her, sitting gracefully with her hands folded, legs crossed, in her black spaghetti-strap dress. The elegance of the image took her breath away, and she immediately knew it was the one she wanted enlarged and framed to place on the walls of her home - she even knew the perfect spot. It was a timeless keepsake of a moment that had already left an indelible mark on her heart.

Jimmy, as she affectionately called him, quickly became a close friend and generous supporter of her and her two sons. However, he never mentioned he was married. Assuming he was single and available, Bobbie never asked about his relationship status.

CAPTURING HISTORY:
A LEGENDARY CAREER BEHIND THE LENS

Meanwhile, Jimmy's photography career flourished as he became the go-to photographer for Detroit's most prestigious events. Jimmy didn't just witness history—he captured it. His lens immortalized legendary Motown figures like Berry Gordy, the founder of Motown, Stevie Wonder, Diana Ross and more. He even served as the private photographer to the legendary Motown producer and songwriter Sylvia Moy, who penned iconic hits like "My Cherie Amour" and "Uptight (Everything's Alright)." At the heart of Detroit's cultural renaissance, Motown's sound transcended the city's borders, bringing songs like "My Girl," "Ain't No Mountain High Enough," and "Dancing in the Street" to audiences across the globe, uniting people through music.

Jimmy's work extended beyond music, chronicling Detroit's pivotal moments and iconic figures. He photographed legendary performers like Ray Charles and Sammy Davis Jr., who graced stages at Detroit's most notable theaters, including the Fox Theatre. He also captured pivotal moments in history, photographing civil rights leaders like Martin Luther King Jr. and Malcolm X, capturing the spirit of their fight for justice and equality.

With his camera always around his neck, Jimmy documented pivotal moments for a prominent Black newspaper, the *Michigan Chronicle*. His lens captured powerful images of people from diverse nationalities and religious backgrounds uniting in marches, holding picket signs demanding fair wages, better housing, and an end to police brutality—issues central to Detroit's unrest. Many of these demonstrations occurred in Black Bottom, a predominantly Black neighborhood hub for African American culture and activism.

In 1967, Jimmy's camera documented the Detroit Rebellion, an uprising that exposed the city's deep racial and social tensions. Through his photographs, he preserved the pain, strength, and hope of a community striving for change. He also highlighted Detroit's transformation, capturing the construction of several iconic landmarks including the Renaissance Center, a towering symbol of the city's ambition and renewal.

He was welcomed into prestigious spaces to photograph prominent political figures like Mayor Coleman Young at the Manoogian Mansion, governors, and influential businessmen – his photography serving as a testament to Detroit's strength and cultural impact, connecting the city's vibrant past to its enduring legacy.

With his established reputation, Jimmy brought Bobbie to prestigious events where she became an integral part of his business. Poised behind a table, her beehive hair immaculate, she welcomed potential buyers who admired his photographs. Her beauty and charm drew crowds, helping Jimmy sell his images and connect with clients at workshops, exhibits, and social gatherings.

As they approached the table, Bobbie transformed into a natural-born saleswoman. "Hello, and thank you for stopping by James D. Wilson's Custom Photography," she'd say with a warm yet commanding tone. Gesturing toward a photograph, she'd confidently address a passerby, "You, sir," this photo is exactly what you need. It's not just art; it's a piece of Detroit's history that will elevate any room you place it in." Her assured demeanor made buyers trust her instinct, often realizing she was right before they even knew it themselves.

BOBBIE AND JIMMY: A RENAISSANCE MAN'S REQUEST

Despite their polished connection, Jimmy and Bobbie's relationship was far from simple. Fiercely independent, Bobbie often acted on instinct, making decisions that revealed the complexities of her life. After having a third son with another man - a relationship that ended shortly after the child's birth - Bobbie proudly showed off her son to everyone, often bringing him to her classes while pursuing her education. Through it all, Jimmy's unwavering support stood out; he continued to care for Bobbie and her children, as if they were his own. Their bond was one of rare devotion, marked by contradictions and shaped by the intricacies of their choices.

My mother often said she chose the fathers of her children, ensuring they had qualities that would produce emotionally intelligent, talented individuals who could positively impact the world. She believed all of them fit this category, including Jimmy, which is why she was open to his special request to have a child with him.

Bobbie also admired Jimmy as a true Renaissance man. He spoke multiple languages, played musical instruments, pursued higher education, and became a pioneering college professor, instrumental in establishing the photography curriculum at a Detroit college. Beyond his achievements, Bobbie was captivated by his soft, wavy hair - a nod to his Cherokee heritage – his charm, and his unforgettable smile.

Jimmy's first marriage had produced two children, but his wife refused to have more - reportedly because their children had inherited his darker complexion rather than her lighter one. This rejection deeply hurt him. When he shared this painful story with Bobbie, she sympathized with his desire for a larger family. His unwavering financial support and dedication to her children endeared him to her, sparking her own desire to have a child with him and fulfill their shared longing for more children.

UNVEILING THE TRIANGLE OF BETRAYALS

Bobbie became pregnant with Jimmy's child, and true to his nature, he attended every doctor's appointment and eagerly prepared for their baby's arrival. Years later, she told me that during those moments, she would have had nine children for him– until she discovered his unfaithfulness.

While pregnant with me, my mother uncovered a devastating truth: Jimmy was still married, and he and his wife were also trying to have children together. Now carrying his child, Bobbie, with the confidence and boldness that defined her, decided to confront his wife directly about her relationship with Jimmy.

Knocking on the door, she stood firm as the woman answered.

"Are you Jimmy's wife?" Bobbie asked, meeting her gaze.

"Yes, I am. Who are you?"

"I'm Bobbie," she said, her tone steady. "I'm carrying Jimmy's child. Listen, Jimmy can't have us both. He must make a choice - either you leave, or I'm leaving, but he can't have us both."

The tension between them was thick, with neither woman backing down. Both were determined to claim him, leaving behind wounds that would not easily heal. Shortly after the confrontation, Bobbie began to feel unsafe as the strain surrounding their relationship and growing family had escalated into something darker.

Over time, my mother became increasingly disillusioned as she uncovered more of Jimmy's hidden life. His unwavering support for her and her children couldn't mask his pattern of pursuing multiple women. He was simply a man who would never be faithful. Yet, despite the betrayals, they chose to focus on what mattered most—the children.

THE CHOSEN DAUGHTER: BORN FOR PURPOSE

When my mother gave birth to me, I became the dream she had always wanted—a little girl to dress in ruffled dresses, lace-trimmed socks, patent-leather shoes, and bows in her hair. My father named me with great care, choosing a French first name and a Spanish middle name as if weaving the beauty of different worlds into my identity. He often sang to me – his version of the famous Beatles song, "Michelle." According to my mother, I was the apple of his eye, and the perfect culmination of their hopes and dreams for a brighter future together.

My father wanted to make their relationship official and asked for her hand in marriage. Perhaps blinded by his charisma, success, and his steady financial support, my mother believed Jimmy when he convinced her that he was no longer married. Accepting his proposal, they wed in a small church ceremony but doubts soon immerged. Maybe she sensed he wasn't as free as he claimed, or possibly the tensions between them simply grew too heavy to ignore. Whatever the case, their union lasted only a year before ending in divorce. Yet, despite everything, Jimmy continued to provide for her and her children.

Seeking a fresh start from the heartbreak and drama of her life with Jimmy, she left Detroit and moved to Fort Wayne, Indiana, with her children. The move brought her closer to her brother and sister, who may have encouraged her to take this leap. Above all, she was determined to build a more stable life for herself and her children.

CHAPTER 3:

BREAKING FREE: A NEW START IN FORT WAYNE, INDIANA

"See, I am doing a new thing! Not it springs up; do you not perceive it? I am making a way in the wilderness and streams in the wastelands."
(Isaiah 43:19, *NIV*)

Fort Wayne was a stark contrast to the bustling vibrancy of Detroit. Rows of modest homes lined the streets, and the nearby factories hummed softly in the background, a steady rhythm of work that seemed to seep into every corner of life. The Hanna Addition neighborhood, where many Black families found community, was alive with the voices of children playing on a lazy Sunday afternoon. Yet, there was a stillness to Fort Wayne, as if the city itself held its breath, aware of the struggles carried by those who lived there.

For Bobbie, it was a place of both hope and apprehension. She moved us here to start over, but the quiet streets of Fort Wayne also mirrored her loneliness and the weight of raising four children on her own. I was too young to remember the move from Detroit, but the memories I would carry from Fort Wayne would be life-altering.

BOBBIE FINDING INDEPENDENCE

No distance could keep Jimmy away from Bobbie as he began frequent two-hour drives from Detroit to Fort Wayne to visit us. Though I was his only biological child, he treated all of us as his own, fulfilling his need to be close to Bobbie and the family he had grown to love.

Yet, with everything they had in common, it was hard to understand why I could feel the anger in my mother's words when my father visited us. At times, she would speak to him through a cracked door, a physical barrier symbolizing the hard, cruel truth: he no longer had total access to her heart or her home.

'What do you want now, Jimmy?' she would say, her tone sharp and defensive. 'I have sent you letters, and you have not answered them. You know full well I need more money. Look, if you don't want to be in our lives, you just need to say so!'

Her words carried a weight of deeper wounds, as she came to terms with the man she loved having a weakness – he couldn't share his heart with just one woman. Despite their distance, Jimmy continued sending weekly checks to ensure she could provide for her children's needs. As she moved forward, she began dating again but kept our lives private, never allowing her relationships to intersect with her children's lives. As a child, this felt normal. As an adult, I admired and respected her choice to prioritize our well-being over the presence of outsiders.

A MOTHER'S UNIQUE LOVE AND RULES

My mother poured her love and energy into all her children. As her only daughter, she delighted in dressing me in frilly dresses and twirling me around the living room, her laughter bubbling joyfully. "I always wanted a little girl to spoil," she'd say, ensuring every detail of my outfit was perfect. In those moments, I was the princess of our tiny kingdom, the center of her pride and joy.

Mother had a way of commanding loyalty and keeping control over our lives. She would call us into her room one by one and say, "You know you're my favorite, right? I can always count on you." Her voice was soft, reassuring, as if sharing a secret meant only for us. She knew singling us out made us want to please her and hold on to that special place in her heart.

She also had separate rules for her children. As her daughter, I could do no wrong. One evening, despite being told to leave her jewelry alone, I draped myself in her treasures, pretending I was just like her. When she returned and she caught me, I braced for her wrath, but she only chuckled softly. "Darling, look at you – so beautiful, just like your mother," she said, kissing my forehead. Moments like these endeared her to me even more.

My mother never spanked me or my youngest brother. To her, we were the golden children. However, my two oldest brothers couldn't escape her corporal punishment. "If I don't beat y'all's butts, the police officers will," she'd yell, her frustration erupting like a storm. I'd hear the clang of a skillet or a sharp reprimand. Her anger wasn't about unwashed dishes or an unkempt house - it was something deeper, something I was too young to understand.

ADVENTURES WITH MY BROTHERS

My older brothers and I were inseparable, each other's closest allies, and I looked up to them. The oldest, with his caramel complexion and short, muscular build, had a smile and personality that could light up the world. He was especially creative, often practicing with his nunchucks like the next Bruce Lee or sketching superheroes on his sketch paper. His drawings, brimming with imagination, hinted at a quiet hope for rescue, though we didn't realize how much our lives were on the brink of change. My middle brother, tall, dark, and handsome, carried a cheerful demeanor and compassionate heart, balanced by a thoughtful seriousness about life's important matters. Both brothers were equally good-looking and were athletic and popular, excelling in track, basketball, and football, which made them even more the center of attention at school.

My youngest brother with his light complexion, sandy brown hair, and big brown eyes, had a playful, mischievous personality that often led to snitching on our oldest brothers to our mother. His naughtiness sometimes felt like an attempt to reclaim his place as the youngest, when he received the most attention. Although we generally got along, he loved testing my patience and boundaries. One time, he hid my favorite baby doll in a floor vent. Furious, I grabbed a wooden board and swung with all my might, not realizing it had a nail in it.

"Wham!" It landed above his right eyebrow leaving a scar he carries to this day. Let's just say he never touched my toys again.

Despite the occasional sibling rivalry, my brothers and I shared endless laughs within our adventurous world. My oldest brother was the master of pranks and was always coming up with creative ways to make us laugh. Once, he created a game called the "breath-holding contest," claiming it would test our lung capacity. After his countdown, we all filled our lungs and began. My youngest brother and I were the first to give up, followed by my second oldest brother. My oldest brother lasted over two minutes – until we discovered he'd been cheating, sneaking small breaths when we weren't looking. We laughed until our sides hurt, marveling at his cleverness.

I often got swept up in my brother's adventurous schemes, like when they turned our staircase into a makeshift slide, sending me flying down on a large piece of cardboard - giggling my heart out as their fearless guinea pig. Or when my oldest brother played tricks on my siblings and me, lying on the railroad tracks and making us cry as we struggled to pull him off, terrified a train might come. He'd eventually get up laughing, leaving us frustrated but relieved. Those moments were filled with innocence and togetherness, capturing the pure joys of childhood.

SUPERNATURAL RESCUE THROUGH THE FLAMES

We moved often from one apartment to another, never fully settling. In one of those apartments, something happened that left no doubt in my mind God's angels were watching over me.

As the little sister, I looked up to my three older brothers - especially my youngest brother with admiration. For some reason, whatever he told me to do, I would do it without hesitation. Maybe I wanted to earn his approval or simply be a part of his world. This blind trust sometimes led me into dangerous situations, like the time my father visited and took us to a hotel for a staycation. We were all having fun by the pool, and I was zooming around on my Big Wheel - the plastic tricycle every kid wanted - when my brother told me to ride it straight into the pool. Without thinking twice, I pedaled right into the deep end, oblivious I couldn't swim. Sinking fast, my two oldest brothers jumped in and pulled me out just in time.

The same pattern of following my youngest brother's lead unfortunately set the stage for what happened next. One afternoon, while our mother cooked in the kitchen and my two older brothers were downstairs, he wanted to share his fascination with fire by teaching me how to strike a match. I was only four, sitting cross-legged on the bed, watching as he demonstrated, "See? Easy." Then he handed me the box, leading me to try it on my own while he went to the bathroom.

On my third attempt, the match lit with a hiss. As the flame crept toward my fingers, I panicked and dropped it onto the mattress. Within seconds, flames erupted and encircled me as smoke filled the room. Frozen in fear, I couldn't scream or move, I felt completely helpless. Suddenly, my youngest brother burst into the room and pulled me to safety, running through the flames as if supernaturally protected. Firefighters arrived just in time to rescue us through the second-floor window, saving us from what could have been a tragic ending. Although the experience was terrifying, my brother's fascination with fire didn't end there, and I continued following his lead. More apartments would catch fire due to our reckless curiosity, yet through it all, God's protection remained steadfast.

Despite these incidents, our mother never sat us down to explain the dangers of fire or to warn us not to play with matches. She had a laid-back approach to parenting, trusting we would learn through experience. She often said with a chuckle, "I didn't talk to you about wetting the bed. I knew you would grow out of it. And if you were grown and still wetting the bed, you'd figure out it was time to go to the bathroom. I just let kids be kids." In her mind, childhood was a journey of discovery, and she believed we would eventually outgrow our reckless curiosity. I sometimes wonder if she ever imagined how far our 'discovery' would take us.

GLASS SHATTERED, LIFE PRESERVED

It seemed like the devil knew my bright future and was trying to kill me before I could even get started on my journey. One day, God used my father to rescue me during what I believe was one of my greatest brushes with death. I was in the kitchen playing around as children often do, my little hands eager to explore the mysteries in every cabinet. While my family members were in the other room, I opened one of the cupboard doors, excited to see what treasures it contained. My eyes lit up as I spotted a glass pitcher, so fancy, I couldn't resist picking it up. I held it carefully, turning it at every angle, mesmerized by the way it sparkled.

Suddenly, my mother entered the kitchen to check on me and froze. "Michelle, put that down right now!" she shouted, her voice sharp with panic. It was as if she had a premonition or a vision of what would unfold before it even happened. Startled by her tone, my hands fumbled, and the pitcher slipped. It shattered on the floor into what seemed like a million pieces. In my fright, I lost my balance and fell backward, landing directly on the jagged shards. The glass pierced my left leg and sliced through my flesh near the bone. I was in shock as blood poured from the deep gash.

"Jimmy, come help Michelle!" my mother screamed. "She's had an accident! There's blood everywhere." My father came running into the kitchen and grabbed a stack of newspapers nearby, wrapping them tightly around my leg to stop the bleeding. He carried me to the car while my mother and brothers stayed behind. At the ER, the doctors worked quickly to assess the damage. After hours of surgery and over 90 stitches, the doctors finally finished.

One surgeon, looking solemn, turned to my father and said, "Had the glass penetrated just an ½" deeper, she would have lost her leg." The words hung in the air, heavy with what could have been. My father nodded, his face a mix of relief and gratitude. They placed my leg in a cast and gave strict instructions for my care to my father, who stood by my side the whole time. As my leg healed, I had to learn how to walk with the cast. My full recovery time was three months, including regaining strength and mobility. Although I bear a long scar on that leg from that day, it is a physical reminder of how God saved my life once again for His greater purpose.

CHAPTER 4:

QUALITY TIME WITH MOTHER AND LESSONS FROM BIG MAMA IN THE DEEP SOUTH

"These commandments that I give you today are to be on your hearts. Impress them on your children. Talk about them when you sit at home and when you walk along the road…"
(Deuteronomy 6:6-7, *NIV*)

After years of moving, we finally settled into what would be the last home we lived in as a family unit. It wasn't tucked away in a quiet neighborhood with cul-de-sacs and winding streets; instead, it sat along a busy road where traffic seemed endless. The house was a simple two-bedroom, single-story home with three stairs leading to a front porch with a wraparound white wooden banister. The slightly warped door opened to a haven filled with laughter, tears, and whispered dreams, where creaking floors and drafty windows held the memories of our family's life.

A MOTHER QUITE UNIQUE

My mother was my constant source of strength, her gentle demeanor was like a warm hug on the coldest days. We shared a bedroom, and our nightly ritual was one of my favorite times with her. "Come on, baby, it's time to go to sleep," my mother said gently. I'd climb into bed, snuggling close as I listened to the rhythm of her breathing as she rested from the day's cares. She always slept on her right side, her arm tucked behind her head, as her right hand reached for mine. I'd hold her hand tightly, my small fingers wrapping around hers. That simple touch – firm and familiar – was my anchor.

I felt comforted and reassured, knowing no matter what, she would be there to guide me through the darkness – through life.

Mother had a flair for the dramatic. In her mind, she was an Academy Award-winning actress, always living out a performance on stage — and her children were her eager audience. One day, she called us into the living room to witness her latest debut. I remember her sitting on the sofa with tears in her eyes, showcasing her uncanny gift for crying on cue, which always made us rush to her side in alarm.

"Mama, why are you crying? What's wrong?" we fretted, crowding around her, desperate to know what had happened. And she would wail louder until we felt her emotion and wept. Then, instantaneously, the sobs would vanish, and laughter would ensue. She would dole out embraces like they were sweets at a carnival. In retrospect, maybe she was using her acting talent to cope with her emotions, a silent plea for help we didn't recognize or understand at the time. As a single mother, she must have felt the weight of immense pressure, perhaps reflecting on her failed relationships or dreams she had set aside to raise her children – a sacrifice that brought with it heaviness, sadness, and even moments of depression.

WISDOM IN THE LITTLE THINGS: THE BATHROOM TALK

Yet, despite her burdens, Mother was a master of multitasking and never compromised on giving her children the individual attention they deserved. Each week, she set aside 15 sacred minutes of uninterrupted space – what she called "quality time" - for each of us. A tradition where we had her complete focus to ask questions or do something we loved together, free from distractions.

She would create a cozy atmosphere and ensure no other sibling was around to interrupt. It was our moment to shine, and we cherished every moment.

One day, my mother took me by the hand and led me into the bathroom. "Come here darling. It's time for us to talk," she said, motioning for me to walk with her to the bathroom. She often called me by sweet names like "Baby", "Darling", and "Baby Doll", her words warming my heart like a soft embrace.

Closing the door behind us, I stood before her as she sat on the toilet lid, her expression serious yet gentle. "One day, when you're around 12 or 13, something special will happen," she began. She went on to explain I would start a cycle called menstruation. "It's a sign you're growing up," she said, holding my hand as if anchoring me to the moment.

Though my five-old mind didn't grasp everything she explained, I listened closely as she told me about the changes my body would go through. The tone of her voice made it feel sacred, even if I didn't fully understand everything. When she finished, she smiled softly and squeezed my hand.

"You'll remember this when the time comes," she whispered.

And I did.

As we opened the door, my brothers were crouched by the keyhole, mischief written all over their faces. I shot them a glare, protective of the precious moment I had just shared with our mother. Their giggles quickly faded as I walked past them, holding the lesson close to my heart.

LESSONS FROM BIG MAMA:
THE TRACKS OF SEGREGATION

Mother was a steadfast presence in our lives who never truly left our side except when we visited her mother, affectionately known as "Big Mama." I never understood why they gave her that nickname; she wasn't a big woman. She was petite, probably 120 pounds, with a caramel complexion. Her bifocal glasses magnified her eyes, and her greasy curls bounced as if fresh from pink sponge rollers. Big Mama's essence filled the room, radiating the southern hospitality she served up every morning alongside oven-fresh buttery biscuits.

Big Mama, lived in Bruce, Mississippi, in a small rural country town with a tightly knit community where everyone waved and greeted their neighbors with a smile. The city, nestled in the rolling hills of Calhoun County, exuded a sense of simplicity and charm with its red dirt roads, cozy country homes, and expansive farmland. Time moved slower, and the sound of cicadas often filled the humid air during long summer evenings.

There was a local grocery store, a post office, and plenty of churches that served as the backbone of spiritual life. The lasting effects of segregation were still evident, shaping the community's dynamics and interactions. I remember Big Mama telling me never to cross the railroad tracks just over the hill because, on the other side, there was a community of people I didn't belong to. Blacks lived on one side of the tracks, and Whites lived on the other side of this stark color divide. It felt as if crossing those tracks could mean life or death; like there was an invisible wave of hatred, as tall as a mountain, lingering on those tracks, daring anyone to cross.

Though I never went near them, I came to hate that line of cold steel, noticing how the houses were larger on the other side and the community seemed bustling with more activity and businesses catering to its people. Why do certain individuals have special privileges just because of the color of their skin? I pondered silently within myself. I listened to Big Mama and never crossed those railroad tracks, no matter how much curiosity tugged at my heart. I knew Big Mama's rules weren't meant to hurt me – they were meant to protect me.

As I think about them now, I almost liken them to the Red Sea in the story of Exodus – the barrier God parted so the children of Israel could cross over to freedom to escape Pharoah and his army. Deep down, I wished that stretch of iron and wood could be parted in the same way, bridging the gap of racial disparity with liberation and unity for all people. I longed for a world where the division didn't exist, where there was no longer separation, but instead, connection and equality.

A FEAST OF LOVE AND TRADITION

No matter how harsh and divided the world was, Big Mama's modest two-bedroom home, situated on a dusty back road, was a place where love thrived, and lasting memories were made. As you walked up the steps and past the screened in front door there was a cozy living room. My grandmother's bedroom was just to the left, and a narrow hallway led to the kitchen where she dished up her famous southern delicacies. A small bathroom was tucked away to the side with another bedroom next to it.

Big Mama spent most of her time in the kitchen, pouring love into every meal she cooked from smothered pork chops to fried chicken, fresh vegetables from her garden and an assortment of tasty desserts. There were times she made dishes I didn't like – food I ate anyway, out of respect for her.

One day, while I was kneeling before the coffee table, she handed me a plate and said, "Here you go, baby, eat up." The plate held a small serving of chitterlings, commonly known as chitlins, with their distinct aroma hitting my nose.

"What's this, Big Mama?" I asked hesitantly, poking at the food with my fork.

"Chitlins," she said matter-of-factly, wiping her hands on her apron. "They are good. Put some hot sauce on it, and you'll be fine."

I stared at my plate, unsure, with a slight frown.

She chuckled and waved a hand. "Baby, you don't know what you're missing. This here is soul food. It'll stick to your ribs and keep you strong."

Chitterlings, made from pig intestines, are considered a delicacy in the South, but their history is rooted in the painful legacy of slavery. Enslaved people were given discarded animal parts — the scraps deemed unworthy by their enslavers. Yet, through resilience and ingenuity, they transformed these leftovers into nourishing meals, turning survival into tradition.

Big Mama, though not a slave, grew up in the shadow of systemic racism and Jim Crow laws. No doubt, the lessons she passed down to me were deeply rooted in the wisdom and strength of her mother and grandmother, women who had likely lived through or had a direct awareness of slavery. These traditions, born of necessity, became symbols of survival and pride — values she instilled in me to ensure I, too, knew our history of ingenuity and endurance.

THE RICH CULTURE OF SOUTHERN WORSHIP

Big Mama and I would go to church together, an experience unlike any I had with my mother. I was christened as a baby at the Catholic Church

– a significant spiritual milestone my parents valued deeply. While I don't remember it, I'm grateful I was dedicated to Jesus Christ at the start of my life. Big Mama's church, however, was entirely different – vibrant and alive with joyful expressions of faith that filled the air. The gospel music spilling out from the church just up the road seemed to draw us in, serenading and beckoning us all at once. It was a sound symbolic of the rich culture of the South. The drums, guitars, and piano created an infectious rhythm that, even as a child, I couldn't help but clap along to.

I remember the congregation jumping, shouting, and calling on the name of Jesus with an energy that filled the air. Songs like 'What a Mighty God We Serve' and "Amazing Grace" flowed from the pews with such power they seemed to rise straight to heaven. Even at five years old, I knew God was smiling, and I felt God's presence moving in that church.

Big Mama was well-known and highly respected in the community, so walking into church with her meant I had the privilege of sitting in special seats near the front, with a clear view of the preacher. His hour-long sermon, filled with uplifting Bible stories and heartfelt prayers, stirred the congregation to trust God not only amid their personal struggles, while also rising together in their collective strength.

After the church service, people lingered, greeting one another with warm smiles and hugs. As Big Mama introduced me to her friends, proudly declaring me as Bobbie Jean's daughter, I felt their gaze searching for traces of the beauty, poise, and charm they admired in my mother. Being her daughter in that moment felt like wearing a crown, and I basked in the love and admiration extended to me through her legacy.

I often heard things like, "Look at Bobbie Jean's daughter. My, my, my. You're just as beautiful as she is."

THE JOYS OF PECAN TREASURE HUNTING

When we weren't attending church, Big Mama kept me busy with plenty of activities, which I thoroughly enjoyed because they gave me a glimpse into her world. She would take me to pick pecans on Miss Louise's farm, where she worked as a maid. Big Mama was a master of many trades—her hands knew the rhythm of scrubbing floors, the precision of ironing, and the art of bringing forth life from Miss Louise's Garden. Big Mama taught me how to select the sweetest pecans off the trees and the ground when allowed in the pecan field. She'd point to a branch and say, "Now, baby, see that one? It's still green – leave it be. You want the ones that are brown and just starting to crack open. That's how you know they're ripe." As I placed each pecan into her gathering bag, she'd smile and inspect them with sun kissed hands worn from years of hard work –weathered with creases deep and defined. Though strong and steady, her fingers carried the unmistakable tenderness of someone who had spent a lifetime creating, nurturing, and providing.

"That's a good one. You're getting pretty good at this, baby." I would smile, knowing I was doing my part to help my grandmother.

My favorite part was the treat that came afterwards. Big Mama would expertly crack open a pecan and carefully pull out the meat for me to taste. "Here you go, baby," she'd say, handing me the small treasure that warmed my soul. The nut was buttery and sweet, a reward for my hard work. It was well worth it because I was at my grandmother's side, learning valuable lessons only she could teach.

I didn't think much of it then, but now I wonder if Big Mama taught my mother how to pick pecans, tend to gardens, and appreciate the land's beauty. Was I walking in the same footsteps, unknowingly reliving my mother's traditions, perhaps at the same age she once had shared with Big Mama long ago?

A RED BICYCLE AND FAMILY TIES

Outside the pecan fields, life in the community felt timeless, with children playing barefoot in the yards, climbing trees, and riding bicycles down the roads. To my surprise, my father sent me a huge box of clothes as tall as me to Big Mama's house and outfitted one of her bedrooms with a white canopy bed and matching dresser. I felt like a princess, yet I always carried a heart of thankfulness in my quiet observance of God's blessings.

The highlight for me was the red bicycle my father bought for me, complete with a basket and colorful fringes hanging from each handlebar. I had longed for it, and now, my father, who had flown down from Detroit, was teaching me how to ride it down Bruce's dusty roads.

"Keep your balance, Mich Mich," he'd say, steadying the seat. "And keep looking forward – that's it. You've got this. Keep pedaling. I'm not going to let you fall." His encouragement carried me forward, both on those roads and in life.

Soon after, my brothers joined me at Big Mama's house, and my father took the opportunity to capture moments of all of us together. He lined us up for pictures—my two oldest brothers standing proudly in the back, me in the front, and my youngest brother standing beside me. My father must have taken dozens of pictures that day, each a snapshot of our rare times together.

Later, we visited my mother's youngest sister, Aunt Marie, and her five children, who lived two hours away in Memphis, Tennessee. I enjoyed playing with my cousins in their warm and welcoming household.

True to form, my father, always with his camera in hand, stood all of us kids on the front porch, capturing that special moment. That day, with my long thick hair styled in three ponytails adorned with yellow barrettes, I wore one of the outfits my father had purchased for me—a white faux fur coat with a matching muff for my hands, a knitted hat and scarf, yellow pants, white boots, and a bright smile to match.

We enjoyed that day of laughter, pictures, and good food, spending time with Aunt Marie and Uncle Roger, who always greeted us with plenty of kindness and good home cooking.

ANGELS PROTECT ME FROM A STRANGER'S TRAP

After leaving Memphis, my brothers and I settled back into the simplicity of Bruce, Mississippi. One day, my youngest brother and I walked to a store near Big Mama's house when an elderly man in a long Cadillac parked outside caught our attention. His suit was neat and his hat - perhaps a fedora - sat at a perfect angle. He watched me intently, then motioned for me to come closer so he could give me some candy. Curious and unaware of the danger, I took a step toward him. My brother quickly grabbed my arm and whispered; we're not supposed to talk to strangers. His words snapped me back, and we hurried into the store, leaving the man and his unsettling stare behind. I shudder to think what could have happened if my brother hadn't stopped me. It felt as though an Angel had been standing guard, creating an invisible barrier between us and the man. That day reminded me God's protection was ever present, shielding me even in the smallest moments of danger

Not long after, my father left to return to his life in Detroit, and my brothers soon went back to Fort Wayne to be with our mother. I, however, remained with Big Mama for a couple more weeks, soaking in every moment of summer before it ended. There were still more adventures, and I couldn't wait to see what was in store.

SHIELDING BIG MAMA FROM DANGER

Similarly, Big Mama poured her love and wisdom into me through her enormous garden, which offered her the land's riches. It yielded every vegetable you could imagine - turnip greens, tomatoes, okra, string beans, and everything else. I always went into the backyard with her to pick the day's vegetable for whatever dish she was preparing. I was glad to help her shuck the corn, shell the peas, peel the collard, and turnip greens off their stems, knowing soon, we'd sit down to a heartfelt meal we would enjoy together.

Big Mama didn't only rely on her garden to feed the family—she loved to fish in the nearby creeks. With her cane pole in hand and a bucket at her feet, she'd sit on the creek bank for hours, waiting patiently for the tug of a fish on her line. She'd catch anything that could be cleaned, fried, and served with cornbread on the side.

One day, I tagged along, happy to sit by her side while she worked her skills with the fishing line. The air was thick and warm, the quiet hum of nature broken only by the sound of water lapping against the creek's edge. As I sat watching her, something caught my eye.

"Big Mama," I said, trying to keep my voice calm, "you're sitting on a snake."

She didn't believe me at first and laughed it off. "Don't be messin' with me, now, chile" she said, adjusting her hat and keeping her eyes on the water.

Yet I wasn't joking. "Big Mama, Look down."

When she finally did, her eyes got wide. Somehow, with the calmness she could summon, she eased herself off the snake without so much a scream. The snake slithered away, and she turned to me with a mix of disbelief and humor. "Well, I'll be," she said, shaking her head. "Guess he thought I was keeping his seat warm."

We both laughed about it later, though it was one of the few times I saw Big Mama truly surprised. That day, she didn't catch any fish, but she proved again how unshakable she was—even when the ground beneath her was crawling with danger.

As the summer ended, I returned to my mother's house, back to the familiar chaos of life with my brothers. The lessons and moments I shared with Big Mama stayed with me, etched into my heart like footprints on a dusty road.

BIG MAMA'S CELEBRATION OF LIFE

Years later, at Big Mama's funeral at Jackson Missionary Baptist Church, - the same church I attended with her as a child - I stood before her casket as a young woman, trying to be a pillar of strength for our family, especially for Aunt Marie, who had cared for her until the end. I took in the richness of the memories we shared when I was a little girl and celebrated the life and legacy, she left behind with relatives who had flown in from all over the United States.

Yet during the solemn occasion my thoughts drifted to my mother. My mother wasn't there. No one knew where she was. During the funeral services and the repast that followed, a small part of me hoped she might surprise us all in grand fashion, bursting through the doors to pay her final respects to her mother—however, she didn't.

The family had, by this point, accepted the twists and turns of her life. Yet there was still a deep void in my heart, wondering why she had chosen to be absent at such a sacred passage. Did she even know her mother had died?

After the service, I was snapped back into reality as a couple of men introduced themselves to me and subtly hinted, they could have been my father, wistfully implying they had wished to be the one my mother had married. It was then I realized how much admiration my mother still commanded, even after years away from Bruce, Mississippi. Her beauty and charm had left an indelible mark on the hearts of those who had known her.

CHAPTER 5:

GOD'S BLESSING IN DISGUISE – THE JOURNEY TO THE CHILDREN'S HOME

"Even if my father and mother abandon me, the Lord will hold me close."
(Psalms 27:10, *NLT*)

SALT OFFERING: A CLEANSING BEFORE THE RESCUE

"God, in His infinite mystery, delights in revealing the miraculous by unveiling new facets of His boundless character and limitless personality in ways that defy human logic. His greatness is never confined to the expectations of man, for He often moves through the unassuming simplicity of childlike faith untainted by doubt and fear that demands His greatness to show up. It is through this pure and unshaken trust that He transforms ordinary acts of faith into extraordinary moments of cleansing, healing, and redemption - reminding us His ways are higher, His plans are greater, and nothing is ever beyond His reach."

- Michelle B. Wilson, author,*In Search of a Mother's Love.*

The start of God's redemptive plan for all our lives was unthinkable, even heartbreaking at first glance, but necessary for His ultimate purpose to unfold. At the time, we couldn't see it. – just as Joseph, betrayed by his own brothers, was thrown into a pit and heard whispers of their plot to kill him. What seemed cruel and unimaginable was, in truth, God's preparation to save a nation and restore even the very family that had wounded him. In the chaos, God was orchestrating a healing far beyond human comprehension to save our family as well. I now see His hand at work in ways I never imagined.

Even as a little girl, long before I could articulate destiny or understand redemptive pain, there were glimpses. Whispers in the stillness. Moments when something unseen would stir my heart toward trust – even in the simplest, most unexpected ways.

Growing up, although my family didn't attend church, I felt an undeniable awareness of God's presence. I was six years old, standing outside our Indiana home, the world around me blanketed in snow. The sky was gray and heavy. The cold blew through my coat as the wind whipped around my small frame – and yet, somehow, there was a warmth inside me. A knowing.

Standing near the tree on the side of our house, my tiny hands filled with salt, I felt compelled to trust. To believe without understanding, that God was nearby. There was no voice, no sermon – just a deep, quiet urge. Something stirred within me, a whisper urging me to pray.

Until now, I had never seen my mother or father praying to God. Yet, here I was, standing outside with salt in my hands, offering what must have been my first real prayer prompted by the Holy Spirit—initiated by God Himself.

I closed my eyes and, with a faith larger than the size of a mustard seed, whispered a simple prayer to God, "Dear God, make the snow go away." I threw the salt into the air to seal the prayer with an "In Jesus' name. Amen."

The salt scattered like tiny stars, disappearing into the wind. As I returned inside my humble home, I knew God would answer my prayers and didn't give my act of faith another thought.

The next morning, I opened the door and stood in stunned amazement.

The snow was gone.

Every bit of it melted away as if it had never been there. It was a miracle in my young eyes. It was as if it had never snowed. At that moment, I felt a joy I had never felt before. In my mind, I had a special connection with God I kept secretly tucked away in my heart.

Although I didn't have a personal relationship with God, nor had I accepted Jesus as my Lord and Savior, this was, without question, a pivotal moment in my life that marked the beginning of my journey of trusting God. It sealed the beginning of my faith journey.

It was the first time I stepped out, trusting God for something small – yet meaningful. That's where it all started. The planting of trust. The birth of belief.

As a child, I didn't understand the act of throwing salt into the air while praying or what it could mean. Now, as an adult, I can see through scripture it symbolized faith and purity. Like Elisha, who used salt as a symbol of cleansing and transformation, trusting God to answer his act of faith, my childlike prayer carried the same essence of innocence and trust.

In 2 Kings 2:20-22, (*NIV*) Elisha says,

"'Bring me a new bowl,' he said, 'and put salt in it.' So, they brought it to him. Then he went out to the spring and threw the salt into it, saying, 'This is what the Lord says: I have healed this water. Never again will it cause death or make the land unproductive.' And the water has remained pure to this day, according to the word Elisha had spoken."

Reflecting now, I realize my innocent act was never just about the snow.

I was offering something unseen. Something holy. Perhaps, without even knowing it, I was releasing something greater – an unspoken prayer, a hidden act of faith that would ripple through time – a seed God would use as a catalyst for transformation, healing and redemption in my family's story. Even then, He was answering prayers I didn't yet have the words to speak.

Much like Joseph, who couldn't have known the pit was part of the path to the palace, I could not have known a handful of salt flung into the winter air was part of a much bigger story.

THE KNOCK THAT CHANGED EVERYTHING

What began with a child's unspoken act of faith was about to collide with heaven's intervention. The next movement in God's redemptive plan came not with a whisper, but with a knock. A sound that shattered the fragile illusion we called life, tore open the secrets we had buried, and marked the day everything changed. As social workers quickly led my mother away into the bedroom we shared, we stood frozen, watching helplessly as the delicate walls of our world crumbled around us.

The air grew heavy with unspoken grief. I couldn't tell whether my mother's stoic expression was a sign of resignation or a silent surrender after years of emotional turmoil. Perhaps, the burden of being a single parent had finally crushed what remained of her strength. Or perhaps something even deeper was unfolding. Whatever the case, that day marked a turning point in our lives, and we were forced to confront the harsh reality of our situation head-on.

The sorrow my mother must have carried – losing her four beloved children in a single, irreversible moment – is a depth of pain I can scarcely imagine. It shattered whatever fragile beauty she had managed to build from her broken pieces. Even Saber, our loyal canine companion, must have been sent to a shelter I pray led him to a loving home where he could live out the rest of his years wrapped in kindness.

My mother's love for us was a unique and potent force, burning with a ferocity that only she could give. Yet, as strong as her love was, it wasn't enough to shield us from what was to come. Her pride, once the backbone of her survival, had quietly refused to seek help until it was too late. This was her untold story, a secret she harbored deep within. And on the day heaven sent that knock to our door, her hidden story was forced into the light. The life we knew ended with that sound – and a new chapter of redemption, still unseen, began.

THE SILENT RIDE TO THE CHILDREN'S HOME

As social workers quietly questioned our mother behind closed doors, the decision was made none of us could undo. One by one, we were led away – beginning with my two oldest brothers who were placed in the first police car. Their faces resigned but their eyes betraying the fear we all felt. My little brother and I were placed in the second police car, where we clung to each other as though we were all the other had left in the world. The stillness in the car was deafening, broken only by the rhythmic hum of the engine—a sound that seemed to echo the unanswered questions circling in my mind.

Allen County Children's Home was an emergency shelter facility, a place meant to provide safety for youth aged 6 – 18 who had endured abuse, neglect, or delinquency. My three older siblings and I would soon be added to that number.

As the car drove through the unfamiliar streets, the weight of separation from my mother settled heavily in my heart. The world outside blurred into shades of gray, matching the emptiness I felt inside. Eventually, the monotonous motion of the car lulled me to sleep, but it wasn't the kind of sleep that brought peace. It was restless with fears and the unshakable uncertainty of what awaited us at the end of this ride.

When we arrived, I opened my eyes to see a cluster of red brick buildings with gray roofs sprawled across acres of land. This would be our home now. The car door opened, and we stepped out, holding onto the few belongings we could take. Wiping the sleep from my eyes, I held on tightly to my tan plastic bunny rabbit - the only belonging I was allowed to take into this unknown world. No suitcase, no extra clothes, just the outfit on my back ....and the memories of my mother in my heart.

THE ROLLER SKATES AND THE MAKE-BELIEVE BIRTHDAY

The officer gently guided me and my brother up the steps to the looming entrance of the children's home. I held on tight to my brother's hand, both of us freshly removed from the only world we knew – one of chaos, survival and silence.

The shelter doors creaked open, swallowing our small bodies into a new kind of unknown. No one had explained why we were there. All we knew was that everything familiar had vanished, and we were now in the hands of strangers.

The world inside the children's home was loud, busy, and overwhelming. Children moved in every direction, their faces etched with stories of loss, resilience, and uncertainty.

As my eyes adjusted, I spotted a little girl clutching a staff member's hand. She was leaving, her arms overflowing with treasures: a baby doll, roller skates, and other toys. My gaze fixated on the roller skates – white with tan wheels and long white laces. I'd never roller-skated before, still I wanted nothing more at that moment.

In my six-year-old mind, I hatched a perfect plan. Excitement bubbled up, erasing my worries momentarily, "My birthday is coming!" I blurted out, hoping it would be my golden ticket to getting skates like hers.

The intake worker leaned in, intrigued. "Oh, when is your birthday, honey?" she asked, her eyes sparkling with curiosity.

"Next week!" I declared with a huge smile, as I volunteered information on what my presents should be. Truthfully, I didn't know when my birthday was; I only cared about those shiny roller skates and the pretty baby doll the other girl held.

For a fleeting moment, God gave me the gift of turning my attention to the simple hope of getting roller skates, rather than the devastating reality that I had been ripped away from my mother. In the middle of chaos, my innocent hope transformed the overwhelming noise around me into something lighter. A pair of roller skates would make everything okay again – at least in my little mind – even though no one promised me they would come. It was a fragile thread of joy I clung to, a small reminder that even here, even now, dreams still exist.

CRYING UNDER THE PIANO: THE LAST VISIT

Soon, my delicate sense of security would be shattered when I found out the children's home separated the boys from the girls. As I waved goodbye to my brother, my heart ached. He eagerly joined our two oldest siblings in the boys' quarters, while I was taken away to the girls' dormitory, feeling more alone than ever.

The enormous room I entered felt foreign, with rows of neatly made beds lining both walls, much like the dormitory in the movie, *Little Orphan Annie*. The cheerful resemblance did little to comfort me. I was six, but lost and afraid. During the uncertainty, one teenage girl who sensed my fear became a source of comfort. With quiet compassion, she became my guardian angel, making sure I was safe in a world that felt foreign and unforgiving.

The first few weeks blurred together in a haze of tears and sadness. On the first day, I wandered into the lobby, desperate to escape the overwhelming turmoil. I spotted a large black piano, and without hesitation, crawled underneath it – searching for a place to anchor my soul while quietly wishing I could disappear.

I sobbed uncontrollably, my mind spinning with questions - Where was my mother? Why weren't we together? The case manager eventually found me, her voice laced with both concern and urgency. Yet, no amount of coaxing could quiet my cries. Hours passed before I was finally persuaded to return to my dorm, yet the heaviness in my heart remained heavy.

The next day, I crawled back under the piano, searching for solace in the shadows of confusion. Then, unexpectedly, I felt familiar arms wrap around me – strong, tender, and unmistakably hers. My mother.

"Bobbie," a staff member had said earlier, "your daughter has been crying under the piano inconsolably. She needs to see you."

I don't remember seeing her face or hearing her approach. She simply crawled beneath the piano and pulled me close. For a moment, the pain quieted. I can't recall if she spoke, or if she cried - but none of that mattered. Her presence was enough.

Her visit was brief, and it would be the last time I would see her. When she left, it felt as though a door had quietly closed on my life. Something within me shifted. The tears dried up, and in their place, a quiet resilience settled in. Maybe it was her love that remained…or perhaps something greater, watching over me.

AN UNEXPECTED CELEBRATION: A GLIMMER OF JOY

The children's home ran on strict rules and ridged routines. We earned tokens by completing daily chores - tokens we could use at the general store to buy clothes, candy, toys, and toiletries. The thought of what I might one day afford kept me going, even though deep down, I doubted I'd ever save enough for the things I longed for most —a pair of white roller skates or a beautiful baby doll.

One day, a group of girls in my dorm pooled their tokens and surprised me with a surprise party. I'm not sure if they felt sorry for me, yet I believe it was God who moved in their hearts to bless me.

As the door to our dorm swung open, I froze.

"Surprise!" they shouted.

I stood in shock - streamers, cake, gifts – everything was for me. Joy rushed in like a wave as I opened each present, surrounded by their sincere smiles and laughter. I struggled to find the words to express my gratitude. Then, among the gifts, I saw her – the baby doll I had dreamed of.

I turned to them and whispered my thanks. For a moment, the weight of my reality lifted. I would carry this memory into the darker days ahead - a reminder that God could bring joy even into the most barren places.

CHAPTER 6:

THE ENEMY'S TARGET: MY VULNERABLE SOUL

"...The enemy shall come in like a flood, the Spirit of the Lord shall lift up a standard against him."
(Isaiah 59:19, *KJV*)

Each morning, we gathered on the hard classroom floor to learn the basics of reading, writing, and numbers. Occasionally, I caught glimpses of my brothers across the room. They seemed more at ease that I was – maybe because they had each other. However, I felt alone and unsure how to process what was happening around me.

Recess offered a brief escape. I remember one afternoon when I raced my youngest brother down the long sidewalk and won. That rare victory filled me with a flicker of joy. Yet, even in that moment, sadness overshadowed me.

My mother was nowhere to be found. Her absence grew louder with each passing day, a growing ache I couldn't quiet. Being separated from her and labeled an orphan, left wounds I didn't have language for. I clung to moments of kindness, but the deeper trauma had already taken root. It lived beneath the surface.

The children's home became the birthplace of a war I couldn't name - spiritual warfare that wrapped itself around my soul. I didn't know what to call it. But I felt it's weight.

Something dark moved quietly in the background, waiting for me to break.

Trauma cracked open my young soul, leaving me exposed to the enemy's earliest assaults.

Emotional. Spiritual. Identity–based.

Rejection. Isolation. Abandonment.

Fear. Shame.

A million unnamed arrows, each aimed with precision.

Issues lying dormant, waiting to stagnate my future. The children's home wasn't just a place of transition - it was a battlefield. And I was already under attack.

The enemy targeted me young - planting lies before I even knew how to fight back.

THE WAR BEGINS: THE DIABOLICAL STRATEGY

Before the children's home, rejection hadn't taken root in me. Even with the instability of my mother's care, I still belonged to someone. Her parenting – though imperfect – anchored me.

When she was suddenly removed from my life, that anchor was violently ripped away. I was left uncovered, and emotionally unguarded. That's when the enemy moved in - swift and calculated - like a skilled predator who knew his prey had been left exposed.

I was uncovered.

Looking back, I see how vital a parent's presence is to a child's sense of identity and self-worth. Without Mother, I lost my grounding. I became an open target for the enemy, who wasn't merely after my emotions, but my destiny. The enemy struck early, attempting to shape how I saw myself long before I understood who I was in God.

At night, I lay awake, staring at the ceiling, drowning in unanswered questions, the dark felt too wide. The silence, too loud.

And the questions came:

Where is my mother?

Why hasn't she come for me?

Has she forgotten me?

Does anyone see me?

The walls weren't just encircling my body - they were suffocating my soul. Loneliness wrapped around me like a thick fog, pressing in with a weight I couldn't name.

The silence wasn't just an absence of noise. It was the sound of neglect, of unanswered cries, of silent prayers I wasn't sure any one was listening to. It was grief without language.

I wasn't just lonely.

I was spiritually unprotected. Emotionally unguarded. Physically unseen.

The enemy didn't see a helpless child - he saw a ferocious threat to his kingdom – a future warrior. So, he struck early, planting seeds of destruction before I had the wisdom to recognize his schemes. His goal was clear: to trap me in cycles of pain, trauma, and rejection - replaying them until they became my truth and rendered me powerless.

You are unwanted.

You are unworthy.

You are unloved.

I didn't know it then, but I was in the midst of a spiritual war – one not fought with swords or fists - it was waged against my mind, and my emotions, and distorted my identity. The enemy wasn't trying to kill me physically. He was trying to destroy my destiny. To steal my voice. To rewrite my identity long before I discovered who I was in Christ. To destroy my ability to believe I was anything more than what my circumstances told me I was.

His strategy was subtle, but deadly: to blind me to who I was in God, so I'd never walk in the authority heaven had endorsed me to walk in. If he could convince me I was worthless, he could keep me from ever believing I was chosen – handpicked by God for a greater purpose.

WORDS SPOKEN IN DARKNESS THAT
SHAPE DESTRUCTION

At night, the dormitory came alive. The teenage girls huddled in corners, whispering secrets and trading stories soaked in rebellion, pain, and the neglect that had bought them to the children's home. One girl stood at the foot of my bed nearly every night. Pregnant, defiant, her fiery red hair catching the dim light like a warning flare. She spoke freely about her boyfriend, her choices that led to her pregnancy, and the taboo subject of sex.

Something in me shifted. A knowing. A warning. Deep down, I felt I wasn't supposed to hear what she was saying. At six years old, I didn't know how to shield myself. Her words weren't just stories; they were spiritual doorways. Portals of rebellion, lust, and perversion. I didn't recognize it as the time, but unclean spirits latched on, slipping through the cracks of my wounded soul. These weren't just conversations – they were weapons, and I didn't yet have the armor to defend myself.

Scripture warns us, "Do not be misled: Bad company corrupts good character" (I Corinthians 15:33). I hadn't sinned - but I had been exposed. And that was enough. Enough for the enemy to plant the seeds of destruction that would grow into internal wars I'd fight for years.

The Bible also says, "Death and life are in the power of the tongue..." (Proverbs 18:21). Words carry spiritual weight. They are either vessels of truth and life – or arrows of destruction. As a child, unguarded and unseen, those words entered my spirit and sowed confusion, emotional struggle, and spiritual bondage.

NO WEAPON FORMED WILL PROPSER

Even as the enemy sought to rewrite my identity and taint my purity, God had already authored a greater one – one of redemption, healing and restoration. The enemy's aim was to fill my emptiness with everything except God. Still the truth is: only God could make me whole.

The enemy's power is limited. Yes, sin gives him legal access, however, God's grace is greater. Through repentance and surrender, every foothold the enemy gains can be broken. That's why Ephesians 4:27 warns, "Do not give the devil a foothold." God doesn't call us to purity just to avoid shame – He calls us to it because purity protects. It guards the sacred spaces of our soul and keeps us aligned with His Spirit.

The enemy had a plan: to reroute my future, rob me of my identity, and separate me from God's purpose. Even as I look back on every door the enemy tried to open, I now see the deeper truth – God's power to shut those doors, heal my wounds, and restore what was broken.

Redemption didn't just save me—it awakened me. It gave me clarity. I finally understood that God's call to holiness wasn't about just about following rules but walking in true freedom – the kind of freedom that brings ultimate peace.

"Don't you realize that your body is the temple of the Holy Spirit, who lives in you and was given to you by God? You do not belong to yourself, for God bought you at a high price. So, you must honor God with your body" (1 Corinthians 6:19–20).

The redemption God offers doesn't just heal our wounds—it reclaims our identity and sets us on the path to walk fully in His purpose. The enemy's oldest trick is to corrupt innocence—especially in childhood—hoping to send us on a lifelong search for fulfillment in everything but God. Only God can satisfy. Only God can restore what's been lost. And in time, He would show me just how powerful His redemption truly was.

UNSPOKEN WORDS FOR A FORGOTTEN CHILD

Another tactic the enemy used to distort my identity was silence - the absence of life-giving words spoken over my fragile, searching soul. No one on staff ever pulled me aside to say, "You are loved," or "God has a plan for you." No one told me that even though I was an orphan—unsure of where my mother or father was—there was a God who saw me.

No one reminded me God longed to be my mother and my father, the One who would adopt me into His family and give me an identity beyond my circumstances. They didn't see the invisible scars the enemy had etched across my heart, scars that cried out for someone to notice, someone to care.

No motherly figure ever pulled me close to whisper words of comfort or pray strength into my heart. No one ever said, "You are more than this moment, and your future is brighter than you can imagine. You will impact this world monumentally for Jesus Christ!" Instead, the silence screamed. It echoed in empty rooms and long nights, slicing through my soul louder than any voice could have.

My soul cried out in agony for anyone to believe in me and guide me toward my destiny, which I couldn't see yet desperately hoped existed.

And so, my tender soul began to crumble from within. I sought refuge in a secret world—a quiet inner fortress where I was unreachable, where I convinced myself, I was safe from harm. If those entrusted to protect me had failed, how could I trust anyone else? In the shadows of this imaginary refuge, I was in control. I learned to protect the last pieces of myself, even if it meant hiding away forever.

THE ADOPTION THAT ALMOST WAS

Then, one day, something unexpected happened.

I was told to wear my best dress. Then I was called into a room where a woman with gentle eyes and soft blonde hair knelt before me and said, "Hi, Michelle, my name is Anne."

She wanted to adopt me and my younger brother. She visited often, bringing small gifts, brushing my hair, gently trying to reach the parts of me I had already started hiding.

When she took me to McDonald's, hoping to break through my silence, I could barely eat or respond to her questions. Her efforts were genuine, yet my young heart was guarded.

Still, Anne began the adoption process, hopeful to bring me and my youngest brother into her family.

However, Indiana law prioritized placing children with relatives. When my mother's sister and brother stepped forward, the plan shifted. My youngest brother and I were sent to live with our aunt, while my two older brothers went to live with our uncle.

It wasn't the ending Anne had hoped for. And it wasn't the reunion with my mother I desperately needed.

It was just another door that almost opened – and didn't.

CHAPTER 7:

THE ROAD TOWARD UNCONDITIONAL LOVE IN THE MOTOR CITY

"For I know the plans I have for you," declares the Lord, "plans to prosper you and not to harm you, plans to give you a hope and a future."
(Jeremiah 29:11, *NIV*)

LEAVING THE CHILDREN'S HOME: THE SEEDS OF BATTLE TAKE ROOT

Leaving the children's home didn't mean leaving the war behind. The seeds the enemy had sown - rejection, fear, abandonment - were still buried deep inside. I wasn't walking away from the battlefield; I was carrying it with me.

The whispers of unworthiness, the wounds of silence, the unseen scars – they all followed me. And now, those battles would no longer be contained within the walls of the children's home. They would spill into the real world, shaping my journey, testing my identity, and haunting every attempt to belong.

The day I left felt surreal. I packed my few belongings – including my skates I had longed for – and hugged the teenage girls goodbye.

As the car pulled away, I turned to see the staff and other children waving from the doorway, their outlines blurred by tears and memory. A swirl of emotion filled me with sadness, fear, and a flicker of hope.

I didn't know where life was taking me, yet I knew this:

I wasn't just leaving with skates. I was leaving with an inner toughness, a growing instinct to survive.

Still, that toughness came at a cost. I was already learning how to wall myself off – layer by layer – from a world I didn't trust.

As the car drove toward my new life, I whispered silently, "Maybe one day, my mother will come back for me."

A TEMPORARY HOME WITH RELATIVES

When we arrived at my aunt and uncle's home, they welcomed us warmly. My aunt bore a striking resemblance to our mother, though her skin was lighter and her voice full of love.

With six children of her own, the home was full of life. I stayed with my cousins; my brother bunked with the boys.

Life in my aunt's house marked a new chapter – one filled with unfamiliar faces and even a different rhythm. Still, we were grateful for the shelter and care provided. My uncle, a hardworking mechanic, often slipped us small amounts of money and words of encouragement. His acts of grace were quiet, but powerful. His kindness made us feel seen in a way that took away the sting of us being orphans. My aunt, who carried the weight of long workdays and many responsibilities – showed her love through discipline, helping us realign with the structure and values we'd been missing.

After a few months, just as we were settling into this new life, everything changed again. My aunt must have called my father. Then, one afternoon, he showed up, his warm smile reassuring. We learned we were leaving with him and climbed into the backseat of his car. Beside him sat a newly discovered half-brother, who had a faint resemblance to my father.

THE JOURNEY INTO THE UNKNOWN

My brother and I sat quietly, as we began the three-hour journey from Fort Wayne to Detroit.

My father had traveled this road many times to visit us. But this time was different. This time we were fragile, displaced and now his.

No doubt, he had heard that our mother was missing, and now the children he once cared for from a distance would soon be his full responsibility, living under his roof. Not for a weekend. For good.

The late afternoon softened as we drove, slowing giving way to dusk. I stared silently out the window, trying to process the whirlwind of emotions inside me. The world rushed by. Trees. Signs. Sky. My mind unsure.

No one spoke.

The air was still. The only sound was the low hum of music crackling through the speakers.

Within a year, my brother and I had endured more than most children do in a lifetime – removed from our mother, placed in a children's home, moved to relatives, now starting over with a father we barely knew in a new state.

The weight of it was too big for my little body. Too heavy for my small heart. It was a lot for anyone to carry—especially for two young children.

The sun slowly set behind us as we crossed state lines, leaving behind our two older brothers and our beloved mother. We didn't understand why they stayed. We only knew this: we had each other.

I felt like a ragdoll - tossed from place to place, forced to adapt without breaking.

No one asked how I felt.

Maybe they didn't know how.

So, I held my confusion close, swallowing the storm inside me.

Strangely, a calmness washed over me as the vibration of the tires on the road lulled me to sleep.

ARRIVING AT A NEW REALITY

When I woke, we were parked outside a brightly lit diner—a classic 24-hour spot where coffee pots never ran dry.

My father stepped out and disappeared inside.

Moments later, he emerged – but he wasn't alone. Walking beside him was a beautiful woman whose presence felt - different. She was petite, with caramel skin, flowing black hair, and delicate features that radiated kindness.

"Hi, how are you two?" she asked, her voice warm, her smile wrapping around us like a soft blanket.

We both murmured a shy "hello," unsure of who she was but sensing she was important.

After dropping our half-brother off, we continued driving. I assumed we were taking the nice woman home - until I asked.

"Are we going to drop her off at her home?" I said suddenly, even surprising myself – after barely speaking a word the entire ride, and now this.

She turned to me and smiled gently. "I live here, sweetheart."

Her words landed softly, but with quiet finality. I couldn't yet process what they meant.

MORE THAN A HOUSE: A POSSIBILITY FOR HOME

Then we turned down a street lined with stately homes and pulled into a long driveway beside a massive red-brick house.

It looked like a mansion.

As we exited the car, my eyes widened in awe. The glowing porch lights illuminated the massive white columns that framed the home. The yard was manicured, and the row of bushes trimmed with care lined the red tile porch.

Towering before us, the three-story home was covered in windows and dressed in elegant drapery. It felt like something out of a storybook. And for the first time in a long time, my heart dared to believe: maybe this is good. Maybe this is safe.

We stepped inside of the grand foyer, enclosed by a stunning French glass door with a crystal lever handle, and burgundy tiled flooring. Past the small waiting area was a green carpeted staircase that seemed to stretch to heaven. It felt endless. Regal.

The home was immaculate, curated with sleek modern pieces that seemed both timeless and intentional. The furniture belonged in a museum.

My father, a gifted artist, had styled every corner like a gallery:

- A Milo Baughman rosewood-encased sofa
- A red Womb chair
- A Herman Miller black leather lounge chair with a molded wood backing

My attention was particularly drawn to a striking coffee table. Its base, a cluster of slender golden rods, converged gracefully at the center and flared outward beneath a glass top. Later, I'd learn it was one of Warren Platner's designs for Knoll.

His artwork graced the walls – abstract swirls of movement and color, each piece layered with meaning. Like his black and white painting whose intersecting lines captured the tension and imbalance of systemic racism, highlighting how deeply it affected the lives of Black Americans. Family portraits lined the staircase, capturing moments of connection and history.

To the left, a formal dining room stretched wide, its mirrored walls, reflecting endless space. Down the hallway, more rooms whispered of elegance and mystery.

Built in 1921, the house stood tall at 3,500-square-feet-imposing yet warm as if to say:

You are safe here.

You can breathe now.

You may begin again.

And for a fleeting moment, I let myself hope.

Maybe this place could become home.

Maybe, for once, I could let go of survival.... and rest.

CHAPTER 8:

"ANGEL MOTHER" – A MOTHER'S LOVE BEYOND MEASURE

"Love bears all things, believes all things,
hopes all things, endures all things."
(I Corinthians 13:7, *ESV*)

THE CHOICE TO LOVE BEYOND PAIN

It was nearing midnight, and exhaustion weighed on all of us. The kind woman led my brother and me to our bedroom, where neatly folded pajamas, awaited us - a simple gesture that spoke volumes. That night, wrapped in warm blankets, I drifted into the deepest sleep, comforted by my brother nearby.

The next day, she called me downstairs. Standing on the staircase, she held a large bag.

"Go ahead, take a look," she said, her smile steady as she lovingly handed me the bag.

My heart raced as I opened it and looked inside at brightly colored clothes, each one perfectly my size. I pulled out outfit after outfit and could hardly contain my joy. Though I lacked the words then, my heart swelled with gratitude.

Two weeks later, she asked what we wanted to call her.

Without hesitation, my brother said, "Angel Mother."

From that moment, forward, she became our Angel Mother – a title that felt like a claim to the motherly love we so desperately needed. A covering. A miracle.

BEAUTY FORGED BY FIRE

"My beauty didn't come cheap. It's God's masterpiece, shaped by the hands of time and wrapped in the uncertainties of life - a mosaic of strength, sacrifice, and silent battles won in the shadows. It radiates a luminous resilience, not because it was unscathed, rather because it endured – refined by fire and still standing radiant for all to see. My beauty cost me everything."
- Michelle B. Wilson, author, *In Search of a Mother's Love.*

Angel Mother's beauty carried an unspoken depth - one that went beyond flawless skin or striking features. It was wrapped in quiet dignity. It was sculpted by survival, resilience, and silent battles. Her past was marred by betrayals and wounds unseen, yet she chose love over bitterness. Her elegance wasn't just in her appearance but in her unwavering strength and grace etched into every movement, every gesture.

Perhaps that's why she stayed.

Not because she thought she was unworthy of more –

Rather because exhaustion can distort reality and silence the will to fight.

A rescuing hope can also make you run into the arms of a complicated love - not one disfigured by fist or fury, but by a silent erosion of the soul. When you've escaped the fire, even a smoldering ember can feel like safety.

Dysfunction wears a smile. And sometimes, what doesn't bruise the body still wounds the heart. Love wrapped in charm but riddled with betrayal is its own kind of slow death.

She didn't wear her pain outwardly - it was woven into the fabric of her delicate poise. She had learned how to smile through sorrow, how to hold her head high despite the weight pressing down on her.

Yet, her toughness never hardened her. It only made her shine brighter.

A brilliance born not from ease – but from fire.

If life tried to break her, it had failed. Rather than diminish her, every trial carved out something even more striking in her essence.

Her presence commanded attention – not just because of her high cheekbones, radiant smile or the effortless elegance, but for the light that lived within her. There was a quiet magnetism that drew you in and a beauty that couldn't be ignored.

A striking photograph hung above the fireplace—one I often paused to admire.

In it, she wore a flowing green pleated gown with multicolored accents, the fabric cascading around her like a light. She radiated timeless beauty, the kind that didn't need embellishment to command attention.

She wasn't merely photogenic.

She was magnetic.

My father saw it too. Long before that portrait was framed, he had captured hundreds of images of her. She had trained at the Robert Powell Modeling School, and for him, she wasn't just a beautiful woman—she was his muse.

The camera loved her. More importantly, so did he - in his own complicated way.

Her elegance was undeniable - not in competition with my mother's, but distinct. Divine - in a league of its own. In both women, beauty wasn't just worn—it was lived.

THE INTERCESSORY PRAYER FOR MOTHER THAT CHANGED EVERYTHING

Yet even more beautiful than her outward appearance was her heart.

Though she wasn't a regular churchgoer at the time, her spirit was in tune with Heaven's frequency. And she would prove that in a way I never expected.

One evening, she called us into her bedroom.

"Come here, babies," she said softly. "Kneel, because we're going to pray. I want you to repeat after me."

She knelt at the foot of her bed, folding her hands near her chin. My brother and I followed her lead. Her voice was steady, full of conviction.

"Heavenly Father, thank you for your blessings. Bless our mother. Wherever she is, bring her safely back to us one day. In Jesus name, Amen."

At the time, I didn't grasp the depth of her gesture.

She had no reason to pray for the woman who had caused her so much pain. No reason to lead us in intercession for the very person who had confronted her while carrying me in her womb.

And yet, here she was – kneeling in humility, rising in power - teaching two children she didn't give birth to how to love through prayer, how to forgive through faith.

Her words became ours. And when I opened my eyes, I looked at her in wonder.

She wasn't just selfless. She was different.

Like an angel walking the earth.

That prayer did more than comfort – it activated something eternal. It planted another kind of seed – the tender beginning of my calling to intercede for lost souls, starting with the one who had given me life.

THE PAIN THAT ECHOED THROUGH GENERATIONS

Her family, however, struggled to understand her choices. To them, we were a painful reminders of the heartbreak Angel Mother had endured through my father's infidelities. And now, instead of leaving that past behind, she invited the pain into her home.

I was the child of the man who had betrayed her, and the truth was not easily forgotten. They struggled to accept us, not out of cruelty, but out of a deep, unresolved hurt. Their rejection was real, and so was their pain. To them, the love and devotion she poured into us could have been theirs.

Yet Angel Mother chose love, even when it didn't make sense. Even when it cost her dearly.

She could have turned away and said no. She could have let bitterness close the door. Instead, she opened her heart and let God's grace do what pride and self-preservation never could – start the journey of generational healing.

Her choice to embrace us was more than kindness - it was a lesson in unconditional love that would prepare me for my own journey of extending sacrificial love.

ANGEL MOTHER'S BEAUTY SHOP: WHERE HANDS HEAL AND HAIR GROWS

"Favor is deceitful, and beauty is vain: but a woman that feareth the Lord shall be praised."
(Proverbs 31:30, *KJV*)

My father worked at Chrysler in Highland Park while pursuing his master's degree in fine arts and humanities at Wayne State University. Focused and determined, he studied through every lunch break, a book in one hand and a sandwich in the other. It was during one of these moments that Angel Mother's mother, a co-worker, noticed him. Drawn to his kind demeanor and relentless drive, her suggestion would change their lives forever.

"I have a single daughter. I think you two should meet."

At the time, both my father and Angel Mother were coming out of failed marriages, each carrying the quiet hope of a fresh start. When they met, kindness and gentleness drew them together. Soon, they married, blending their families – my father's two children from his first marriage and Angel Mother's daughter from hers.

Always an entrepreneur, my father believed in ownership. He had built a successful custom photography business, so, when Angel Mother shared her dream of opening a beauty shop, he supported her without hesitation.

A trained model from the prestigious John Robert Powell School of Modeling, Angel Mother had walked the runways in Detroit. Yet, her true calling was cosmetology. With training from top schools in Boston, Chicago, and North Carolina - including Virginia Farrell and Dudley Cosmetology University – she had already built a reputation for her "hair-growing hands." Now, it was time to open her own shop.

She found the perfect location on Fenkell Avenue and opened her beauty shop she named, "Net Set Hair Fashion," also known around town as the Net Set. Her creative genius was evident from the moment you stepped inside. Delicate nets draped the entrances and workstations, while seashells—white and glistening like pearls—adorned the space. The shop radiated a tropical beach vibe like you'd been transported to a serene Hawaiian oasis.

Angel Mother poured her heart and soul into the Net Set, and her talent as a hairdresser quickly made it a success. The shop's eight booths were always filled because hairstylists knew working under her meant thriving. She generously shared her expertise, keeping her team ahead of industry trends. More than a salon, the Net Set became a hub where beauty, business, and community converged. Her reputation as a skilled beautician—and her warm, welcoming personality—drew clients from far and wide, eager to experience her anointed touch.

I'll never forget my first experience in her chair, perched on stacked telephone books so my head could reach the shampoo bowl. By now, Angel Mother had given me my endearing nickname, "Mademoiselle Michelle," or my favorite – "Missy." Every time she said those names, her voice was filled with love and affection, making me feel special, as though I truly mattered in her eyes.

"Come on, Missy, and sit on these books," she'd say with a laugh, carefully draping the black cape around my neck after wrapping it in paper neck strips. I was so ticklish I'd squirm and giggle uncontrollably.

"Still ticklish, Missy?" she'd tease with a knowing smile.

"Yes, ma'am," I'd laugh, clutching her hand as she secured the strip.

Her hands were heavenly washing away more than just the day's dirt. It was something deeper, something healing. The rhythmic lather, the warm rinse, the deep conditioning—it felt like a quiet, unspoken kind of love. And when she finished styling my hair, I felt brand new.

I would observe the busy hum of the shop—women chatting, laughing, and basking in the warmth of her presence. As they sat in her chair and received the final curl from her sizzling curling iron, she'd style it out with care, then hand them the mirror so they could admire the finished look – crowned with that signature touch only she could give. Clients often lingered long after their appointments, soaking in her joy. She made everyone feel like the most important person in the room.

I had my weekly appointment with Angel Mother and without fail, after every visit, I'd look up at her and say, "Thank you." She'd nod, smiling softly.

"You're welcome, Missy."

My heart was full of gratitude for every gesture of love she freely shared and I made sure she knew it.

As I revisit that season, I realize how much she gave—not just to me; to everyone around her.

Angel Mother wasn't just a skilled businesswoman and a talented hairdresser; she was a beacon of love and grace, creating a space where everyone felt seen, cared for, and uplifted. Her ability to give so selflessly was a testament to the depth of her beautiful heart.

HOLIDAYS: JOYFUL SEASONS OF CHILDHOOD

"And the angel said unto them, Fear not: for, behold, I bring you good tidings of great joy, which shall be to all people."
(Luke 2:10, *KJV*)

Our first Christmas in the new home wasn't magical in the traditional sense—it was something deeper. For the first time, we weren't spectators but participants. Angel Mother handed me a box of ornaments, giving me the honor of decorating the tree. My little hands placed red and gold balls on the branches while garlands and tinsel shimmered beneath twinkling lights. My father crowned the tree with a brilliant star, its glow whispering promises of hope.

Red stockings hung above the fireplace, each stitched with a name. Seeing mine filled me with warmth—it meant I belonged. Inside were simple treasures: peppermint sticks, walnuts, oranges. The scent of pine and cinnamon filled the house.

Christmas morning arrived with a mix of excitement and curiosity. We didn't rush to tear open a mountain of presents; instead, Angel Mother and our father encouraged us to savor the moment. They taught us the importance of moderation, reminding us that the season wasn't about excess rather gratitude and togetherness, and celebrating the birth of Christ.

My father - wanting to capture our first Christmas together - set up his camera on an automatic timer. He positioned my brother and me in front of the tree as I held on to Yellow Doll - my beloved crocheted doll with the bright yellow dress and yarn hair. He stood behind us and smiled.

Click.

The shutter froze the moment in time—a memory of love, of new beginnings, of family.

One of my favorite toys was a talking robot, that taught me science, math, and history basics, sparking a curiosity I hadn't known. My brother received a train set and an art kit.

Every holiday became special. Easter egg hunts, laughter, pastel-colored dresses. These moments weren't just traditions—they were healing. They proved joy could rise from loss and laid the foundation of the love I had always longed for.

CHAPTER 9:

ECHOES OF AN UNSPOKEN CRY

"The Lord is close to the broken-hearted and saves those crushed in spirit."
(Psalm 34:18, *NIV*)

"The human heart is astonishingly resilient – built to endure, to rebound, to beat on through the storms of life. Yet in the fragile hands of trauma, even the strongest spirit can begin to fray like a thread unraveling. For a child – especially one too young to name their pain or chart the path to healing – the damage doesn't scream; it whispers. The wound hides in plain sight, quietly scripting the chapters that follow, shaping a life in shadows long before the light ever returns."

– Michelle B. Wilson, author, *In Search of a Mother's Love.*

SCHOOL DAYS: A CRY FOR HELP

I began the second grade with Mrs. Lee Davis, a teacher whose warmth became a refuge. Although she didn't know my story, it was like she sensed the heaviness of my burdens, and her kindness reached the silent ache inside me. Her classroom felt like a sanctuary, where I was chosen, seen, and celebrated for things like handwriting and reading – simple affirmations that soothed wounds I couldn't name.

Beyond that room, the ache of separation still followed me. Though life with Angel Mother and my father was stable, my heart remained tethered to what I'd lost - my mother's absence, my older brothers' distance, and the quiet sorrow of not seeing my youngest brother in class. I felt adrift, struggling to connect beyond the walls I'd built for protection. I clung to academic perfection, hoping good grades could steady the ground beneath me.

Angel Mother filled our home with warmth – dinners cooked with care and my school lunches packed with love. Yet even in abundance, scarcity had left its imprint. I ate more than I needed, as if excess could silence the fear of going without. Only God saw the storm raging inside me beneath my calm exterior.

When I received my first report card, my heart pounded with anticipation. A row of S marks – Satisfactory – lined the page. Joy swelled in me. Maybe now I'd earn approval, to quiet the lies that whispered I was unworthy.

"Great job, Missy!" Angel Mother beamed.

My father, ever the educator, studied the card and nodded, "This is what I expect from you."

His words taught me: success was the only currency that mattered.

For a moment, I basked in their praise, feeling worthy, if only briefly. Still, beneath the surface, there was a silent ache that never faded. I had learned how to hide it. Yet, at school, emotions surfaced, raw and unfiltered.

One day, the principal, a frail woman with greying hair and a dress that looked stitched from faded curtains – stepped into our classroom. My classmates snickered at her tired appearance. Yet, something stirred in me. Compassion surged, and I felt an instinctive need to protect her from their ridicule. When she left the room, their laughter lingered like smoke, and tears welled in my eyes before I could stop them.

"Why is Michelle crying?" someone whispered.

Yet, I couldn't explain. How could I? The grief was deeper than words. My world had altered too suddenly, and my heart was still catching up. I was still in shock – not just from the changes in my life – but from the instability of the past that clung to me. The world around me seemed harsher because of it, every moment a reminder of what I had endured.

Later I would understand this sensitivity was a gift—a budding discernment, a deep empathy that allowed me to feel the emotions of others as if they were my own. At the time, it felt like a curse.

Then one day, my teacher gently pulled me aside.

"Michelle, why are you crying so much?"

I froze. Could I tell her the truth? That I missed my mother? That I didn't know where she was? That I longed for her to come back? The words stayed trapped in my throat.

"Did someone threaten to hurt you?" she asked, her concern genuine.

I shook my head.

"Then why all the tears?"

Finally, I whispered, "I'm in a new school," hoping it would satisfy her.

She nodded, however her searching eyes told me she wasn't convinced.

When my next report card came, the academic praise remained – but now, a new comment appeared: "Needs improvement in behavior."

The words stung. My pain had betrayed me. I was no longer the perfect student. I was broken in the eyes of others.

Yet, my father and Angel Mother never mentioned it. Perhaps they explained to her the massive changes I had endured – perhaps they told her about my mother's absence. Because after that, she never asked again. Even as the tears continued, her questions stopped. Yet, the students continued to notice.

"Michelle is crying again."

Then, something unexpected happened - my father enrolled me in the school choir. I had never sung before, yet as I slipped into a crisp white shirt, black skirt, and polished black shoes, I felt a glimmer of something new.

As we sang the rhythmic beauty of *Edelweiss* and *You Are the Wind Beneath My Wings*, something awakened inside me.

For the first time, I felt my voice mattered. My presence mattered. As our harmony rose, the weight inside me lifted. For a moment, I wasn't the girl with hidden tears – I was a girl who could soar through the gift of music.

SHE AIN'T YOUR MAMA: THE INVISIBLE WEIGHT OF NEVER BELONGING

"And I am certain that God, who began the good work within you, will continue His work until it is finally finished on the day Christ Jesus returns."
(Philippians 1:6, *NLT*)

"She ain't your mama," one of the kids who was visiting our home blurted out, shattering the fragile illusion I clung to. Their words struck like a hammer against thin glass, cracking the safe world I thought I had finally entered. I wasn't prepared – not in that moment when I had just begun to feel seen, even safe. Yet, their dagger dragged me back to a harsh truth: I was living in a house that wasn't fully mine, with a family that didn't fully welcome me.

A woman in the family, old enough to be my mother, often made her disdain of my presence clear, "Why are you always under her?" she once asked me with a sharpness I didn't understand. I was too young to grasp the depth of her bitterness, still, I felt the sting of her hatred. Her words became another brick in the growing wall of rejection I was building around myself – quiet, invisible, and weighty.

The rejection had roots deeper than Angel Mother's home. I still lived in the aftermath of being locked in a basement with my brother, listening to the laughter of other children playing just outside the window above us. I still heard the echoes - being called greedy, and the aching sense that my presence was a burden, not a blessing. Overtime, I learned to shrink myself, to become nonexistent. Being undetectable felt safer than risking more rejection.

When Angel Mother's family visited, I made myself scarce. I waited until the kitchen was empty before quietly slipping in to eat. In my young mind, being seen eating was another opportunity for judgment – another reason to be disliked.

I never felt truly welcomed. I'd enter a room and feel it shift – smiles tightened, laughter dimmed, conversations paused.

"They talk about you really bad," someone close to their circle once confided. Deep down, I already knew. The atmosphere said what words never had to. Their presence made it clear: You don't belong here.

And yet, I didn't understand why.
What had I done to deserve their scorn?
Why did my presence stir so much discomfort?
I carried these questions in silence never daring to lash out. Just an aching wonder that never found a clear answer – at least not until years later.

PHOTOGRAPHS OF A MISSING MOTHER:
A DAUGHTER'S ESCAPE

Even with the steadfast love of Angel Mother, the rejection and my longing for acceptance only deepened. I craved the comfort I once knew with my own mother – a place where I felt seen and accepted without question. Though I had no idea where she was, something inside me told me she wasn't dead. She couldn't be.

I clung to the only tangible connection I had left – photographs of her.

They were more than just pictures; they were my lifeline. Each image, taken by my father, captured glimpses of the woman who had once held and cherished me. They became a window into a world I longed to return to; of a mother I desperately wanted to embrace again.

When emotions overwhelmed me – when sadness lingered too long or anger burned too hot – I retreated to my room, with my secret diary in one hand, and her photographs in the other.

There, I poured out my frustrations in private, my emotions spilling onto the pages in ways I couldn't express aloud. My diary became my outlet, and when the words weren't enough to release my pain, I turned to the photographs.

One picture captured her youth and elegance in a single frame — standing outdoors by a fence with shimmering water in the background she wore a lace scarf draped lightly over her hair. Her simple, white spaghetti-strapped sundress caught the light with her hands folded gently in front of her. The breeze seemed to carry her happiness, sealed forever in her radiant smile. I often stared at that picture, wondering if she was truly happy when it was taken, or if she had mastered the art of hiding her pain behind a smile like I had begun to do.

I would trace her face with my fingertips as if touching the photo might somehow bridge the distance. Sometimes, I'd flip the picture over and write desperate messages on the back:

"Mama, come home."

Or simply, "Mama."

They were more than words. They were my prayers. My pleas to God, my whispered hopes that somehow would cross the distance between us and bring her back to me. In those moments, staring at her frozen smile, I could almost feel her presence - if only in my imagination.

Looking back, I realize now: it wasn't about what she did or didn't do. It was the unbreakable, God-ordained bond between a mother and a child - a bond that defies logic, distance, even absence. Though Angel Mother loved me deeply, a part of me still longed for the woman who had given me life.

The photographs anchored that search. They reminded me: I was her daughter and that I truly belonged to someone without question.

Her story was written into mine.

And somehow, even in her silence, she had never fully left me. Even in my loneliest moments, she was still there - captured in the frame, forever watching over me.

LESSONS IN HARD WORK, LOVE AND QUIET STRENGTH: A SONG FOR NANA

"Train up a child in the way he should go, and when he is old,
he will not depart from it."
(Proverbs 22:6, *KJV*)

Then there were chores.

Weekends carried the rhythms of discipline and responsibility. Angel Mother ensured I learned the value of hard work, assigning long cleaning missions throughout our vast home, where windows stretched high, and staircases wound endlessly. Her standards were high, yet her motives were all about love and instilling in me the importance of order and routine.

"Missy", she'd say, "Always make up your bed. It's the first thing you do in the morning. It helps to start your day off right."

She taught me the precise art of how to make nurse's corners – sheets tucked so tightly the mattress looked dressed for inspection in military barracks. There was satisfaction in the order, in the way discipline settled chaos around me. Her lessons didn't stop at cleaning. She made sure I knew how to cook as well, guiding me through recipes and techniques that would serve me for a lifetime. I learned how to make her rich poundcake, slowly blending butter, powdered sugar, flour, eggs, and flavorful extracts into something mouthwatering. Afterward, I'd scrape the bowl with my finger, enjoying the tasty cake batter. And after what seemed like an eternity, it was finally ready to slice – and I savored the light, fluffy goodness of that homemade delicacy, each bite tasting like love baked into tradition.

One of my most time-consuming tasks I loathed was sweeping down twenty green carpeted steps with a hand broom, then scrubbing the glass panels that overlooked the backyard, bordered by intricate wrought iron. I used Angel Mother's secret formula - warm water and vinegar – that left them spotless, so clear I could see my reflection in them. To Angel Mother, these weren't just chores; they were lessons in responsibility, and pride in one's home.

"Missy don't forget the corners," she'd remind me. "Dust hides there."

And yet, during the structure and routine, there were still moments of childish wonder - like when I would crack open the cattails near the window. Their long brown spikes looked exactly like hot dogs on sticks, and I couldn't resist bursting one open and watching a cloud of feather-like fluff floating lazily in the air. These moments of joy, nestled within the day's demands, gave me a fleeting sense of childhood innocence.

Each day in that house felt like stepping into a living mystery - full of hidden corners, secret pathways, and small wonders, like the laundry chute just outside my room where I dropped clothes down and peeked through, hoping to catch a glimpse of where they'd land, only to later discover them in a basket in the basement as I learned to wash clothes; or the intercom system I loved to play with, pressing buttons and calling out to my brother - or anyone who might be listening - just for the joy of being heard in another room. It was a vibrant house to grow up in, and it made ordinary days quite adventurous.

Then came Nana.

My paternal grandmother moved in with us. Her light complexion, high cheekbones and long, braided hair paid tribute to her Cherokee roots. She carried an air of mystery, never revealing much about her past, yet her presence commanded quiet respect.

Nana was a woman of deep conviction. An ordained minister, she devoted herself to helping the poor, praying for the sick, and visiting the forgotten in the nursing homes. Though she spoke little, her compassion spoke volumes

Still, she held on to old traditions wrapped in superstitions – like reading tea leaves or interpreting the meaning behind dropped silverware.

"A spoon means disappointment is coming. A fork and knife mean unexpected company."

At the time, I didn't question it. Perhaps it was her way of keeping the past close while walking in her faith.

Our moments together were simple yet sweet. After I'd finish cleaning, her living area, we'd settle in to watch her favorite games shows like *Wheel of Fortune*, and she'd sit there in her familiar button-up gown, worn soft with time.

It was in the kitchen where she came alive. She taught me how to make golden corn fritters, perfectly crisp and sweet when drizzled with molasses. On holidays, she baked trays of homemade yeast rolls, fluffy coffee cakes, and peach cobblers, gifting them to friends and neighbors - a quiet act of generosity that spoke volumes.

Yet her strength was tested. Cancer or some other disease had eaten through her hip bone, leaving one leg shorter than the other and her body in constant pain. She leaned on a walker, sometimes crying out when the pain gripped her. And with each scream that was normally twice a day, I could feel her suffering with a tenderness I couldn't name.

Though we never had deep conversations to reveal the depths of her life's journey, I now understand the lesson she lived before me - resilience in silence, generosity in action, and the unspoken power of faith.

One memory of Nana remains etched in my heart shortly before she passed away. She had been bedridden for a while and one day, she called me into her room with a special request:

"Sing to me."

I didn't even know she knew I sang, and I certainly didn't think I had a special voice nevertheless, I obliged her request for me to sing the song, "Holy, Holy, Holy, Lord God Almighty."

As the words and melody filled the room, her eyes closed, and a peaceful smile spread across her face. It was as though the words wrapped her in comfort, a sacred exchange between us, and perhaps the most tender of all our times together.

Although I didn't realize it then, that moment was a farewell, a granddaughter singing her grandmother into the arms of God. It was a glimpse of redemption, love, and our eternal connection.

GREATER IS HE: BREAKING FREE
FROM SIBLING INFLUENCE

"Ye are of God, little children, and have overcome them because the One in you is greater than the One in the world."
(I John 4:4, *KJV*)

My brother had a magnetic pull – mischievous, persuasive. If he said, "let's do it," I followed without question. One day, he hatched a new "mission"—a prank to scare Angel Mother as she returned home from work. Although something in me hesitated, I gave in to the thrill of adventure. Angel Mother often carried large amounts of cash and a pistol for protection.

It was late one night, and we crouched near the garage, making eerie noises as she got out of her car. Her voice rang out – firm, sharp, unshaken.

"Who's there?"

Panic surged through us as we confessed, "It's us!"

She scolded us sharply, "Don't you ever do that again."

It wasn't the first time I blindly followed his lead. Once, he convinced me to sit with him on our third- floor roof. As cars passed below, people shouted, "Kids get down; it's not safe!" We stayed, suspended between childhood daring and real danger.

The worst came with a cruel set up.

"When Angel Mother comes home, ask her, 'Can I have an orange, Orange Face?'" he said, giggling.

As she walked up the stairs, I repeated his words. Her warm smile faded instantly.
She knew.
My brother burst into laughter in the background. I got my first spanking ever – and my first awakening.
"Missy, you can't do what your brother tells you to do anymore. Greater is He that is within you than he that is in the world."
I stared confused.
Who was the "Greater One" she spoke of?
I only knew I had been punished for following someone I loved and trusted. Her words settled in my heart, waiting to bloom in the years to come.
That day marked a shift. I never blindly followed my brother again. Her words became a banner over me, rising in moments when my identity felt threatened, or my faith was tested. They whispered in storms I'd face later – rejection, confusion, compromise – and reminded me of a truth I couldn't yet articulate:
There is something greater in you. Walk in that.
Yet my brother still found ways to tease and taunt me.

I remember an episode of *Charlie's Angels* called "The Séance," where Kelly, played by Jaclyn Smith, had flashbacks of a cruel woman named Beamish who locked her in a closet and stole the only thing that brought her comfort - her doll, Lilibet.

As a child, watching that scene unraveled something in me. I hadn't been locked in a closet—but I had been locked in a basement. And in that moment, I was Kelly—frightened, voiceless, clutching my innocence in the face of authority that felt more terrifying than tender.

Somehow, my older cousin and brother sensed that fear and used it against me. "Come here, Beamish," they'd taunt, mimicking the voice as I held back tears. They turned my fear into entertainment, and what felt like a joke to them became a spiritual wound for me—another seed of rejection, watered by mockery and masked in laughter.

Yet God saw me. He saw the little girl afraid of being locked away and forgotten. And He never let her go. He's redeeming the memory—not by erasing it, but by reclaiming it.

In later battles, Angel Mother's words echoed within me: "Greater is He that is within you…" And they gave me strength to keep going.

A HEART TO SEEK HIM: BIBLE QUIZZES AND GROWING IN INNOCENT FAITH

"You will seek me and find me when you seek me with all your heart."
(Jeremiah 29:13, *NIV*)

Even though our family didn't attend church regularly, I felt an unexplainable awareness of God's presence. It was like a quiet pull toward something familiar. I didn't yet understand what it meant to walk with the Holy Spirit, but I knew I wanted to know more about Him.

I was overjoyed when my father and Angel Mother gave me a children's Bible that became my treasure. Its brown cover, vivid illustrations, and large print made the stories come alive. I read it constantly, underlining verses and writing in the margins with childlike devotion. Though I didn't fully understand everything, the words filled me with a peace I couldn't explain, as if God had tucked Himself between the lines, waiting for me to find Him.

One day, while flipping through radio stations, I stumbled upon a children's Bible quiz show. Each week, the host tested our Bible knowledge and encouraged us to search the scriptures for answers. After each broadcast, quiz booklets arrived in the mail — like treasure maps guiding me deeper into the stories of Noah, King David, and Queen Esther. I wasn't old enough for Bible school, and these quizzes became my sacred classroom. The more I sought Him, the more He revealed Himself to me — and the more I wanted to know the Author behind the words.

Then something unforgettable happened.

While visiting, my father's brother, Uncle George, in Lansing, my brother and I walked down the street when an elderly man stepped out of his house, holding a small, worn, brown leather Bible. His voice was gentle but purposeful.

"This is my personal Bible," he said. "I've marked verses that have meant the most to me. God wants me to give this Bible to you."

I took it – confused, honored, unsure what to say. I didn't know then what I now believe: God revealed something about my life to him — a calling to preach the gospel I wasn't yet aware of.

I crossed out his name, Mr. Maness, and wrote my own, careful to add the date. I read his notes as if they were personal letters. That little Bible became more than a gift – it was confirmation. A holy seed planted in my childhood, quietly preparing me for the road ahead.

Even in my innocence, God was speaking. And somehow, even then, I was learning how to listen.

DANCE SCHOOL DAYS: FINDING JOY IN MOVEMENT

"Music is one of the greatest gifts God has given humanity. In the melody of the notes and the inspirational words that are sung, our souls can release the burdens of every pain inflicted by life, leaving us with a renewed hope to live life in a brand-new way."

— Michelle B. Wilson, author, *In Search of a Mother's Love.*

Soon, a world of wonder was about to unfold – where pain gave way to movement, and I discovered joy in the rhythm of choreographed routines, satin-lined costumes, and the quiet magic of dancing before a cheering crowd.

It all began when I was nine. I slipped into white tights, a black leotard, and ballet shoes, stepping into a family tradition - Toni's School of Dance Arts. Saturday mornings became sacred: the static hum of the record player, the instructor's calm yet firm commands, - "First position, second, third" – and rows of girls lined against mirrored walls with wooden banisters, practicing pliés, relevés, and sautés until they became second nature.

Ballet gave me posture and poise, however, my spirit longed for something less restrained. Tap and jazz awakened me. Inspired by Shirley Temple, I embraced the rhythmic joy of shuffles, ball changes, and flaps. These classes ignited a spark, offering a freedom ballet couldn't.

The highlight of each year was the annual recital at the majestic Detroit Masonic Temple. It's gold revolving doors, grand staircase, and velvet halls made me feel royalty. Performing on the iconic stage, where legends like Sammy Davis Jr. once danced was unforgettable.

Backstage, dressed in sequins and feathers, I felt the flutter of nerves and excitement. When the curtain rose and the music played, our tap shoes echoed against the wooden stage like declarations of joy. We danced with everything in us, and the audience clapped with equal measure.

Over the next five years, I immersed myself in dance, donning beautiful costumes and performing memorable choreographed routines before proud parents. My father snapped hundreds of photos. Angel Mother beamed from the audience, her love steady and full of pride. Though I didn't know it then, these dance school days were laying a foundation—confidence, discipline, presence. They taught me to move with intention and grace.

The stage became more than performance; it became a preview. A rehearsal for the future spotlight moments when I would be called to rise, to speak, to sing, to lead. Though the dance ended, the rhythm stayed. And when life would later press in, I'd return to that inner stage—where courage first found its voice through music and movement.

LEAVING ANGEL MOTHER'S HOME: LOSING STABILITY, FINDING GOD

*"Praise the Lord, who is my Rock. He trains my hands for war
and gives my fingers skill for battle."*
(Psalms 144:1, *NLT*)

After just four years of stability, my world fell apart once again at the age of eleven.

The days leading up to my fifth-grade graduation should have been a time of joy, but instead, they were marked by a suffocating stillness. The discovery of my father's new infidelities affected all our lives and left a wound no word could mend. Angel Mother, strong yet weary from betrayal, faced an impossible decision - she could no longer share a home with him. It was also decided my brother and I would leave with him.

The decision felt like exile.

As I stood in my bedroom – my safe-haven for so many years – I took in every detail, memorizing it as if I might never return. My fingers lingered on the walls, tracing the memories that had shaped me within the four corners.

Then, across the hall, I saw her.

Angel Mother – seated on the loveseat in the bedroom she and my father once shared. Her shoulders bent under the invisible weight of betrayal, with silent tears rolling down her cheeks.

I quickly turned away.

Her grief was too raw and unguarded – too sacred to witness. Although I wanted to run to her, to stay, to undo it all I felt helpless – I was just a child. A child being pulled away from the safety of her arms and the place I wanted to call home.

Descending the staircase felt like walking into an uncertain future. The house, once filled with warmth, now echoed with the emptiness of goodbye. The security I had known crumbled beneath me, replaced by an unsettling unknown. Yet, I clung to a single hope - God would guide us through this storm to solid ground.

That goodbye fractured something in me, yet it also awakened something resilient. I was being trained—though I didn't yet know it—for spiritual battle. My fingers, once skilled in folding nurse's corners and turning Bible pages, were now being taught how to fight in prayer, how to hold on when everything was slipping.

And though I walked away from Angel Mother's house, her imprint never left me. Her strength, her convictions, her tears—they traveled with me, stitched into the very fabric of who I was becoming.

REFINED BY FIRE

"See, I have refined you, though not as silver; I have refined you
in the furnace of affliction."
Isaiah 48:10, (*NIV*)

Our new home - a corner unit in a freshly built townhome complex on Detroit's east side – felt unfamiliar, foreign. Gone were Angel Mother's delicate touches, the warmth that had once made a house a home. My father tried to create a sense of normalcy, yet we all felt the void left by her absence.

Then came another shift.

A new woman entered our lives – soon to become my father's wife – and the atmosphere changed. Their arguments flared over the smallest things: a chair out of place, a word spoken too sharply. The air thickened with tension. My brother and I became unwilling spectators in a play we never auditioned for, caught in the crossfire of two people trying—and failing—to build something from brokenness.

One night, it all exploded. A knife was drawn in the heat of an argument, and my father left with a cut lip. I sat with him in the emergency room under sterile lights, wondering how my world had turned into this—a child watching chaos unfold under the guise of family.

And then there was him.

A man who was down-and-out came to live with us – never fully part of the family, always slightly in the shadows. Something about him always made me uneasy. I avoided him when I could, trusting the instinct in my gut. One day, while I was alone in the basement, he approached me. At first, it sounded like advice. Then his words twisted, became suggestive, wrong. I froze—too confused to speak, too shocked to run.

I never told anyone.

Our home life was already fragile. Stirring more trouble felt like dropping a lit match into an already burning house. Instead, I kept my distance, pretending it had never happened.

Yet even in silence, God was nearby.

MY BEDROOM: MY SANCTUARY OF PEACE

Though my world had become unstable, threatening, and loud with arguments and unspoken trauma, I clung to the only peace I could find. I retreated to my bedroom, the only place that still felt safe and sacred. There, I wrote prayers in secret, cried invisible tears, and whispered for rescue.

I didn't know it then, but I was being refined. The fire meant to consume me was forging something stronger—an inner strength, sharp discernment, and a voice that would one day speak healing into broken places.

And in time, what the enemy meant for destruction, God would shape into strength.

Writing became my meditation, my escape. My pen became my unspoken prayers.

"Dear Lord, please rescue us. When is this going to end? Will I have to live like this forever?"

Though I didn't realize it then, God was already answering me—not by removing me from the fire, but by refining me in it. His grace surrounded me, not always in the form of rescue, but as endurance. He was shaping something in the shadows, strengthening muscles I didn't know I had. I was learning how to fight—not with fists instead with prayer.

There I learned how to anchor myself in God's voice, even when every other voice around me was tearing something down. It was where I learned to listen for whispers of hope when the world around me felt chaotic.

God held me in that room—shielding me in silence, protecting me, speaking to me in written prayers, reminding me that even in this, I was not forgotten.

What felt like isolation was consecration.

And the battles I faced in secret became the training ground for the calling I'd one day walk in publicly.

CHAPTER 10:

THE CROWN, THE CALLING, AND THE COMING OF AGE

"Before God unveils the next level of destiny, hell often tightens its grip. The warfare isn't proof you've missed the mark - it's the scent of precious oil from your pressing. When the enemy senses promotion, he stirs confusion. Take heart: the relentless shaking isn't your ruin - it's the sound of monumental gates opening."

– Michelle B. Wilson, author, *In Search of a Mother's Love.*

Elementary school had been anything but a place of refuge. I spent much of it in tears, still in shock from everything I had endured. Loneliness lingered in every hallway. And now, as I stepped into middle school, the battle was about to intensify. The bullying would become relentless which signaled escalating spiritual warfare.

I buried myself in schoolwork, hoping achievement would bring belonging. Instead, it painted me as a target.

"Michelle turned in her homework two weeks early. You should be more like her," my teacher announced.

"Why don't you crucify me?" I thought silently to myself.

The glares from my classmates were immediate, a silent yet sharp reminder my achievements made me a target.

My father, a gifted scholar, presented our class with a lecture on our rich African heritage during Black History Month. "We came from kings and queens, a proud people who contributed greatly to the world's innovations," my father exclaimed.

Days later, my teacher announced, "If anyone should win the Black History contest, it's Michelle." What was meant as affirmation only deepened the isolation.

Each compliment drove a deeper wedge. I found myself shrinking, wishing I could disappear. The more I achieved, the more their disdain grew.

Then came the day of the chant.

"QUEEN OF SHEBA": THE BLESSING OF REJECTION

It all began like any other—thirty students sitting in a classroom, waiting for the teacher to return from a brief errand. The moment the door clicked shut, a familiar hush fell over the classroom and the taunting began.

"Queen of Sheba, Queen of Sheba, Queen of Sheba," they chanted, their voices rising in unison like a drumbeat.

The words struck like arrows, each syllable pounding in my ears. It was as if I had been transported to a battlefield, the echoes resembling the call of African war drums. I tried to hold back my tears, still they came anyway, streaming silently down my face. The humiliation was overwhelming. Though I didn't know it at the time, God's presence surrounded me. It was as if invisible arms were holding me up, shielding me from the full weight of their cruelty.

I began wiping away my tears as I heard the teacher return. His presence was a welcome relief, like a friend stepping into the middle of a battle to shield me from further wounding. As he resumed the lesson, the atmosphere returned to normal, as if nothing had happened.

Years later, during a time of healing prayer, I asked God to reveal any lingering wounds. This memory surfaced, and He spoke something profound:

"What they meant for evil, I used for good. Those chants were not mocking you—they were prophetic words; a declaration of the destiny I have prepared for you."

Curious, I researched the Queen of Sheba. She was not merely a historical figure – she was a woman of great wealth, wisdom and influence known for seeking out King Solomon's wisdom and bringing rare and precious gifts.

"Then she gave the king 120 talents of gold, large quantities of spices, and precious stones. Never again were so many spices brought in as those the Queen of Sheba gave to King Solomon."
(1 Kings 10:10, *NIV*)

What my classmates had chanted to shame me, God used to mark me. I wasn't being broken. I was being called.

Despite the relentless bullying, I refused to let it define me. I didn't retaliate, nor did I confide in anyone about the cruelty I endured. Instead, I poured myself into my studies, earning a place on the President's List for all A's year after year. Though the weight of rejection pressed against me on every side, I clung to an unspoken strength – one I now recognize as God's hand upon my life.

ENTERING WOMANHOOD: MY MOTHER'S MISSING GUIDANCE

"She is clothed in strength and dignity; she can laugh at the days to come."
(Proverbs 31:25, *NIV*)

I had learned to block out the chaos around me, to focus on what mattered. Yet even as I matured in wisdom, I was unprepared for the changes happening in my body. One day, I felt something strange. I was twelve, caught between childhood and something entirely unknown.

I called my father, hesitantly telling him what had just happened. His face lit up – not with concern, but with joy. Then he spoke about the sacred rite of passage.

"In Africa," he said, beaming, "when a girl reaches this stage, the whole village celebrates! It's a sign she has become a woman."

Through his words, I envisioned it:

A sun-drenched village where women in vibrant wraps danced in a circle, their feet pounding the earth in rhythm with the djembe drums. Laughter and ululations filled the air as elders adorned the girl with beads, placing a golden sash over her shoulder to mark her transition. Platters of sweet fruits and roasted meats were passed around, while mothers and aunties clapped their hands and sang songs of womanhood, wisdom, and lineage. The girl - now seen as a young woman was no longer a child in the eyes of her people – she was a blossoming flower in the garden of womanhood.

The more he spoke, the more I wondered, was I about to be celebrated like the girls in our homeland? I interrupted his thoughts, gently pulling him back to reality.

"So…what do I do next?"

His face softened, and with a smile, he told me to go see my grandmother, who lived nearby. She handed me what I needed and said only, "Now you are stepping into womanhood. Take care of yourself because you can get pregnant."

Her words fell heavy. I wasn't thinking about sex – I was simply trying to survive the storms of my life.

Sitting alone in my room, a memory surfaced - a conversation with my mother when I was just five. She had told me about this moment, preparing me long before I could understand. I wished she was there to share in this experience, to help me navigate the path ahead, and provide the comfort and assurance only a mother could give. What should I expect? How would things change? Her absence left a void, a missing place in this transition. Yet, even without her there, her words had prepared me. Somehow, she knew.

THE SEEDS OF MY BUDDING MEDIA CAREER: LOOK OUT, OPRAH

"And I have filled him with the Spirit of God, with wisdom,
understanding, knowledge, and all kinds of skills."
(Exodus 31:3, *NIV*)

While many search for years to find their calling, mine began to whisper early, this is the way; walk in it. And so, I did. By the time I was twelve, doors were already opening, confirming my steps were being divinely ordered.

Like many aspiring media professionals, I admired Oprah Winfrey. She was a cultural phenomenon, captivating millions with her authenticity, intellect, and compassion. Watching her, I dreamed of storytelling, not for fame, but to inspire others with hope.

My father, a photographer and arts instructor, played a role in nurturing this dream as well. His work brought him connections in radio and television, and he ensured my summers would never be idle.

One day, he asked, "Dr. Barbara Wilson needs kids to ask questions on her radio show about finances. Do you want to do it?"

Without hesitation, I said, "yes."

That night, I wrote my question with care, as if it held the weight of my destiny. On the day of the show, I stepped up to the microphone, heart pounding. The guest smiled at my question, and the praise I received ignited a renewed confidence I needed. Though I wasn't sure about a career in radio, I felt the thrill of connecting with an audience.

Another summer, I joined a youth video production program. Our team chose to create a documentary on Detroit's Arabic community, and for the first time, I stood in front of a camera as a host and reporter. At a local restaurant I interviewed the owner about his homeland while savoring his signature dishes. The *kibbeh*, with its crispy golden shell and flavorful lamb filling, was unforgettable. The *tabbouleh*, a bright mix of parsley, mint, and lemon, was refreshing. And then there was the *baklava*—a decadent pastry layered with honey and pistachios that melted in my mouth. Submersing myself in a culture I had never explored before was exciting.

At Detroit's cultural festival, I immersed myself further in the Arabic community. Standing in front of the camera, delivering openings and segues,

I felt a deep connection to storytelling and knew I was in my element. When we completed the documentary, our instructor praised our work – we were the only group to finish, and the praise we received was invigorating. These experiences weren't just about learning new skills—they were shaping my identity and preparing me for something greater.

Doors continued to open.

Another family friend, Dr. Mary Wilkes, invited me to be a part of a teens tv show, T*een Profile*. Every week, I took on different roles, honing my skills. One episode stood out: I performed in a *Star Trek*-inspired segment, my face painted silver, fully immersed in the creativity of it all.

God was planting seeds.

From radio to documentary to television, He was shaping me. I wasn't just learning skills—I was becoming who I was called to be.

What began in whispers became a divine rhythm. And though I didn't know it, I was already walking the path He laid before me.

CHAPTER 11:

JOURNEY OF FAITH: THE DOORS OF THE CHURCH ARE OPEN

"If thou confess with thy mouth the Lord Jesus, and shalt believe in thine heart that God hath raised Him from the dead, thou shalt be saved."
(Romans 10:9, *KJV*)

Chaos had become my constant companion at home. Daily arguments between my father and his wife, police visits, and the weight of shame made me fear this tumultuous life would be my reality forever. I longed for peace - something only God could give.

Weekends with Angel Mother became my refuge. Though carrying her own heartbreak, she found solace in the Lord - re-committing her life to Jesus at Little Rock Missionary Baptist Church. Her transformation was visible: her eyes sparkled with renewed purpose and her spirit was lighter.

The first time I stepped inside the church, I was mesmerized. Majestic stained-glass windows cast vibrant hues across the congregation. Towering pipe organs hummed with the rich, soulful melodies of classic gospel hymns, filling the sanctuary with God's powerful presence. Angels adorned each pillar, as if watching over worshippers. And there, at the end of a regal burgundy stone aisle, stood the pulpit – beckoning. sacred.

Rev. Jim Holley, the church's senior pastor was a spiritual giant. His presence commanded attention, and his words carried power. He was more than a preacher - he was a beacon of hope to the disenfranchised, extending benevolence through food drives, outreach programs, and support for the struggling.

Angel Mother's devotion to her faith was inspiring, and I longed to experience the peace she had discovered. I was only 12, yet I knew I wanted what she had – an unshakable connection with God. One Sunday, my brother, cousin, and I made a pact; the next time the pastor opened the doors of the church, we would walk forward.

That Sunday, dressed in our best, we sat in anticipation. Rev. Holley delivered a fiery sermon that stirred the hearts of everyone in the room. At the end of his sermon he extended the invitation declaring, "The doors of the church are open," I knew it was time.

As our eyes met, silently confirming our pact, we began our journey. My heart pounded as I walked down the long aisle, the weight of the moment settling over me. It felt like the heavens were watching, cheering us on as we approached the altar. With every step, I sensed I was crossing into my destiny. I knew my life would never be the same again.

When we finally stood before the congregation, with Angel Mother beaming with pride,

Rev. Holley led us in the prayer of salvation.

"Lord Jesus, I believe You are the Son of God. I repent of my sins and ask You to come into my heart. Be my Lord and Savior. Thank you for saving me. In Jesus' name, Amen."

As I repeated each word with sincerity, my heart overflowed with a peace I had never known. At that moment, I knew I had made the best decision of my life: to give my heart to Jesus and to draw closer to God.

It was more than a moment; it was a major decision that would shape the rest of my life and draw me into a deeper purpose I had only begun to understand. Unbeknownst to me then, Angel Mother's example and devotion would help propel me to the heights of becoming the woman of God He had called me to be.

THE GIFT OF THE GOLDEN CROSS

At twelve, Angel Mother gave me more than a necklace.
It was a small golden cross, a 14-karat whisper of heaven.
It wasn't just a gift; it was a seed, planted in the soil of my becoming.
My first treasure of belonging to God.

I wore it close, always — fingers tracing the metal as if I could touch God
through it, as if faith had form and weight and could anchor me
when the world felt uncertain.

Each time it brushed my skin, I remembered her gift — not just the necklace,
but the invitation it carried:
to believe,
to hold on,
to grow in grace.

And I did.

Because Angel Mother didn't just give me gold — she gave me a reason to
reach for something eternal.

ROOTED IN FAITH:
FINDING BELONGING IN THE CHURCH

"Train up a child in the way he should go, and when he is old,
he will not depart from it."
(Proverbs 22:6, *KJV*)

Church became my second home. Where the sting of rejection once lived,
I found open arms. It was a gift from God – sacred ground where, for the first
time, I truly felt seen, known and accepted. Five days a week, I was there -
eager to learn and serve.

"Missy, make sure you have your clothes ready for church tomorrow. Did
you iron your skirt?"

"Yes, Angel Mother," I replied, my heart full of gratitude for her presence in my life again. I was excited to learn all I could about God. I was also truly grateful for a place where I could discover my talents and use them to glorify God.

At the start of each service, the deacons opened each service with hymns that swelled through the sanctuary:

"Guuiiiiiide meeeee, O great Jehovaaaaaah,
Pilgrimmmm through this barreeeeen land…"

Deacon Willie's voice soared with passion and conviction, drawing every soul into focused reverence for God. His fervor fascinated me, but I didn't fully understand why they dragged out the words or what they meant.

The adult choir, fiery and full of passion, would raise voices in worship. Tambourines rang out as the congregation stood on their feet, hands clapping in rhythm. During offering, Angel Mother always pressed dollar bills into my hand, whispering,

"Never come to the church without giving something to the Lord."

She was teaching me worship wasn't just singing – it was also a monetary offering to God.

After announcements were made and another song rendered, Rev. Holley would then take to the pulpit, his voice thunderous. I noticed most of the congregation was made up of women, drawn not only by his compelling presence but also by his powerful, passionate preaching.

"He died, but that's not the end. Sunday morning, He got up. Tell your neighbor, 'He got up!'

The congregation erupted in unison, shouting with such fervor it felt as though Jesus Himself were delivering the sermon.

CALLED TO SPEAK, MOVED TO SING

Rev. Holley guided many on their faith journey and he especially provided a platform for the youth to use their gifts and talents for God. I never volunteered—yet, when called upon, I felt compelled to say yes. Whether it was reading scripture, reciting a rehearsed speech, or inviting the church to support our youth activities, I knew these moments were shaping me and building my confidence to become a young leader in the church.

Standing behind the pulpit in front of our vibrant church community of 300 was another story. Despite my efforts to appear calm, the pressure to be perfect often overwhelmed me. My hands would drip with sweat, as I'd take one deep breath, holding it as if it could steady my nerves. I slowly released the air, letting it anchor me as I shared my speech. This simple routine became my way of staying calm under pressure, allowing me to push through my fear and deliver what I needed to say with excellence.

Afterward, people praised how poised I sounded. One friend slipped me a note that read, "Nice speech, little peach." It made me smile, affirming the direction God was leading me toward—a media career that would soon become clearer in unexpected ways.

In Sunday school, I competed to recite all 66 books of the Bible – winning two years in a row. By the third year, I was playfully told to let someone else win. Nevertheless, I didn't let that deter me from my pursuit of knowing everything about God. Each victory was a testament to my growing hunger for His Word and desire to dive deeper into my faith.

One of the highlights of my time at church was joining the "Youth for Christ" choir, a transformative experience that gave me a sense of purpose and belonging. Youth leaders, Gwen and Margaret, welcomed me with open arms.

Behind Gwen's strictness, was a deeper kindness and genuine care for everyone she encountered. Her unwavering support showed me an acceptance and unconditional love I rarely experienced elsewhere. Through her mentorship, God began to heal the deep wounds of rejection I had carried for so long, even as her family welcomed me and treated me as one of their own. Their love touched parts of me I didn't know were still broken.

From a young age, music became a refuge for me – a sacred space where I could express what words alone could not.

I found immense joy in singing hymns and the latest popular Christian songs with my soprano voice, proudly wearing our signature uniform: a knee-length black skirt, crisp white blouse, and polished black shoes. Later, we transitioned to light blue robes, which added a sense of reverence to our worship, making my experience with the choir even more glorious.

Every fourth Sunday was the youth choir's time to shine. The anticipation of our grand entrance march brought excitement and nervousness. The harmony of our voices and the rhythm of our steps created a moment of worship that filled the sanctuary with reverence. I always worried about staying perfectly in step. The aisle seemed endless as we proceeded in unison, our voices soaring beautifully to the tune of:

"We're marching to Zion, beautiful, beautiful Zion.

We're marching upward to Zion, that beautiful city of God."

We sang many memorable songs that brought the church to its feet as we worshipped God.

"Come on children sing for God." the church mothers would exclaim proudly as they waived their hands in praise.

One of our favorite songs to perform was "I'm Looking for a Miracle" by Detroit's own Clark Sisters, a praise song that charged the congregation every time we sang it.

"The sky is the limit to what I can have.
Just believe it and receive it. God will perform it today. Hey Hey!"

Every time I sang in our church choir, God shaped me profoundly and beautifully, gently pushing me further out of my comfort zone. Through each note and every performance, He forged within me the heart of a leader and the foundation for my calling.

Unlike school, where I often felt invisible or out of place, I was seen, valued, and embraced as part of something bigger. The church became my refuge where I could grow spiritually and emotionally.

THE RHYTHM OF CHURCH LIFE

Being part of the choir was more than just singing; it allowed me to expand my horizons. We embarked on field trips, including a memorable visit to Georgia to honor Martin Luther King, Jr's. memorial. It was more than a trip—it was connection to a legacy. I saw myself in that story: a young voice rising from hardship.

Angel Mother joined the adult choir and even led solos. I clapped the loudest, pride swelling in my chest. I never dared sing a solo, but I loved standing behind others, cheering them on.

When she began teaching Sunday school, I was in awe. Watching her speak life and truth into children reminded me how God was using her—not just to shape others, but to continue shaping me.

After service, the fellowship hall overflowed with laughter and the aroma of baked chicken, macaroni, green beans, lemonade, and dessert. It wasn't just food—it was family, healing, belonging.

LONGING FOR MORE OF GOD

Despite the joy I found in church, a deeper longing stirred within me to feel Him move in my soul. As I watched others "catch the spirit"—jumping up and down, shouting with unrestrained passion, and weeping loudly as though touched by the very hand of God—I couldn't help but wonder what it felt like to have such a profound encounter. It was silently understood that those who experienced this were seen as truly serious about their walk with God.

Ushers rushed to fan and comfort the overwhelmed, dressed in white uniforms. I watched, yearning—not just to know about God, but to feel Him.

Little Rock became the launching pad for my spiritual awakening. Through Angel Mother's faith, God planted seeds that would one day bloom. I didn't yet see the full picture, but I knew this was where purpose was born.

REUNITED AS SIBLINGS

My older brothers, now grown, came to stay. Handsome, confident, adored by the girls—they brought laughter back into our lives. Angel Mother welcomed them like sons. We spent Sundays in church, followed by restaurant meals with no limit. For the first time in years, life felt light again.

Still, some things were never said.

We didn't speak of our mother. Where she was. Why she never came back. Only hushed questions:

Who called the police?

Did someone make her leave?

Yet no answers.

So, we coped by pretending she was away on a long trip.

We were used to her absence now. Yet, the silence left wounds, buried deep, waiting to surface later in fractured places of our souls.

Still, for a moment, we were together. And that was enough.

ANGEL MOTHER'S CADILLAC RIDES AND BIBLE LESSONS

Angel Mother always invited me to ride on errands, and I gladly went, cherishing every moment with her. Our times together always felt special, holding moments of profound spiritual influence I held dear.

Her Cadillac—so long it seemed to stretch a mile—glided smoothly through town. She always had her tall, light brown coffee cup clipped to the window ledge, sipping it as we rode.

Our soundtrack wasn't music; it was J. Vernon McGee, his distinct unwavering voice filling the car with scripture and wisdom. Angel Mother treasured his teachings, and though I didn't always want to listen, I knew better than to ask to change the station.

McGee's program, *Through the Bible,* spoke urgently about sin, holiness, and Christ's return for a church without spot or wrinkle. I didn't always understand, but I listened. Seeds were being sown.

At the end of each broadcast, a hymn would play:

"Jesus paid it all,
All to Him I owe.
Sin had left a crimson stain,
He washed it white as snow."

Those car rides became a sanctuary. No stained-glass windows or pulpits—just truth, love, and faith riding side by side. Angel Mother didn't just teach me about God—she showed me how to walk with Him.

Those moments—her quiet strength, that old hymn, McGee's unwavering voice—are still with me. They were the steady, sacred rhythms that helped build the foundation of my faith.

CHAPTER 12:

SHAPED BY FIRE: MIDDLE AND HIGH SCHOOL YEARS: THE ROAD TO DESTINY

"Fire does not destroy gold; it refines it. Pain does not diminish purpose; it reveals it. The greatest callings are forged in the hottest fires – where rejection, affliction, and trials burn away everything false, leaving only what is true, what is strong, what is destined. Pain and Rejection are not signs of failure; they are marks of divine greatness within you. God often chooses those who have walked through the fiercest battles and endured the deepest wounds.; the outcasts and misunderstood to carry His reflection. Like Lazarus, He calls them to 'come forth,' shining His glory through their brokenness and using them to accomplish His greatest triumphs for the Kingdom of God."

— Michelle B. Wilson, author, *In Search of a Mother's Love.*

SET APART AND CHOSEN - NOT "WEIRD"

The school bus rumbled down its usual route, a low hum of voices filling the air. I sat near the front, away from my peers, staring out the window. Solitude had become my hiding place. My silence, my preference for stillness, and the unrest I couldn't name made me an easy target.

One memory still echoes:

"She's weird."

The words hung in the air, sharp and deliberate. I didn't turn around, didn't react – but it stung.

Years of navigating rejection had taught me how to mask my emotions, how to keep moving forward no matter what. Those words pierced my heart in a way I couldn't explain. Still, their laughter rippled from the back of the bus, confirming the label they had agreed upon:

"Weird."

Their carefree laughter felt worlds apart from my reality. Maybe they had the stability of both parents, a foundation I longed for but couldn't grasp. The truth was, I carried a story that set me apart, even at my young age.

And in that moment, I wondered:

Was I really that different?

Deep down, I longed to reach out, to be a part of their world, to feel like I belonged. I wanted to laugh with them, to be carefree – but I didn't know how to truly laugh anymore. I carried the heaviness of rejection, of instability, of trying to fit into a space that never seemed to be mine. I felt safer in my own thoughts, navigating my existence within the quiet of my mind. Still, her words stuck to my soul like a brand. Every rejection that followed seemed to echo those words.

For a long time, I wore that label like a badge of shame. I tried to blend in, to find my place, yet I never truly succeeded outside my church. It wasn't until years later I realized being different wasn't a curse—it was a calling. While others targeted me for not fitting in, it reflected the greatness of God within me – something that was so blinding it made others unknowingly feel insecure.

Those who stand alone often reveal a strength others may lack, especially those who rely on the crowd for validation. God had set me apart for a purpose far greater than I could understand or imagine. God often calls the misfits, the outcasts, and the overlooked – because what the world rejects, He redeems for His glory.

What others saw as "weird," God saw as chosen.

I see now that even in isolation, God was with me. He was using those moments to prepare me, to shape my heart and spirit for a greater purpose.

LOOSE WHEELS AND MISS AMERICA DREAMS

The feeling of not belonging didn't end at school. Even at home, tension simmered beneath the surface.

One afternoon, I laced up the latest gym shoe roller skates, eager for one of my favorite pastimes. Skating brought me joy - it was one of the few things that made me feel truly carefree. I loved the rush of the wind against my face as I glided down the street, the rhythmic sound of the wheels rolling beneath me.

Angel Mother had bought me a pair of ice skates, and I cherished every moment spent at Hart Plaza ice skating rink in downtown Detroit. There was something about skating on all four wheels though that made me feel more secure.

However, this day was different.

I pushed off and immediately felt something wrong—the wheels wobbled beneath me. In seconds, I was on the ground. A sharp sting shot through my legs as pavement scraped my skin. The bolts were too loose. Too loose to be accidental.

I said nothing, but suspicion stirred.

Still, the sting of the fall was nothing compared to what followed. My father, who was grooming me to compete in the Miss America pageant, was more upset about the potential scars on my legs than the emotional pain I had endured. That moment deepened the perfectionism and insecurity I would carry for years.

I never knew for certain what caused the fall that day — whether it was an accident or something more intentional. The experience left me feeling vulnerable in a way I couldn't quite explain. It wasn't just the physical pain; it was the realization that life, and family relationships, can be unpredictable and messy.

The real injury wasn't the fall—it was the message: my pain didn't matter.

Much of our family tension had little to do with me. We all carried silent wounds; unspoken hurts passed down like heirlooms. Yet it caused strained relationships. Whether it was my father placing me at the front of the line, insisting that I be the first to learn new skills, or telling my grandmother I especially needed to be taught how to cook, his favor toward me was undeniable.

My father's esteem toward me, though never intended to cause division, became a source of tension within my family. What I once viewed as ordinary moments - him guiding me, pushing me to excel - were seen by others as special treatment, as evidence that I was different, set apart. And with that distinction came the weight of being misunderstood, much like Joseph in the Bible who was favored by his father. I've since learned that others' actions weren't driven by hatred towards me but their own hurts and insecurities.

Yet, through God's grace, I've come to understand and forgive.

RUNNING FOR VP: FINDING CONFIDENCE

Navigating through school was always a challenge for me. I often felt like an outsider, watching the popular kids move through life with a confidence I hadn't yet found.

For years, I had watched from the sidelines, hesitant to step into the spotlight. Yet as my final year of middle school approached, something shifted.

I decided to run for class vice president.

When a classmate found out, she quickly jumped into the race, certain she'd win. I knew I was the underdog. I didn't even know if anyone would vote for me—but I was determined to try, to step into the light even if rejection followed.

Then came the results. My name was called.

"Michelle Wilson for Vice President."

I had won. My heart smiled.

It was a turning point. A moment that whispered, There's something in you worth noticing.

LESSONS FROM THE DARKROOM: SEEING MYSELF THROUGH MY FATHER'S EYES

Though I struggled to fit in at school, I always knew I had a special place in my father's heart. His love and encouragement reminded me I was made for something extraordinary.

As a respected photography instructor, he had a gift for capturing beauty in the ordinary. His students often chose me for their portrait assignments, and he proudly framed their work—silent affirmations that, to him, I was special. No doubt, those students earned A's.

I often joined him in class, listening to his lectures on photography, African history, and life. Afterward, we'd step into the darkroom where the real magic happened.

The turnstile door creaked. Pitch blackness. The scent of the chemicals filled the air. There, I learned how to develop film using enlargers, chemical baths, and running water. It was mesmerizing to watch blank photographic paper slowly transform into a vivid image, coming to life with each swish in the chemical bath.

Though I faced loneliness in other areas of my life, these moments with my father gave me a sense of belonging. They were a reminder I had a place in the world, even if I hadn't fully discovered it yet.

Perhaps that's why I was so drawn to exploring new places and meeting new people - always searching for something more. A fresh start. One of those after school adventures led me straight into the office of a city council member.

THE HEARTBREAK OF HIDDEN TRAUMA

"And we know that in all things God works for the good of those who love Him, who have been called according to His purpose."
(Romans 8:28, *NIV*)

Even in moments of triumph, I carried a silent weight—too heavy for a teenager. It wasn't just the absence of my mother that shaped me, but the silence that followed. The unspoken wounds. The unanswered questions.

I buried myself in academics, hoping success would quiet the ache. Yet emptiness isn't erased by effort. It lingers.

I often sensed others expected me to fail, to become another statistic. Determined to break that narrative, I vowed to remain pure until marriage— both as a stand for myself and a shield against repeating the broken cycles I had witnessed.

Angel Mother praised this, though it only deepened my fragile place with others.

Still, beneath my quiet obedience were memories I never voiced.

An older man I once visited for chores told me to pick something up off the floor—then reached for my blouse, exposing me. I froze. My innocence, once again, disrupted.

The world whispered a toxic lie: "Your worth is in your body."

Each inappropriate touch, every stare or crude comment chipped away at my identity.

I hid in baggy clothes.

I hid in silence.

One person even told me, "Men will only want you for one thing." That sentence branded my soul.

I withdrew.

Believing silence was survival. Yet even in the quiet, God was speaking.

God was inviting me to see myself as He did—worthy, whole, and deeply loved.

The shame and rejection I carried were never meant to be mine. He was setting the stage to restore what had been stolen, using every moment of heartbreak as part of a redemptive story that would one day inspire others to find hope and healing in Him.

GROOMED FOR MINISTRY:
AN ANOINTING I NEVER KNEW I HAD

My bedroom became my pulpit – a world of books, studies, prayers, and solitude where I could process life's challenges to share with invited guests.

When my brother's girlfriend visited, our conversations would unexpectedly shift. She'd open up, tears forming as my words healed places she hadn't expressed aloud. I never meant to counsel her. Something in me spoke to pain I didn't yet understand. God was using me—long before I knew I was being used.

Even my brother noticed:

"Don't make her cry," he warned.

This wasn't manipulation. It was ministry – an anointing I didn't yet recognize that God placed within me to help others. Unfortunately, no one around me, including myself, knew how to cultivate or nurture this calling. At that point in my life, the enemy had convinced me I was too broken to contribute anything meaningful to others, let alone walk in ministry.

I was laser-focused on media though.

Television. Storytelling. Not church pulpits. Still, God had planted something deeper. And the enemy saw it too—which is why the war over my identity began so early.

John 10:10 wasn't just a scripture. It was my reality. The enemy had tried to steal, kill, and destroy my destiny before I even knew what I carried.

Still, God was already dropping clues—like breadcrumbs, leading me toward a multifaceted calling: a career in media, a voice in ministry, and the creative spark to bring new ideas to the world. Each role was a part of the divine blueprint he had crafted for me before I was even born.

And maybe that's why the fire came early—because what I was called to carry wasn't just for me. It was for others.

The lessons I was learning—compassion, empathy, obedience—weren't wasted. They were preparing me to serve.

How could I minister to the broken if I hadn't first been broken myself?

A SWEET 16 SURPRISE: A BROTHER'S HEART OF LOVE REVEALED

My brother wasn't the emotional type, but that didn't mean he didn't love me. There was a quiet bond between us. We were the two who had stayed together after the children's home—survivors of instability, clinging to each other in the emotional current.

When my 16th birthday approached, I asked for Nike gym shoes. Simple. Practical. He went far beyond that.

He threw me a party.

He called my classmates. My mind raced with worst-case scenarios: What if no one came? What if I ended up embarrassed and alone? To my surprise, many showed up and the night went better than I imagined.

My brother fired up the grill. He baked the cake. He gave me something I hadn't felt in a while—celebration without fear or judgment. A moment to just be.

After the party, I thanked my brother. Still, in typical fashion, I couldn't resist adding, "I really just wanted a pair of gym shoes."

Still, I saw the deeper meaning behind his gesture. The shoes were never the point. His actions spoke the words he struggled to say; I see you. I care.

THE WINNER IS: A BRIGHT FUTURE
IN MY TELEVISION CAREER

My love for media wasn't just a passion - it was a calling, one that crystallized in high school.

During my senior year, I enrolled in a vocational-technical school specializing in television production. Mr. Smith, my instructor, identified untapped potential in me – skills and promise I had not yet recognized in myself. His passion for teaching and dedication to his students provided me with countless opportunities to explore all aspects of media. From learning how to operate television equipment to editing and production, I discovered a world that felt like home.

At the of the year, my school project – showcasing the vocational programs – became my defining moment. As the reporter, I poured myself into it, capturing the stories of students across disciplines through my interviews. When the final edit played, something clicked. This was where I belonged.

This labor of love stretched me in ways I hadn't expected, helping me discover talents I never knew I had like reporting. I edited the segments, and the final product was a triumph. Mr. Smith's faith in me solidified my passion for media and gave me the confidence to dream bigger.

However, success often invites envy. One day, I entered class to find crude messages on the chalkboard—false, insinuating things about Mr. Smith and me. I refused to let the lies take root, and he addressed it. I stayed focused.

Later that year, Mr. Smith invited me to a prestigious video awards ceremony. My family arrived late, and I missed receiving one award in the reporter/host category—but just in time for another.

The next category—educational videos—was announced. To my shock, I was a nominee. I didn't expect to win, yet when my name was called as the winner, I was ecstatic. I walked onto that stage, accepted the Crystal Pyramid Award, and delivered a heartfelt acceptance speech. Standing there, a quiet assurance came over me signifying I was stepping into something bigger than myself.

This wasn't just an achievement – it was another confirmation I was headed in the right direction.

Years earlier, I had been eager to date, however, my father advised, "Men will always be around. Focus on your education." I took his words to heart, devoting my energy into my studies and dreams of a future in television.

I envisioned myself as a national news anchorwoman, breaking records as one of the youngest in the industry or even hosting my talk show. Pioneers like Barbara Walters, Oprah Winfrey, and Carole Simpson—the trailblazing African-American ABC News anchor who made history moderating a key presidential debate, inspired me. These groundbreaking figures were role models, fueling my determination to work harder than ever to achieve my dreams.

And in that moment, standing under the stage lights, I knew - I wasn't just chasing a dream. I was walking into destiny.

TWO PROMS AND A DEBUTANTE
COTILLION TRADITION

Despite the challenges of high school, moments of joy still broke through—especially two proms and a debutante cotillion.

I went to two proms during my high school years, one for each of the two schools I attended. My church mentor Gwen hand-sewed a stunning peach dress, that radiated elegance and complemented my brown skin beautifully. The bodice was fitted with a sweetheart neckline, delicately adorned with shimmering sequins that caught the light with every step I took. The skirt flared into gentle chiffon waves, flowing gracefully as I walked. She smiled warmly as she finished the final fitting, her eyes brimming with pride.

"Ok, Beauty," she said, her voice filled with genuine affection.

On prom night, as I stepped into the limousine with Jonathan, my date, I glanced back at Gwen. She waved me off proudly, reassuring me I was loved and supported. Even amid such celebratory moments, I carried with me the values instilled by my faith—remaining steadfast in my choices and conscious of my behavior.

After graduation came something even grander—the Debutante Cotillion. It was a grand event meant to introduce young women to society, showcasing their grace, poise, talents, and aspirations. My father was thrilled about this opportunity, seeing it as a steppingstone to his dreams of me competing in the Miss USA pageant. Even though, it wasn't my aspiration, I embraced the experience to please him.

Weeks of preparation followed—ballroom dancing, public speaking, talent rehearsals. Margaret, another mentor, let me practice in her home and even lent me a beautiful leather outfit for the talent portion, where I performed a dramatization of creation—my faith expressed through movement and story.

My sponsor for the event, Charles Harrell, the owner of a Black-owned Chevrolet dealership, generously supported me throughout the process. My escort for the evening was Terry, a friend from middle school who was not only one of the most handsome men there but also an exceptional dancer.

The night of the Cotillion was nothing short of a fairy tale. My family turned out in full support, dressed in their finest attire as though attending a royal wedding. Angel Mother radiated beauty in a light green floor-length gown, its diamond-sequined collar catching the light with every turn. Her hair was styled in an elegant updo, framing her beautiful face gracefully. My father, dignified in a classic tuxedo, stood tall, his pride evident in every glance. Even my middle brother attended along with my youngest brother and his girlfriend. Some of Angel Mother's family members attended offering a moment of unity that touched my heart.

My gown, also designed by Gwen, was a masterpiece. The pure white ball gown featured a fitted bodice with intricate pearl-encrusted lace, while the full skirt flowed like a cascading waterfall of satin, giving me the air of a princess. I wore elegant long white gloves that added a touch of timeless sophistication to my ensemble, perfectly complementing the grace and poise of the occasion. My hair was styled in soft curls that flowed past my shoulders, and my natural make-up shimmered delicately under the lights, enhancing the glow of the evening.

As the debutantes lined up in their signature white gowns, we held our heads high, ready for our formal introduction to society. The young men in their sharp tuxedos stood on the opposite side, awaiting their turn to join us for the dance. My heart fluttered as my name was announced:

"Introducing Michelle Wilson. She studied media and journalism and will be attending college to pursue her dreams of becoming a national news anchorwoman."

As everyone clapped, I walked down the runway, feeling the weight of my family's pride and expectations. First, I danced with my father, whose face beamed with joy. As we glided across the floor, I felt cherished with a father's love. Afterward, I danced with my escort Terry. The weeks of rehearsals showed in the ease of his steps as he led me through the waltz with quiet confidence. Beneath the soft lights and gentle music, his steady hand and warm smile made the moment special – an elegant close to a night I would never forget.

During our time, countless photographs were taken, including one of my father and me dancing together. The picture of his proud smile said it all as he and I graced the pages of the local Black newspaper, a quiet moment of honor that spoke louder than words.

Though I didn't win the crown, I walked away victorious. The night wasn't just a celebration—it was a declaration.

I was stepping into purpose.

THE LONG-AGO PRAYER OF A CHILD IS ABOUT TO BE ANSWERED

On the surface, my life looked victorious—my father's favor, winning class vice president, television awards, being introduced to society in an elegant white gown on Cotillion night, and the unwavering love of Angel Mother.

I had every reason to feel confident. Yet, despite every victory, deep inside, I still felt invisible. Still questioned my worth. Still wondered if I truly mattered. No achievement was able to silence this whisper: If you were valuable why wasn't she here?

That's the silent war of abandoned children. It doesn't matter how much success they achieve - without the foundational love of the one who was supposed to cherish them first, they question their own worth. The truth is, no matter how much love surrounds a child, there is something deep within them - a tether to the past, an invisible cord that still longs for connection to where they came from. It isn't about rejecting the ones who raised and loved them. It's about finding the missing pieces of themselves.

Some call it abandonment wounds. I knew it as a void no award, no favor, no accomplishment could fill.

And yet, something was shifting.

The door to my past was about to open. After eleven long years, I would stand face to face with the woman whose absence had shaped my entire existence.

Would I find answers? Or more aching questions?

CHAPTER 13:

ELEVEN YEARS LATER: THE RETURN OF MOTHER

"He will restore the hearts of the fathers to their children and
the hearts of the children to their fathers."
(Malachi 4:6, *NASB*)

When I was 13, my father made a statement that stayed with me: "Your mother will probably return to your life when you're 18," with a prophetic assurance that made me pause.

I couldn't tell if it was just intuition – something deeper. Did he know something he wasn't saying? My brothers and I often speculated—maybe she was in jail. Maybe she'd disappeared into a new life. I tucked the thought away. Hoping for something that seemed impossible felt too risky.

And yet, when I turned 18, his words came to pass.

It was a bright, peaceful day in Detroit when Gwen, my church mentor, invited me on a road trip to Lansing. Gwen had become a quiet anchor in my life—a nurturing presence who filled the space where close friendships should have been. Her kindness softened the sting of rejection. She reminded me that I wasn't forgotten. So, when she asked me to accompany her while she took a weekend class, I jumped at the chance. It offered something rare: peace. A few precious days where I could simply exhale, feel safe, and not worry about being misunderstood or rejected.

The next morning, while Gwen was away at class, the phone rang. I answered.

"Hi, Missy!"

It was Angel Mother. Her voice, as always, brought warmth. I could feel her smile coming through the phone.

"Hi, Angel Mother."

She paused, then asked, "What's something you've always wanted?"

Caught off guard, I said, "A bike?"

She chuckled. "No, something else."

I thought for a moment. "A leather jacket?"

There was a long pause, her voice softening like a breeze before a storm.

"Well, your mother has been found."

The room froze.

"She called your father at work and left several messages. Jimmy had her sister, your Aunt Earmy, call back to confirm it was really her. And it was. She's coming to Detroit next month to see you and your brothers."

I couldn't speak.

I had dreamed of this moment since I was six years old. For years, Angel Mother had led us in prayer, asking God to protect her and bring her back. Now, those whispered prayers were being answered.

Beneath the excitement, rose a flood of questions.

Where had she been?

Why now?

Did she miss us—or did she need something?

Was this reunion truly a miracle… or a disruption?

My father often spoke of her with a mix of admiration and resentment. He'd show me pictures – stunning portraits he had taken of her, as beautiful as a magazine cover. Then he reminded me of the debts she left behind. Afterward, almost like clockwork, he'd add, "You're starting to look a lot like your mother; just don't act like her."

I studied those photographs wondering who was she beyond the flawless images? Did she ever think about me? Did she regret leaving?

I wanted to ask her everything.

I was finally going to have the chance to confront her and find out the truth. A simmering anger bubbled beneath the surface, and I wouldn't back down until I had all the answers.

SEEING MOTHER: THE LONG-AWAITED REUNION

The day finally came.

We were driven to Uncle Charlie's house on Detroit's east side. The air inside the car was thick with anticipation. As we pulled up to the curb, I saw her - standing on the porch, long flowing hair, radiant in a way that matched the photographs I had memorized over the years.

I slowly walked up the sidewalk to the front steps with a mix of curiosity, anxiety, fear and longing – all carefully held in check. As I stepped in front of her, I looked past her smile she offered and into her eyes.

And in that moment, I didn't feel the connection I had longed for. Instead, it felt like I was meeting a stranger.

She welcomed us with kisses and lighthearted greetings, as if the past decade plus one year hadn't carved deep wounds into our souls.

"Hi darlings."

She was animated, cheerful – yet her energy felt disconnected. Her demeanor didn't match the weight of the moment.

Eleven years had passed. Eleven years of birthdays missed, holidays skipped, milestones void of her presence. And here she was, acting as if time hadn't demanded answers.

We sat down for dinner, exchanging small talk. The conversation felt forced as an unspoken wall of memories, questions and hurt separated us. She didn't explain her absence. No apologies. No acknowledgment of the void she had left in our lives. Instead, she moved forward as if the past didn't matter.

She had returned... but not as the woman I had imagined.

That night, after my brothers left, I stayed behind. I wanted more than dinner and polite hugs. I wanted history to be seen. I pulled out my photo album—the one filled with all the moments she had missed.

"This is my elementary school graduation," I said, opening to the first page.

"Here's me singing in the church choir."

"These are my prom pictures... and my debutante cotillion."

She turned each page slowly, eyes scanning the images. Occasionally, she'd smile.

"Oh, baby, you look so beautiful. Mother is so proud of you."

Yet even her warmest words floated like a mist. They didn't reach the places that ached for answers. I wanted her to acknowledge the void, to say something – but she didn't.

Every picture held a secret sorrow - a silent ache for the mother who was never there to share those moments. Behind every smiling pose was a little girl with a deep sorrow – even depression setting in – wondering why her mother wasn't there.

I wanted to ask her—Where were you when I needed you?

Did you think about me?

Why didn't you come for me sooner?

Yet she said nothing. And I didn't press—at least not at the moment.

That night, we lay beside each other, mother and daughter reunited, yet miles apart. I desperately wanted to feel her warmth again. I wanted her arms to wrap around me and erase the years of pain.

Instead, we lay in silence.

As I drifted off to sleep, I knew that rebuilding our relationship would be long and uncertain. For now, I held on to that moment. I was grateful to have her back, even if the bond we once shared felt like a distant memory. Even more so, I was thankful that He had not forgotten the prayer of a seven-year-old girl who once asked Him to protect her mother and bring her back.

God, in His faithfulness, was beginning to restore what had been lost.

I was ready to take the first step toward healing.

And for now, that was enough.

THE COST OF CONNECTION

Something in me needed more than a visit. I needed answers. I needed time. I needed to know the mysterious woman behind the photos and fragmented stories – the woman who had become a ghost in my life.

So, I made the bold decision that shook my family.

I would move to Fort Wayne, Indiana, to live with her while attending college.

It wasn't just about reconnection—it was about resolution. I figured if our relationship dynamic didn't work out, I'd still complete a semester of college and walk away with closure.

Still, not everyone understood.

My father was livid. "You don't care who you hurt," he whispered as I left with my suitcase in hand. The sting in his voice held the grief of a man who had carried the weight of her absence and now feared was being replaced by her presence.

My youngest brother saw it as a betrayal. To him, it was disloyalty to Angel Mother—the woman who had sacrificed and stood in the gap all those years.

I loved Angel Mother deeply and was grateful for her and my father's sacrifices, yet I also knew this journey was necessary for my growth, healing, and closure. This journey alone was mine to take.

Sometimes, the search for wholeness requires you to leave the safety of the known to confront the shadow of what could have been. This was that moment for me.

A FRAGILE BOND

"Sustain me, my God, according to your promise, and I will live;
do not let my hopes be dashed."
Psalm 119:116, (*NIV*)

Our three-hour drive carried a mixture of emotions—an air of excitement for finally connecting with my mother, someone I had longed to know. Yet, there was also a foreboding undercurrent, a quiet warning from God to brace myself for the unknown, anticipating the ebbs and flows of life with her that awaited me.

My mother and I moved into a makeshift living space downtown—an old office building repurposed for her nonprofit, the LaMaster Foundation. Her mission was noble: helping single mothers with food and emergency aid. Yet the space felt like a metaphor—functional, temporary, strangely hollow.

The first room served as her "conference" area. A second room, likely meant for office work, was now our shared bedroom. A narrow hallway led to a half bathroom and a small kitchen. Above us, the attic brimmed with food pantry donations. It wasn't much, but it worked. The same food she gave to others kept us fed, too.

Soon after I arrived, my mother gave me a baby doll. While I appreciated the gesture, it left me puzzled. I was eighteen, yet she seemed stuck in time, seeing me as the little six-year-old girl she left behind. Despite my confusion, I tried to be patient with her. She was trying in her own way. And I wanted—desperately—to understand her.

A COLLEGE DREAM OF ACCEPTANCE

One of the first people I met in Fort Wayne was Lenny, a kind, older man who worked for my mother's foundation. He served as our driver, protector, and friend, often shuttling me to school and my mother on her business errands. His gentle spirit offered a bit of balance in a home that was beginning to feel more unpredictable than I expected.

College felt like a second chance at life. I threw myself into my studies with an excitement I hadn't felt in years. For the first time, I wasn't the outsider – I was accepted by my peers. I wasn't the girl carrying the weight of a motherless childhood. I was Michelle—a young woman with dreams and potential. God was redeeming the years I'd felt unseen, giving me a taste of belonging.

One day in class, we passed around papers, writing anonymous affirmations for each person. When my sheet returned to me, it was filled with words my souls longed to hear:

"You're pretty."

"You're smart."

"I like how you speak."

And then the one that gripped my heart:

"I know someone who would like to meet you."

I clung to that little slip of paper like a sacred scroll. In it was evidence—I wasn't invisible. I mattered. I read it over and over when I needed to believe that I was worthy of being seen.

It felt like the beginning of something beautiful. A new chapter. A new identity.

Yet even dreams built on hope can be shaken—especially when the foundation has cracks you can't see.

THREADS OF HOPE UNRAVELING

At home, my mother tried to involve herself in my life the best way she knew how. One evening, as I was working on an assignment, she suggested, "You should use the word 'dichotomy' here," explaining its meaning and how to use it in a sentence.

Her linguistic skills were impressive. Her intellect undeniable. Yet even her guidance couldn't erase the quiet storm brewing inside me—the ache, the caution, the questions I still carried.

In our tiny makeshift bedroom, the tensions were amplified. Some nights, her mood shifted with no warning—sweet and affirming one moment, then sharp and resentful the next. Her anger often bubbled over into resentment toward Angel Mother and my father for raising us, as though their love for us was a betrayal to her. I never understood why she wasn't more thankful for what they had done - for what she did not do. Yet I never voiced that concern. I never challenged her. I just listened to her rants.

Perhaps she couldn't come to terms with the fact that the very woman she had once confronted while carrying me – the woman she likely saw as her rival – was the one God had chosen to mold and shape me into who He needed me to become. Maybe thinking about us being raised by other people only unveiled her failures. And perhaps that was too much for her bear.

To cope, I kept my Bible—gifted to me by Mr. Maness—tucked beneath my pillow. It became my shield, my sword, my silent prayer for protection.

One moment, she admired me; the next, she treated me like competition. One day, as we walked to the store, men honked at her from passing cars. Without missing a beat, she turned to me and said, "If you look this good when you're my age, it'll only be because of plastic surgery!"

Her words stung. That wasn't a compliment. Still, I swallowed the sting and continued to monitor her behavior.

Every day was an adventure; I never knew what she would say or do. I was caught in a quiet test—of my patience, of my faith, of my desire to believe that reconciliation was still possible. Just as my spirit began to wear thin, God would open a door of connection in the most unexpected and fascinating ways – like a divine thread pulling us back together before the unraveling could go too far.

One of those moments came during a political rally we attended together. She was well-versed in political agendas on both sides of the aisle, able to precisely articulate each party's priorities and policies. At the Allen County Arena, she stood up mid-debate and shouted her opinions with a confidence that turned heads. It was fascinating—and chaotic.

At 18 years old, I had the privilege of casting my first vote, one of the greatest rights afforded by the Constitution. A rite of passage. And a memory I shared with her. She walked me through the process and explained who she believed deserved my vote. It was one of the few moments we felt like mother and daughter, shaping history in our own small way.

Yet even in the milestones, the tension lingered. Our time together was a pendulum swinging between admiration and competition, warmth and coldness, silence and shouting.

The more I tried to connect, the more I realized—I wasn't just navigating a relationship. I was walking through a minefield of unhealed wounds.

FACING THE PAST IN AN UNUSUAL WAY

"The past is never as silent as we think. It lingers in the choices we make, the people we push away, and the pain we pretend isn't there. To move forward, we must unearth what we've buried and confront it with truth and humility. Healing begins when pride is shattered by the courage to say, I was wrong. Forgive me."

- Michelle B. Wilson, author, In Search of a Mother's Love.

Facing the past is one of the most brutal acts of courage a soul can endure. It demands the ripping away of the veil of denial and the confrontation of wounds that shaped your identity and choices. The truth is - buried pain doesn't stay buried. It bleeds through our decisions, taints our relationships, and shows up in the most unexpected places — until we face it.

At the crossroads of healing and hiding, there is a choice: confront the pain or let it control you.

I didn't realize how loudly our past was speaking until it echoed through the screen of a soap opera.

One afternoon, as I passed through the office, I saw my mother watching her favorite characters unfold their drama. I never understood why she was so invested in fictional lives until I realized—sometimes it's easier to escape into someone else's pain than face your own.

As she sat in front of the television, something on the screen caught my attention – a scene that hit painfully close to home. A young woman confronted her estranged mother, her voice trembling: Why did you abandon me?

I stopped in my tracks. My mother watched intently, nodding at the screen.

"That's so sad," she murmured. "That poor girl."

I sat there stunned. That girl is me; I wanted to scream. Don't you see?

Yet she didn't. Or maybe she did—and couldn't bear to admit it. Either way, her silence spoke volumes. She was watching our story unfold, pretending it wasn't her own.

In her mind, there were no missing years, no children left behind. She had built a world in which absence didn't exist. And she wanted me to live there with her—to pretend we had always been mother and daughter, unbroken and whole.

But I couldn't. I had lived those empty years. I had felt her absence at every birthday, every void at every milestone. And I needed her to say something—anything—to bridge the gap.

As time passed, the tension and arguments between us grew. So did the questions. "Why did you leave us?" I demanded one evening, unable to hold back any longer.

Her eyes flared. "You watch your tone!" she snapped. "You don't question me!"

But I had to. I couldn't keep carrying the weight of her silence.

In desperation, I pressed harder, begging for honesty, for explanation, for truth. Instead, her frustration erupted, and her words cut deep, wounding me further. It was as if I was hammering at a wound, she wasn't ready to uncover, and each question only made her more guarded. The pain and frustration I felt were almost too much to bear, still I couldn't stop searching for the answers I desperately needed.

As I gazed at her, I realized the mother-daughter relationship I had once cherished as a child was long gone. Our time together was a tug-of-war between love and pain, hope and disappointment. I wanted so desperately to rebuild a relationship with my mother, but the wounds of the past loomed like an unspoken shadow over us.

Even amid the chaos, God taught me something profound: brokenness can be a fertile ground for healing, and even the most fractured relationships can serve a greater purpose in His divine plan.

LETTING GO OF BROKEN DREAMS

"When the dreams closest to our hearts collapse under the weight of reality, don't stop dreaming. God is not finished. Broken dreams often give birth to greater purpose and freedom we didn't know we needed."
                              - Michelle B. Wilson, author, *In Search of a Mother's Love*.

There are moments in life when we grip our dreams so tightly, we miss what God is trying to do in the unraveling. We imagine how things should be - how the healing will come, how the person will change, how the story will redeem itself on our terms. We build castles in our minds and call them hope.

But sometimes, the dreams fall apart, and we're left mourning what never came to pass.

Yet even in the ashes of broken dreams, God is at work, crafting a plan far greater than we dared ask for.

For eleven years, I dreamed of reuniting with my mother. I pictured her arms around me, her voice calling me, "Darling," the two of us picking up where we left off – as if love could erase abandonment.

These dreams got me through the loneliest seasons of my life. When the ache felt too deep, I'd whisper to myself:

"One day she'll come back. One day it will all make sense."

Despite the tumultuous events that led to her absence, I clung to the belief her return would take away all the pain and disappointments of my life.

Reality often pales in comparison to the fantasies we build.

When the day came, it wasn't the healing I had imagined. It was another kind of ache—the ache of seeing the cracks in someone you once idolized. The ache of realizing that sometimes, the person you need most is still learning how to show up.

Maybe she had dreams too. Maybe she thought my presence would redeem her past, soothe her guilt, or quiet the torment of her own regret.

Two people with broken dreams, each looking to the other for salvation. Yet the weight of our unresolved pain, our issues, was too much for either of us to carry alone. It was as if life had handed us an equation where the sum never equaled the parts. And the common denominator in our struggle was my mother's absence—a wound that had scarred us both in different ways.

The truth is, we were never meant to heal each other. Not completely. That was God's work.

I began to see the emotional chasm between us for what it was—not a lack of love, but a collision of unhealed wounds. And I wanted to get to the root of why she chose to be absent from our lives. We were trying to dance to music we had never learned—each step hopeful, yet misaligned.

And in that fragile space, God gently began to show me - sometimes what we think is restoration is actually revelation.

The dream I had long clung to wasn't just slipping through my fingers. It was being released into God's hands—where it could finally become something divinely orchestrated.

THE LIES THAT SHATTERED EVERYTHING

My college courses became a refuge. I was doing my part—studying hard, showing up, trying to rebuild something sacred. Communication class, especially, felt like home. There, I wasn't just trying to be heard - I was.

I thought things were moving forward.

Yet beneath the surface, a secret was destroying everything I was trying to build.

My mother had promised to handle my tuition. I believed her. Trusted her.

Every warning letter from the school had been intercepted. I was being dropped from my classes due to unpaid fees, leaving me completely in the dark.

Without ever knowing I was in danger; I was dropped from my classes.

My heart sank. All the long hours. The affirming notes. The hope. The new identity I was forming—it collapsed like a house built on sand.

And it wasn't just the tuition. It was the silence.

She didn't just forget a bill. She let me believe a promise she couldn't keep. She wasn't working. She didn't have the money. Yet, I still believed she would find a way. She let me run toward a dream while quietly watching the floor fall out beneath me.

And for what? Hope? Denial? Desperation?

It broke something in me – not just trust but the fragile thread of belief that our reunion had restored anything real.

As tears streamed down my face, I thought about the disappointment and all the things I had hoped for. There was a moment - an outburst of words and threats that pierced deeper than I could have expected. She called me out of my name, lashing out not just in anger, but in woundedness I couldn't heal. I had pressed her with questions I thought she owed me answers to. And in return, she gave me a version of herself I wasn't prepared to see. That moment made one thing clear: love doesn't require proximity when safety is at stake. I had to let go - not out of bitterness, but out of wisdom.

My dreams—of healing, of reconciliation, of rebuilding—had crumbled. I had come to Fort Wayne seeking to rekindle what had been lost - a relationship with the woman who gave me life. Instead, I was leaving with a heavy heart from disappointment and broken dreams.

THE SILENT RIDE BACK TO DETROIT

By now, my father had been called. One of my brothers, after hearing my quiet confession about the tension between my mother and me, summoned him. I imagine the news didn't surprise my father. I had only been in Fort Wayne for six months, however, I'm sure each passing week felt like an eternity to him.

He arrived quietly, without lecture or rebuke. Just a presence. Strong. Still. Silent.

We didn't speak much.

I packed my belongings into the car, heavy with shame, disappointment and a profound since of failure. The trunk clicked shut like the door on a chapter I hadn't wanted to end. The road back to Detroit stretched out like a river of silence, winding through thoughts I couldn't put into words. I stared out the window, tears streaming down my cheeks. My father didn't press. He simply drove – with the patience of understanding.

I had come to Fort Wayne hoping to rekindle what had been lost – to find a version of a mother-daughter healing that could stitch together old wounds with new grace. Instead, I was leaving with severed expectations and a quiet ache that settled into the hollow places of my heart.

The truth, in time, came into focus like sunlight piercing through fog:

My mother had been a lesson wrapped in longing.

A presence I had yearned for.

A puzzle piece I had spent years trying to force into place.

While I had longed for her love, she was still battling demons she had never truly confronted. Demons that distorted her ability to nurture, to lead, to mother. In hindsight, I can see it clearly now: she would never have been the one to lead me to God. Her presence – had it continued uninterrupted – might have delayed my healing, not helped it.

That realization didn't numb the sting.

Instead, it gave me perspective.

God was gently teaching me what no earthly parent ever could - That no human being could fill the aching void in my soul. That no reunion could restore what only heaven could redeem.

A month later, I received a letter from her. It was tender, soft – laced with apology and memory, like an attempt to sew up the edges of something frayed. As I penned my reply, I felt the fragile thread of connection tug again. I told her about my life, my attending school again, my choices. About how I was holding on to my commitment to purity. About the values Angel Mother had instilled in me, and how I was trying to live them out.

We wrote to each other like people wading through a fog, hoping for glimpses of clarity.

The letters became a bridge – not strong, not steady, but something.

In the quiet space of prayer and reflection, I gave it all to God – again.

My mother.

My pain.

My past.

My future.

I still didn't have the answer to all my questions.

Yet, I had peace.

And I had a direction.

I was moving forward – with God.

With every silent tear and whispered prayer, I was rebuilding my life.

One surrendered step at a time.

CHAPTER 14:

FROM SETBACKS TO SUCCESS: THE POWER OF GOD'S GUIDANCE

"Trust in the Lord with all your heart and lean not on your under-standing; in all your ways submit to Him, and He will make your paths straight."
(Proverbs 3:5-6, *NIV*)

THE FREEDOM BUS TOUR: A DIVINE OPENING

Determined to reclaim time and purpose, I enrolled in the college where my father taught. With tuition waived, I was free to focus on my studies, yet old habits crept in—I slipped into a performance-driven rhythm, striving for approval through achievement.

The dream of becoming the youngest national news anchor still stirred beneath the surface, a quiet flame that refused to go out. When my cousin, whom I admired, emphasized the value of internships, I listened—and God opened a door I didn't even know existed.

My father, passionate about Black history and photography, created an assignment for his students to document national landmarks during his Freedom Bus Tour. This journey through African-American legacy – visiting

Black Wall Street in Tulsa, the Edmund Pettus Bridge in Selma, the Martin Luther King Jr. monument in Atlanta, and the National Civil Rights Museum was covered by the local media.

As I waited for my father's return, I noticed a man holding a video camera. Something inside me nudged me to approach him. Summoning my courage, I asked which station he worked for.

"WGPR," he replied.

Without hesitation, I asked if the station offered internships. He smiled, handed me a contact, and said, "Call the station manager, Teresa Cayton."

Excitement surged through me. The following week, I called Ms. Cayton, and in what felt like divine orchestration, she offered me an internship on the spot.

MY FIRST TELEVISION INTERNSHIP AT WGPR

WGPR—"Where God's Presence Reigns"—was a local station rooted in the heart of Detroit's Black community. From its humble building on Jefferson Avenue, the Renaissance Center shimmered behind it like a distant promise. It wasn't NBC or CBS, but for me, it was everything. It was the beginning.

On my first day, I wore my best suit, eager to make a good impression. Ms. Cayton greeted me warmly and gave me a tour of the station. That day, God also placed Monica Wilson in my path. Sharing my last name felt like a divine connection, and we bonded instantly.

Monica swept through the station in stiletto heels, all power and poise, but with a softness that invited trust. She became my mentor, protector, and sister in spirit. For once, I wasn't bracing for rejection. I was growing—watered by kindness, grounded by purpose.

INTERVIEWING "WEEZY" ISABEL SANFORD
FROM THE JEFFERSONS

Months in, Ms. Cayton handed me my first on-camera assignment - cover an American Heart Association event featuring Isabel Sanford—"Weezy" from the hit sitcom, *The Jeffersons*.

My heart leaped. Meeting Isabel Sanford was a dream come true. I had grown up watching her, never imagining I'd one day interview her.

The event took place at the elegant Pontchartrain Hotel in downtown Detroit. As I waited with the videographer, I indulged in a few hors d'oeuvres, trying to calm my nerves. Suddenly, Isabel Sanford appeared. Graceful, composed, and iconic. Steadying my nerves, I introduced myself and began the interview.

She spoke with warmth about her career, her heart advocacy, and the responsibility of representation. That day, I learned that asking thoughtful questions and truly listening would become my greatest tools in media. I left with something stronger than footage—I left with affirmation.

THE MAKING OF A MEDIA EVANGELIST

Over time, I interviewed politicians, entrepreneurs, and community leaders, drawing out their stories with natural ease. Viewers responded positively, and I saw firsthand how God was using my voice to amplify stories that mattered.

Beyond television, I honed my skills in radio, creating commercials and voice spots that showcased my vocal range and creativity. Monica remained my greatest cheerleader, often inviting me to her home, where I met her kind and loving Mother. I also grew fond of her boyfriend, Patrick, who worked at the station. Their relationship was like a love story unfolding – a connection that inspired me and awakened a longing for a similar connection.

REVEALING HIDDEN WOUNDS

Soon, I began dating a charming man who shared my last name - Wilson. My family adored him, especially my father, who jokingly said, "At least you won't have to change your name."

He was handsome, kind, had the greatest personality, and his family loved me as well. He proudly showed off pictures of me whenever other women expressed interest in him. What I truly loved is he respected my decision to wait for intimacy until after marriage.

While he spoke about marriage, we both carried unspoken scars that prevented us from connecting more deeply – though, truthfully, it was more my struggle than his. Despite his devotion, I couldn't fully embrace the love he offered. Although I didn't know it, God needed to do more work in my heart before I was ready to become a godly wife. Childhood wounds made it difficult to trust or commit to love. In the end, our paths separated, still the relationship taught me invaluable lessons about trust, and self-worth, and emotional healing.

After my relationship ended, I refocused my energy on my growing career in media, determined to channel my experiences into something greater. My internship at WGPR was more than just an entry point into television—it was a divine preparation. Each story I covered, every person I met, and every challenge I faced was shaping me for the greater plans God had in store.

CHAPTER 15:

THE DIVINE INTERVENTION: THIRSTY FOR MORE OF GOD

"You, God, are my God. Earnestly, I seek you; I thirst for you, and my whole being longs for you in a dry land without water."
(Psalms 63:1, *NIV*)

Little Rock had been a sanctuary where my soul blossomed, yet in that sacred space, something was missing – a void I couldn't ignore. Every fourth Sunday, I sang in the youth choir, raising my voice in praise to a God - I still yearned to know God more intimately. Church was where I belonged, where I could be myself, flaws and all, and still feel loved and accepted. I was surrounded by people who shared my faith, yet a deep hunger remained.

Matthew 5:6 says, "Blessed are those who hunger and thirst for righteousness, for they will be filled."

I knew I was hungry. I knew I was thirsty. Yet I didn't know how to satisfy that longing.

At the same time, I had just graduated with an associate's degree and faced a crossroads. The nearby universities didn't appeal to me – I refused to compromise my walk with God and longed for a place that would nurture both my faith and my future. Then, one Sunday morning, God answered my desires in a way I never expected.

A DIVINE INVITATION: LEARNING ABOUT ORAL ROBERTS UNIVERSITY

One Sunday morning, a special visitor graced the pulpit - Elder Bill Owens who spoke with conviction about, Give Me A Chance, a ministry opening doors for Black students to attend Oral Roberts University. His words stirred something in me, as if God Himself whispered, "This is the path I've prepared for you."

Here was my answer – a college grounded in Christian values, whose mission was to educate the whole person—spirit, mind, and body. Even when I didn't know where to turn, God had already paved the way to fill my hunger for Him and fulfill my purpose.

Excitement filled the bus as friends from church and I embarked on the journey to Tulsa, Oklahoma. As we pulled up to the campus, awe washed over me. ORU wasn't just a school; it was a place of beauty and serenity.

At the entrance stood the towering Praying Hands sculpture, a 60-foot-tall, 30-ton bronze monument, symbolizing our need to seek God in all things. As we continued down the winding road through campus, I felt an overwhelming sense of peace, as if stepping into a divine covering from the chaos and turmoil of the outside world.

Yet, whispers of doubt lingered. Some had warned me ORU was a cult. As I met other students—bright-eyed passionate believers—those fears melted away. I was surrounded by people who radiated a love for God, a genuine desire to live for Him. Though I didn't fully understand it yet, I was ready to embrace this new dimension of faith.

A LIFE-CHANGING WEEKEND AT ORU

Every detail confirmed I was exactly where I needed to be. The cafeteria, affectionately called Saga, exceeded my expectations, and the worship service Howard Auditorium, was unlike anything I had ever experienced. The atmosphere was thick with God's presence - students crying out in worship, some speaking in languages I didn't understand. Though unfamiliar, it awakened a deep yearning in me.

Later that night, I met with a resident advisor. As I shared my story, especially the pain of my mother's absence, years of suppressed emotions surfaced. For the first time, I allowed myself to feel it all. Tears streamed down my face as I confronted wounds, I hadn't realized I was still carrying. Although it was frightening to allow myself to go there emotionally, it was a confirmation this was where I needed to be.

The RA listened with compassion, then prayed for me. Something inside me began to shift. For the first time, I knew – I wasn't alone in my pain and my heart mattered to God. This wasn't just about college; this was about healing.

FAITH, GROWTH, AND UNEXPECTED TURNS

God was preparing me for more than I could imagine. ORU would stretch my faith, challenge my understanding of Him, and reveal His purpose for my life in ways I couldn't yet comprehend.

Returning home to Detroit, I confidently shared my decision to attend ORU with my father. He smiled, nodded, and supported my choice. Before long, he handed me the keys to a brand new white, 2 door Chevrolet-coupe, a symbol of new beginnings. Packing my belongings, I set out for Tulsa with my second - oldest brother, who loved long road trips. As he drove the 13-hour drive, anticipation filled the air - each mile bringing me closer to the beautiful journey ahead.

CHAPTER 16:

THE RISE OF A PROPHETIC VOICE IN WORSHIP AND MEDIA

"Forget the former things; see, I am doing something new!
Now it springs up; do you not perceive it?"
(Isaiah 43:8-9, *NIV*)

MY FIRST DAYS AT ORU

Autumn met me with amber-gold leaves dancing across the wide, open campus. The Oklahoma breeze carried the crisp scent of change, brushing against my face like a quiet welcome. I stood in my dorm room, not just unpacking suitcases, but stepping into the unknown—a journey God Himself had choreographed. My roommate, Brie, was kind, and we quickly fell into rhythm, easing the transition. Still, beneath the surface, I knew something deeper was being stirred.

I had enrolled in the Broadcast Journalism program with clear intent: to tell stories that mattered. Yet my calling stretched beyond headlines and scripts. I knew the deeper purpose I was called to. I also wanted to use my other talents for God, like my soprano voice, which I had honed and strengthened over the years - especially in my church choir. I was happy to hear about the renowned

Souls A' Fire choir, where Black voices thundered not only in harmony but in worship. It was more than a choir—it was a ministry of God's divine healing to all who heard us.

FINDING MY VOICE IN WORSHIP: SOULS' A FIRE CHOIR

The auditions arrived and I mustered all my courage and showed up. I nervously waited and soon, the director, David Smith, looked at me and said, "What's your name?"

Taking a deep breath, I stepped forward and introduced myself. "My name is Michelle, and I'm from Detroit," I said with a smile.

His eyebrows lifted. "Detroit, huh? Gospel city! Well, what song do you know?"

All eyes were on me, and I felt a certain pressure coming from a city with such a rich history of gospel music helping shape legends like The Winans, Aretha Franklin, The Clark Sisters, and more. Yet as the music minister played song after song, I realized I didn't recognize any of them. My confidence wavered.

Finally, he asked gently, "Do you know 'Amazing Grace'?" "Y-yes," I stammered.

As the piano echoed the familiar chords through the room, I took a shaky breath and sang, my soft soprano voice barely commanding attention. It was trembling but sincere. I left the rehearsal feeling disappointed, convinced my voice lacked the power to stand out. My mind was filled with doubts and worries when I returned to my dorm room. Yet even in my disappointment, I was thankful for the kindness and patience the music director showed me.

The next day, as I nervously scanned the list of accepted choir members, I couldn't believe my eyes. My name was on the list! Michelle Wilson. As my eyes filled with tears, I felt a rush of excitement and gratitude, knowing nothing but God's grace had brought me to this point. My voice wasn't the most polished, yet I had something else to offer—a heart full of faith and a desire to serve God through singing.

Joining the choir became more than just an extracurricular activity - it was a spiritual awakening. Every rehearsal began with an hour of worship, shifting the focus from performance to ministry. One evening, the director paused and said, "This isn't just about performance. We are here to lead people into God's presence." His words struck me deeply.

That moment rewired something inside of me. Worship became my awakening.

THE POWER OF WORSHIP:
CALLED TO THE FOREFRONT

When we ministered at different churches, we didn't just sing - we poured our hearts out to God, drawing people closer to him. It was evident His presence moved powerfully among us, as people wept under the tangible weight of His glory and experienced healing in ways only God could orchestrate. This was all new to me, filling me with a deep sense of awe and reverential fear, knowing I was witnessing something sacred.

During our rehearsals, we were blessed to be visited by many powerful gospel artists and ministers. One memorable moment was when Dr. Iona Locke came to speak to us, encouraging us to see this season of our lives as a special time of preparation and purpose and reminding us to stay grounded in our faith and values. We were also visited by Donnie McClurkin, who taught us some of his most beloved songs. It was clear his success wasn't just due to his extraordinary talent but also to his unwavering discipline. He approached music with a seriousness that left no room for mediocrity, teaching us to enunciate each word with precision and sing with just the right vocal resonance. In doing so, he was imparting the very wisdom that had helped him achieve success in the gospel music world.

What impacted me deeply was when another gospel artist visited and led us in worship. At the end, while he prayed for us, he noticed me standing in the back — hiding, as I often did. He called me forward and spoke over my life, "God is calling you to the forefront. You are not meant to stay in the background. He has great plans for you."

I was stunned. All my life, rejection had made me shrink into the shadows. Yet through this choir, God was gently pulling me into visibility showing me I was seen and chosen by Him.

The choir deepened my reliance on God, allowing me to experience His power in a way I never had before. Even with limited time to study, I remained devoted, and God honored my faithfulness as I achieved the best grades while singing in the choir.

After choir rehearsal or a night of ministering in song, I'd return to my dorm room—tired in body but alive in spirit. The pressure of unfinished homework faded into the background. Somehow, I'd finish it quickly, as if grace itself propelled me. My heart wasn't fixated on academics—it was yearning for God.

I opened my Bible and read it for hours, then I knelt beside my bed, and began to worship. "Holy, holy, holy," I whispered, then cried, then sang. My arms stretched toward heaven, tears streaming down my face as the atmosphere shifted. I wasn't just praying—I was encountering Him. It was sacred. It was personal. I was returning to my First Love, and He welcomed me with open arms.

What unfolded between us wasn't religion—it was a love affair, deeper than anything I had ever known. Many nights, I'd stay up worshiping until 1, 2, even 3 in the morning. And yet, when I woke, it was as if no time had passed. My soul had been quenched. The thirst I had carried for so long was being satisfied in His presence.

God was on my mind constantly—24 hours a day. I talked to Him, and He spoke back in that still, small voice. There was an intimacy between us I didn't know was possible, yet one I had longed for since I was a little girl. I was finally getting to know my God—not just as Creator or Judge, but as Father, Friend, and Lover of my soul.

I wanted everyone to experience what I had found. I started sending my brothers books on how to fall in love with God, how to know Him deeply and intimately. They never responded. I'm sure they thought I had become a fanatic. But I didn't care. I was communing with the God of the universe—and that was all that mattered.

A GLIMPSE INTO THE INDUSTRY: FINDING MY VOICE AS A NEWSCASTER

"The Lord directs the steps of the godly. He delights in
every detail of their lives."
(Psalm 37:23, *NLT*)

Every semester brought new opportunities to sharpen my skills. I dissected news articles pulling apart every line and reconstructing it with the precision of storytellers. In the writing labs, we practiced the delicate art of balancing truth and emotion in a non-bias way—a skill I knew would be invaluable in the future.

I was also drawn to broadcast journalism, where I honed my on-camera presence as a newscaster for our college news station, *ORU Live*. Armed with a microphone and a camera, I roamed the campus, capturing untold stories. This wasn't just schoolwork—it was training for my God-given calling.

I was eager to learn from visiting professionals who shared their insights and experiences who spoke of the industry's harsh realities of fierce competition. They warned us of the thousands of applicants vying for the same jobs and urged us to have a backup plan. Despite these warnings, I trusted in God's divine guidance and believed with hard work and dedication, I would make my mark in this challenging and rewarding industry.

INTERVIEWING PROMINENT CHRISTIAN FIGURES: MY CAMPUS FOCUS RADIO SHOW

Wanting to expand my skills, I created and hosted my own radio show, *Campus Focus*. It became a hub for Christian creatives—singers, preachers, visionaries—to share their stories. I was learning how to amplify other voices while finding my own.

THE LEGENDARY WINANS:
A DEFINING MOMENT IN GOSPEL MUSIC

When the Winans family came to town, I was eager to meet them. Their songs — like "Tomorrow," "Ain't No Need to Worry," and "Millions" — were staples in

African-American churches. Still for me, "The Question Is," held a special place in my heart.

That night, they welcomed me like family. One of the brothers, charming and handsome, teased me with lighthearted flattery, still I remained focused, — capturing the heart behind their music ministry.

The warmth of their welcome reminded me - God was giving me access to greatness, and grace to stand in it.

BENNY HINN: A DEFINING
MOMENT OF TRUSTING GOD

When I learned Pastor Benny Hinn was coming to the Mabee Center, I had just finished reading his book, *Good Morning, Holy Spirit.* Each page was saturated with the anointing of God, confirming Pastor Hinn as a powerful vessel of God's healing touch to the world.

Before the service, I put out a fleece before God:

"If I can interview Benny Hinn, Lord, I'll take it as a sign I'm truly meant to pursue this calling in media."

On the day of his event, I joined the mass choir singing as waves of people fell under the power of God. Even before Pastor Hinn preached, testimonies filled the room - people hearing for the first time, others walking after years in wheelchairs, some receiving healing from terminal illnesses and other healings beyond explanation. Each testimony shared intensified the atmosphere as the presence of God grew more powerful. Then, in a moment that felt both surreal and sacred, Pastor Hinn waved his jacket - and it was as if an invisible current of glory swept across the crowd. Hundreds collapsed under the power of the Holy Spirit, in holy surrender. I sat in awe, having never stepped into an environment so charged with the supernatural. I had never witnessed healing on this level

– so personal, so profound – by the hand of a living God. Uncontrollable tears flowed from my eyes—not just tears of joy for the miracles unfolding before me, but perhaps also the silent cries of my soul, reaching out for the healing I desperately needed. The healing I saw others receiving around me.

After the service, I interviewed attendees for my radio show, capturing their life - changing encounters. One of the individuals I was privileged to interview was Sharon Daugherty, the wife of Pastor Billy Joe Daugherty of Victory Christian Center. She spoke about her faith and the incredible things she anticipated God would do in her family's life and ministry. It was a moment I deeply cherished, as the Daugherty's were highly respected pillars of the community. Still, my goal lingered just out of reach– an interview with Benny Hinn.

As the sun set, Benny Hinn prepared to take the stage again. I stood at the entrance of the VIP area, my heart filled with determination to interview the renowned minister. Security warned me, "Your chances of interviewing him are slim," they told me. Undeterred, I closed my eyes, whispered a prayer for divine intervention, and reminded God of the fleece I had placed before Him.

After his final service, Pastor Hinn stepped through the secure backstage entrance, just moments after concluding the final service. He had been ministering all day, and I knew he must have been tired. He was heading toward his car and just before he reached his vehicle, a security guard pointed in my direction, explaining I had been waiting patiently for hours. Pastor Hinn turned to me and said, "I'll give you five minutes." I felt the heavens open as he walked toward me.

This was my moment. The confirmation I had asked God for.

Clutching my microphone while my college friend stood by with the video camera, I asked about the Holy Spirit's role in the Trinity, miracles, and questions about his book. At the end, he smiled and said words that would stay with me forever:

"Wow, You're good at this. I have never been asked this question before. Keep going."

It wasn't just a compliment - it was confirmation. God had answered my prayer, affirming I was exactly where I needed to be. That night, back in my dorm room, I could hardly sleep. I lay staring at the ceiling, dreaming about my bright future in television.

DR. MYLES MUNROE: A PROPHETIC DECLARATION OF MY CALLING

One of the most profound interviews was with Dr. Myles Munroe, a distinguished teacher and author. After he ministered at a local church, I had the privilege of engaging him in a thought-provoking interview, drawing from his wealth of knowledge and wisdom.

To seal this cherished moment, I asked him to sign his book I had brought with me.

Instead of a simple autograph, he wrote a prophetic message that revealed the breadth and scope of how far God planned to take me in media. He wrote:

"Your future is pregnant with unlimited potential. Never compromise your standards of righteousness."

Then he added something that left me stunned:

"You will work in the professional television medium. Television will be your pulpit, and you will reach MILLIONS for Christ."

I clutched the book to my chest, overwhelmed. Could this be true? Could God have such a monumental calling for someone like me who had been rejected, abandoned, and hidden?

A NEW VISION

As I walked back to my dorm, Dr. Munroe's words echoed in my heart. For so long, I buried myself in work to avoid deep relationships. My classmates even nicknamed me "Michelle on the Run" because I was always moving, never pausing long enough to let anyone close.

God was shifting my perspective.

Every skill I honed, every interview I conducted and every lesson I learned was a part of His divine preparation. I was beginning to see it – television wasn't just a dream It was my calling, my pulpit, my purpose. And God was teaching me to trust Him completely.

CHAPTER 17:

BREAKING TIES, FINDING TRUTH: BAPTIZED IN THE HOLY SPIRIT, AND GOD'S PERFECT TIMING

Jesus explained, "But ye shall receive power after
the Holy Ghost comes upon you.
(Acts 1:8, *KJV*)

BAPTIZED IN THE HOLY SPIRIT

Being on campus stirred a deep hunger in me to draw closer to God, not just to know God, but to truly encounter the Holy Spirit and understand His purpose and power in the life of a believer. I began to dig into the scriptures and often read Jesus' words in Acts 1:8:

"But you shall receive power after the Holy Spirit comes upon you."

I pondered. Hadn't I received the Holy Spirit when I accepted Jesus as my Savior at twelve years old at Little Rock Baptist Church?

AT ORU, I learned while I did receive the Holy Spirit at salvation – because His presence comes to dwell in every believer – there was another level of the Holy Spirit's power available to me. This was the baptism of the Holy Spirit, an experience that empowers believers to walk in greater boldness, spiritual gifts, and intimacy with God.

Salvation brings the Holy Spirit within us (John 14:17), but the baptism of the Holy Spirit is when He comes upon us with power (Acts 1:8). Just as Jesus' disciples already believed in Him yet were instructed to wait for the outpouring of the Holy Spirit at Pentecost (Acts 2), I realized I, too, could receive a deeper measure of His presence to live a more empowered Christian life.

Being baptized in the Holy Spirit with the evidence of speaking in tongues wasn't just about fitting in with my peers. It was about receiving power from God to live a victorious life, to walk in boldness, and to fulfill His calling with greater strength and clarity.

During chapel, I witnessed the Holy Spirit move through ministers like Kim Clement and Marilyn Hickey, whose prophetic words, gifts of healings, and teachings stirred my faith. Yet, I felt like an outsider — especially when I heard others speaking in tongues – this unknown heavenly language that speaks directly to God.

It felt distant to me, like a promise meant for others yet somehow out of my reach.

I participated in tarrying sessions with the Isabell sisters, to seek the baptism of the Holy Spirit. Kneeling in prayer, I repeated phrases, hoping for a breakthrough. Yet hours later, I was left empty-handed. Frustrated, I sought solitude in the Penthouse prayer room of my dorm room building, pouring out my heart to God. I prayed, I wept, I begged — still, nothing happened.

"God makes everything beautiful in His timing." (Ecclesiastes 3:11) became my anchor.

My breakthrough came unexpectedly during a Souls A' Fire choir retreat. In a moment of distraction, I turned too quickly and chipped my front tooth on a stone fireplace. The pain was excruciating, yet I refused to let it ruin my time there.

We all gathered in the main room to pray and sing praises to God. As worship filled the room, I knelt near the piano and prayed for my father's salvation and interceded for my family. In that moment — when my focus shifted from myself to others — a beautiful new language flowed from deep within my spirit. It felt foreign, yet deeply familiar – like it had been resting inside me all along, just waiting to be awakened. As I poured out, I felt lighter…freer…and more connected to God than I had ever known before. It was as if a door had been opened, and I was being gently ushered into a new dimension of intimacy with Him.

I had been baptized with the Holy Spirit.

Overwhelmed with joy, I shared my experience with the group, no longer concerned about my chipped tooth. God had answered my prayers - not in the way I expected, but in His perfect timing. It was as if He was saying:

"When you take your eyes off your circumstances and focus on others, that is when I will move."

This moment changed everything. I now had even more of God's power, guidance, and comfort to walk boldly into my future.

HIDDEN THREADS OF UNSEEN AGREEMENTS

Even when we pursue God's purpose, the enemy works to derail us – often through unhealthy relationships that distract, weaken, or compromise our witness, faith and intimacy with God. This is why we must remain vigilant — praying, reading the Word, and surrounding ourselves with godly friendships that strengthen our walk with Christ.

At ORU, I formed friendships, believing they were God's blessings. Many were, but some were rooted in shared brokenness rather than true healing. We bonded over similar wounds - absent mothers, emotionally distant fathers, and a lingering sense of rejection. Instead of seeking God's ultimate healing, we unknowingly sought comfort in each other's pain, forming unhealthy emotional bonds rather than spiritually edifying connections.

I didn't realize it at the time, these relationships created unhealthy soul ties.

What Is a Soul Tie?

A soul tie is a deep emotional and spiritual bond formed between individuals. These ties can either be healthy - drawing us closer to complete dependence on God - or unhealthy leading us into emotional dependency and spiritual compromise.

<u>Healthy Soul Ties</u>

- Strengthens relationships God ordains (marriage, godly friendships, mentorship).
- Encourages spiritual growth, accountability and righteous living.
- Helps us to fulfill our purpose in Christ pointing us toward healing and wholeness.

<u>Unhealthy Soul Ties</u>

- Formed through shared trauma, emotional dependency, or sin.
- Creates spiritual and emotional entanglements that weigh us down.
- Opens doors to compromise, rebellion, and shame, making it harder to fully submit to God's will.

I thought I was forming healthy friendships, but the enemy was weaving snares that would take years to untangle. These relationships didn't heal me, they reinforced my brokenness.

Breaking free required discernment, repentance, and intentional healthy boundaries. God showed me healing could not come from other broken people - only from Him.

THE PATHWAY TO RELEASE

"Repent, then, and turn to God, so that your sins may be wiped out, that time of refreshing may come from the Lord."
(Acts 3:19, *NIV*)

Recognizing unhealthy soul ties was one thing - breaking free was another. I had to make a conscious decision to repent and close the doors that had been opened through emotional entanglements and compromises.

I prayed for God's forgiveness, still, it wasn't enough to just walk away. I had to make sure these doors remained closed through prayer and seeking God's wisdom daily through practicing healthy boundaries, protecting my heart from reopening toxic cycles, and through accountability - surrounding myself with those who pointed me back to truth.

What felt small and innocent at first had led to spiritual weight and compromise. I knew I had to be vigilant, recognizing when familiar spirits were trying to pull me back into unhealthy patterns. I also had to fight to maintain my purity for the calling God had placed on my life.

THE MR. & MRS. DEGREE:
THE PRESSURE TO MARRY AT ORU

Just as friendships can create unhealthy soul ties, so can romantic relationships built on fear, desperation, or pressure rather than God's leading.

At ORU, many students were just as focused on earning their "Mr. and Mrs." degree as they were on their academic degree. The fear was real: if they didn't find a spouse on campus, they might miss their opportunity to marry a godly partner. This pressure led many to rush into relationships – not out of divine direction, but out of fear and the ticking clock of expectation.

I wasn't immune to this longing, I too desired love, companionship, and a ministry partner - someone who would walk this life of faith alongside me. And there was one man who, in my heart, seemed to fit that role perfectly.

He had everything I admired - a deep passion for God, charismatic personality, and a great sense of humor. And yes, he was very good looking. We spent countless hours studying together, our conversation stretching late into the night, filled with laughter, theology, and dreams of the future careers and ministry endeavors. I found subtle ways to draw closer to him, even volunteering to help him film his ministry outreach events to young adults.

In the end, he chose someone else to marry.

I lay in my dorm room bed that night, tears streaming down my face, mourning what could have been. My heart ached, yet in that moment, I realized something crucial - I had to trust God completely, not only with my future but with my desire for marriage and a family.

THE "GOD TOLD ME YOU'RE MY WIFE" PROPHECY TRAP

As much as I had my own experiences of heartbreak, I also encountered the spiritual manipulation that often came with the pursuit of marriage at ORU.

More than once, I had men approach me, claiming God told them I was their future wife. Some barely knew me. Others made their declarations with confidence and certainty, as if they held a divine contract I simply needed to sign.

God's voice doesn't bring pressure – only peace. And His confirmations don't come through manipulation, confusion, fear or confusion.

I quickly learned to discern the difference between a genuine word from God and the desires of men disguised as prophecy. The fear of being alone had driven many into relationships that weren't rooted in prayer or wisdom, but in insecurity and urgency. And I refused to let fear dictate my future.

THE MAN FROM EUROPE: CHALLENGING BELIEF'S THAT SHAPED ME

While I was sorting through the complexities of love and longing. There was another man who caught my attention – yet in a way I didn't expect.

I met him in my television production class, along with his sister, and we quickly became friends. He was the most handsome man I had ever seen, still there was something beyond his looks that stood out - a quiet authority, a presence that made it clear he carried a divine destiny.

Yet, despite how drawn I was to him, I never allowed myself to entertain thoughts of dating or marriage with him. Not because he wasn't amazing but because he was White.

I had grown up in a home where my father made it explicitly clear – Blacks don't marry Whites. Whites don't marry Blacks. That world simply did not exist in my mind. It was as if an invisible wall had been erected between us, not by my own convictions but by the unspoken rules I had been conditioned to accept.

Still, I couldn't deny he carried something different - a calling, an anointing, a purpose that intrigued me in ways I couldn't explain. Even if I never saw him as a potential partner, I was simply thankful to have crossed paths with someone so uniquely set apart.

As I grew in my walk with God, I came to realize skin color was insignificant compared to the beauty of the heart – something unseen yet deeply valuable. I began to broaden my perspective, understanding that whichever husband God had chosen for me, regardless of his nationality or ethnicity, he would be a part of God's divine plan, and our purposes would align perfectly.

TRUSTING GOD WITH LOVE AND DESTINY

Through every experience - heartbreak, rejection, and even unexpected connections - I was learning my future, my love story, and my purpose were not mine to orchestrate.

The truth was, I had longed for love and a godly husband, but at ORU, I came to understand something greater - God's timing would always be better than my own plans.

I didn't need to force a relationship or fall for prophetic manipulation - I simply needed to trust God, completely and unreservedly.

And that trust would lead me exactly where I was meant to be.

God would later whisper to me if I waited on him, I would have it all – an influential media career, a marriage, and children and success beyond my imagination. Though my desires tried to create its own version of the future, I knew it would be futile. So, I chose to trust God and wait.

Even in the waiting, God was working behind the scenes. My mother, who had been a distant memory, was living in Oklahoma City, just hours away. I didn't know it yet, but God was preparing to bring our paths together again.

This time, I wasn't the little girl longing for her love. I was a young woman on a journey of self-discovery, holding on to the truth that no matter what happened next, God alone was my ultimate source of healing and strength.

CHAPTER 18:

MOTHER'S SECOND RETURN: THE ALTAR AND THE UNFOLDING JOURNEY OF HEALING

"The heart is deceitful above all things and beyond cure. Who can understand it? I the Lord search the heart and examine the mind, to reward each person according to their conduct, according to what their deeds deserve."
(Jeremiah 17:9-10, *NIV*)

MOTHER IS IN OKLAHOMA CITY

Even when my mother returned to our lives, it was as if she never had. Her body may have reentered the scene, but her heart stayed locked behind the doors she'd shut long ago. She moved through life with the same detachment she had when she left—as though none of it mattered. No apologies. No reflection. Just a woman carrying herself like a single traveler passing through a station she'd once lived in.

I stopped expecting anything. Healing couldn't be forced. I had to trust God to move where my hands could not.

Then came the call from my father.

"She's in Oklahoma City now."

Just two hours from ORU.

It had been three years since I last saw her. The mention of her name brought a thunderstorm of emotions—anger, sadness, confusion—and buried beneath them, a flicker of curiosity. Maybe even hope.

I asked my friend Nea to drive. The late-afternoon sun slanted low across the Oklahoma plains, casting golden rays across the highway. The silence in the car was tangible, yet Nea's voice was a spark of light in the stillness.

"Cousin Shelly," she said, lifting the mood with a grin, "What are you gonna say when you see her?"

"I don't know," I admitted, staring out the window as the Oklahoma landscape blurred by.

"Maybe just… 'Hi.' I don't even know what to feel."

She shot me a concerned glance, "God's got this," she said gently. "Just keep an open mind."

When we arrived at her apartment complex, I spotted her immediately. She was walking toward us with a smile, arms outstretched as if all was well.

"Hi, darling!" she called out, like we were characters in a reunion scene she'd written in her own mind.

"Hi," I said flatly.

She exchanged pleasantries with Nea, acting like she had always been a part of my life. Inside, I was seething. How could she ignore the years of absence, the birthdays missed, the milestones never celebrated? How could she pretend everything was fine. Her easy demeanor felt like a slap in the face.

We stood near the car, making small talk for twenty minutes. I was polite but detached. She promised to come to my graduation as she hugged me and said our goodbyes.

SPEEDING TOWARD TRUTH: A SHORT FUSE
AND THE REARVIEW MIRROR

The ride back to campus was different. I had promised to drive, but the longer I thought about the encounter, the angrier I became. My grip on the steering wheel tightened.

"Shelly, slow down!" Nea said, her voice tinged with fear.

I barely registered her words. "I just don't get it!" I burst out. "How can she pretend like everything's fine? She doesn't care about me—she never has!"

"Don't let this get to you," Nea said gently, "God's in control. Just forgive her."

"Don't tell me not to be angry!" I snapped. "You don't understand. You have a mother who loves you!"

The words cut through the car like glass and then silence followed. Heavy. Awkward. Real.

I knew I was being unfair. Nea didn't deserve that. Yet pain isn't logical. It just spills.

That night, I sat on the edge of my bed, knees tucked to my chest, staring at the beige walls of my dorm like they might explain something. My mother was still a stranger. She wasn't the soft, warm vision I saw in other families. She wasn't what I had longed for. She was… gone, even when present.

I had spent years outrunning the ache. Pretending it didn't matter. Still, ignoring pain doesn't erase it. It makes it fester. And I had reached the end of pretending.

LAYING MY BURDENS DOWN AT THE ALTAR

*"In my distress, I called to the Lord; I cried to my God for help. From
His temple, he heard my voice; my cry came before Him, into His ears."*
(Psalm 18:6, *NIV*)

When life becomes weighed down by childhood wounds, the only option is to surrender them to is God. As 1 Peter 5:7 reminds us, we must "cast all our anxieties and fears on God because He cares for us." Matthew 11:28-30 says, "Come to me, all you who are weary and burdened, and I will give you rest."

I desperately needed that rest. The Lord knew I needed healing, and the church was where I could meet God at my point of need.

At ORU, most Black students gravitated toward Higher Dimensions Evangelistic Center, led by Pastor Carlton Pearson. A dynamic singing preacher, whose sermons ignited faith and joy.

One of the most memorable moments of my time was attending the first Azusa conference, an event founded by Pastor Pearson that would grow to draw thousands of people from across the country to Tulsa. The worship, the preaching, and the presence of God at Azusa left me in awe.

It was a historic moment, still my journey with God was about to take a deeper, more personal turn.

My spiritual healing took root at Victory Christian Center, where Pastor Billy Joe Daugherty preached the Word of God with passion and precision. His messages felt personally tailored, delivering profound truth that pierced my soul. The church wasn't just a place of worship; it became a sanctuary of hope and healing for my deepest wounds.

After each sermon, Pastor Daugherty gave an altar call. I found myself walking to the front week after week, surrendering my pain, shame, and fears to God.

I often joked that I should just set up a tent at the altar because I spent so much time there. Those moments were transformative. God was peeling away the layers of hurt, rejection, and abandonment. Through Pastor Daugherty's ministry, I encountered a deeper level of God's love and began to experience more healing.

A NEW SPIRITUAL FAMILY:
GOD'S PROVISION IN FRIENDSHIPS

Outside of church, God continued chipping away at years of rejection, surrounding me with people who embraced me as family. Kim, Nedra, Letitia, and Debbie became like older sisters, drawing me into their world with love and laughter. Nedra often invited me to her home in Texas, where her family welcomed me with open arms. Their Southern comfort meals always wrapped me in warmth and belonging.

Another older student, Carmen, became a mentor to me and others. She celebrated our milestones with thoughtful gifts and words of encouragement. Through her kindness and generosity, I saw God's love reflected in a way that was truly special.

Within these connections, I wasn't just tolerated – I was truly seen, valued, and wanted.

God was healing me, piece by piece, still I wasn't done laying my burdens down. There were still many layers to go.

CHAPTER 19:

FROM GRADUATION DISAPPOINTMENT TO DESTINY: FINDING MY PATH IN MEDIA, MINISTRY, AND MOVIES

"There is surely a future hope for you, and your hope will not be cut off."
(Proverbs 23:18, NIV)

INTERNSHIP AT NBC AFFILIATE

The scent of disinfectant clung to my hands as I scrubbed shower stalls and vacuumed endless dormitory halls—humbling work that helped cover part of my tuition. Yet even as the hum of vacuums echoed down the hallways, my thoughts stayed fixed on something higher. I was planning my first official television internship.

It was during my senior year at ORU that the opportunity came: a coveted position at KTUL, the NBC affiliate. From the moment I stepped into the newsroom, I knew this wasn't just another internship—it was a proving ground. A place where I would learn the language of meeting live deadlines.

The shuffle of reporters preparing live shots for breaking news had me mesmerized. And in the center of it all stood Yvonne Lewis, the weekend anchor. Poised, articulate, and unshakably confident, she took me under her wing.

My first assignment? A feature on the American Red Cross blood drive.

I was nervous. So, I climbed to the station's rooftop. Overlooking the city below - cars weaving through streets and birds chirping in the late autumn sky – created the perfect backdrop. I stood still beneath the open heavens and whispered a prayer.

"God… give me an angle."

And just like that, it came. Blood brothers and sisters. Not just donors, but life-givers. Sacred ties formed through the act of saving another. I raced back inside, my fingers flying over the keyboard. And when Yvonne aired the piece exactly as I had written it—unchanged, untouched—I felt a deep surge of affirmation.

It wasn't just a career milestone. It was a spiritual one. I had asked God to show up. And He did.

GRADUATION DAY: A MOMENT OF TRIUMPH AND DISAPPOINTMENT

"…Well done, good and faithful servant; thou hast been faithful over a few things, I will make thee ruler over many things."
(Matthew 25:23, *KJV*)

Spring in Tulsa was unusually warm that year. The trees on campus swayed lazily in the breeze, their branches whispering over the heads of students who hurried across campus in gowns and caps, faces beaming with dreams unfolding. And for me, it was meant to be the final celebration after years of silent battles and hidden prayers.

I had done it. I had made it through.

My final year at ORU had been marked by breakthroughs. Anchoring on *ORU Live*, I had learned to steady my voice under pressure and grow comfortable in the spotlight. Classmates would stop me in the halls and say, "You're better than some of the weekend anchors." Their words weren't just compliments—they were fuel. Proof that my calling in media was real and undeniable.

Still, what I anticipated most wasn't just walking across a stage.

It was looking into the crowd and seeing her face.

My father and Angel Mother had flown in from Detroit, their joy radiant. Angel Mother even styled my hair with loving precision, the same way she had so many times before—always believing, always investing. She made sure every curl fell just right.

Yet as the graduates lined up and the processional music rose, my eyes searched the rows of family members. Yet as I scanned the crowd for the face I hoped to see – my biological mother – she was nowhere in sight.

She wasn't there.

My biological mother had promised she would come. She had said she would be there for this moment. When I walked across that stage to receive my degree, her absence echoed louder than the cheers of the audience. The sting of rejection resurfaced as I sat in my cap and gown, wondering if she stayed away to avoid facing my father and Angel Mother. Whatever her reason, her absence spoke volumes, and I had to keep moving forward toward the bright future God had planned.

Graduating from ORU wasn't just about academics - it was a spiritual transformation. I left with deep healing, and a calling that grew clearer by the day. As I packed my bags for Detroit, I knew this was only the beginning of a life filled with hope, purpose, and restoration — a journey God had ordained all along.

It was only the beginning.

RETURNING TO DETROIT: FINDING MY PLACE IN MEDIA AND ACTING

"Trust in the Lord with all your heart and lean not on your understanding; in all your ways submit to Him, and He will make your paths straight."
(Proverbs 3:5-6, *NIV*)

I had left with dreams and returned with vision. Though I was coming back to the same city, I was not the same woman.

I took whatever work I could find—jobs that paid the bills while I waited for doors to open. Eventually, I began teaching television production to employees at General Motors, Chrysler, and Ford. Standing in front of professionals twice my age, I shared what I'd learned in school and in the newsroom. Their respect and admiration rekindled a fire in me.

BREAKING INTO BROADCASTING: MY JOURNEY AT CTN

Then, an opportunity opened at WLPC TV-28, a Christian television network, founded by Glenn Plummer. I started as a production assistant for their flagship show, *CTN Live!* and soon Mr. Plummer recognized my potential. He invited me into meetings with executives where I observed his unmatched charisma and deal-making skills. I wore many hats at CTN, from hosting my show *In Your Business* to managing the production staff.

MAKING HISTORY IN THE DIRECTOR'S CHAIR

Within a short time, I became the first female director of *CTN Live!*

The station's flagship show, *CTN Live!* was the heartbeat of our network. Hosted by Plummer, it tackled topics ranging from politics to faith while providing a platform for local gospel artists. The director's role at CTN was no small task. I was thrown into the deep end with a small crew and multiple responsibilities. My first day in the chair was a baptism by fire – dead air, awkward camera transitions, and the intensity of calling shots live while on the air. Still, I found my rhythm.

Directing live television became an adrenalin rush like no other. Mr. Hoadley, Plummer's right-hand man, stood by my side and helped me learn the intricacies of directing. I loved the precision it required: calling out, "Ready camera one, take camera one," and seamlessly switching between angles. The hum of equipment and the focused intensity in the control room felt electric. Within a month, I had found my place, and the fear I once had of directing was gone.

HOLLYWOOD COMES TO DETROIT:
MY FIRST ACTING JOB

"You enlarge my steps under me."
(Psalm 18:36, *NASB*)

While working at CTN, I heard about a movie production filming in Detroit and wanted to audition for it.

The film?

Out of Sight, starring George Clooney and Jennifer Lopez.

I walked into the audition room not with experience—but with presence. I stood tall. My voice clear. My spirit anchored. When they cast me as a reporter by the boxing ring, I knew this was more than a role. It was a glimpse.

On the day of filming, I dressed the part: golden vest, black slacks, Canon 35mm camera slung around my neck, and a small notepad in hand. I wasn't just acting I was inhabiting a dream I'd long carried in silence.

The studio lights illuminated the once – traditional theater, now reimagined theater as a boxing venue with a ring in the center. Surrounded by cocktail tables and glowing lamps, patrons dined as they watched the fight unfold. Camera dollies rolled across concrete. Crew members barked cues and actors took their places. As the scene began, I stood by the ring, mimicking the actions of a seasoned actors portraying journalists—scribbling fake notes, snapping pictures with intention, and soaking up the electricity of it all.

For a moment, I wasn't just a girl from Detroit with a dream—I was living it.

And then came the pull. A holy hesitation.

I watched the scene unfold, its content edgy and sensual—far from the values I had been clinging to. Deep inside, something shifted. A question rose deep within my spirit - one I couldn't ignore:

"Is this where your gift is meant to shine?"

The next morning, I chose not to return. I gave up the chance to be featured in more scenes, risking being cut from the movie. Yet my spirit was at peace.

Months later, a friend called out of the blue:

"Michelle! I just saw you in the *Out of Sight*! movie. Girl, you were on screen!"

The scene had stayed.

Still, more than that, my obedience had been recorded in heaven.

Because the win wasn't being in the movie. It was walking away when God whispered, "Not this door, daughter. Not this one. I have something greater in store. Be patient."

A SEASON OF PROPHETIC PREPARATION AND TESTING

My time at CTN became more than a launching pad—it became a proving ground. God wasn't just refining my skills; He was refining my character and discernment.

There was never a dull moment at the station. It's halls active with clients and guests rushing to the studio to deliver messages, producers juggling script and show demands, and intense production meetings that set the direction for the next three months. I was growing - not just professionally, but prophetically.

Then came the test.

He was charming, wealthy, influential—and married. His pursuit was subtle at first, wrapped in compliments and kind gestures. But soon, the intentions became clear. He told me I was special. That he was in love and soon to divorce. That he could give me the world.

It was the kind of offer many would accept. A life of comfort. Security. Elevation by association.

The Holy Spirit pulled back the curtain. I saw what it really was—a counterfeit path. A shortcut that led away from God's promise for my life, not toward it.

I didn't reject a man. I rejected a mirage.

And that obedience—quiet, resolute—became the soil God would later water with favor.

Through that season, prophetic words began to swirl around me. Guests and clients at the station, affirmed what I had begun to sense - God was preparing to elevate me and open doors only He could unlock. It was a season of sharpening - where I learned to discern His voice, hold fast to my convictions, and recognize the spiritual battles often precede divine transitions.

One guest's prophetic word pierced the deepest:

"God is pleased with you. Stay faithful, repent always, pray especially for your family, and always seek Him. He is about to open doors you can't imagine."

At the time, I couldn't see the full picture. Still, something was shifting. I was being positioned. Pressed. Prepared.

Around that time, I began dating a devoted Christian man—a manager with integrity and a heart for God. He invited me to early-morning prayer meetings, planned thoughtful dates like horseback riding, and even told Angel Mother he wanted to marry me.

By all accounts, he was a good man. Yet, as much as I tried, my spirit didn't settle.

The more I prayed, the clearer it became: "He's not the promise, Michelle. Not yet."

There was more God needed to do. In me. Through me. Around me.

So, I let go. Not out of fear. Out of obedience.

Because sometimes the hardest act of faith is saying no to something good… while waiting on something God.

SPIRITUAL WARFARE: THE VICE GRIP ATTACK

"When the wicked advance against me to devour me, my enemies and foes will stumble and fall."
(Psalm 27:2, *NIV*)

It was supposed to be a restful visit—just a short trip to see my former college roommate in Ohio. Laughter echoed in her kitchen as we reminisced over warm plates of food, old jokes, and the shared memories of college days long behind us.

Yet something unseen was stirring.

In moments of change, when God is preparing to elevate you, the enemy often intensifies his attacks, seeking to derail your destiny. This was one of those moments. I was on the brink of a breakthrough, but the enemy prowled closely determined to stop me from stepping into God's plan for my life.

That night, I sprawled across the guest bed, a neat stack of papers and handwritten notes piled at my feet—plans, dreams, outlines of new television concepts and ministry goals. I had been brainstorming all evening, energized by the clarity I felt about my future. I fell asleep feeling full... expectant... safe.

Until I wasn't.

Somewhere in the early hours, darkness crept in. Not the kind that dims a room, but the kind that tries to steal breath and voice. I was awakened somewhere between a semi-conscious and fully conscious state by an invisible force – its grip intangible, yet unmistakably real. My body was paralyzed, my spirit alert, as if heaven and hell had collided in the room. I couldn't move, but I could feel – a presence pressing in.

Suddenly, something heavy clamped down from the top of my head to the bottom of my jaw. An unseen vice grip. That's what it felt like. A spiritual strangulation—strategic, surgical, targeted. My mouth couldn't open.

I thrashed my head side to side, trying to call on the name Jesus, but no sound came. The weight was more than physical. It was demonic. Suffocating. It was a darkness trying to silence me.

Trying to muzzle my voice.

Yet even in the silence, my spirit cried out. Though my lips were frozen, my heart shouted His name.

Jesus!

And that was enough. Because the enemy can try to paralyze the body – but he can't touch a soul anchored in truth.

When morning finally pierced the shadows, I sat up gasping for air. My notes—those same vision papers I had laid so carefully at my feet—were scattered like confetti across the carpet.

The attack wasn't just on my body - it was on my destiny. It targeted the prophetic office I didn't yet realize I was birthed to walk in. It came for the words – the Word of God – that would one day flow from my mouth like a sword, bringing healing and deliverance to nations I hadn't even imagined.

I shared the experience with my friend, but she had no answers. I turned to prayer. And slowly, understanding came.

This attack wasn't random. The enemy knew what was inside me. He knew the power of the tongue – life and death are in it – and what God had placed in me made the kingdom of darkness tremble. So, it tried to silence me before I ever got the chance to speak.

Up to that point, most of the warfare I'd experienced had come through people – their words, their rejection, their action meant to cut me down. But this…this was different. It was the first time I'd faced invisible warfare. It wasn't just an emotional wound or a spiritual irritation. This was a direct assault on my mind, my mission, and my mantle.

For days after, my thoughts grew cloudy. Confidence began to wane. Doubt seeped into the crevices of my once-clear path. The enemy didn't just want to shake me—he wanted to derail me. To make me abandon the vision God had given because the resistance felt too strong.

It was in this season I clung to Ephesians 6 like a lifeline:

"For we wrestle not against flesh and blood, but against principalities… Therefore, take up the whole armor of God…"

I was learning that life's fiercest battles are often invisible – fought not with fists, but with faith. The armor of God wasn't just spiritual language to me anymore; it became my survival gear. The helmet of salvation guarded my mind against lies. The breastplate of righteousness reminded me I was covered by grace, not guilt. The belt of truth held everything together when deception tried to unravel me. The shoes of peace gave me grounding when fear tried to shake me. The shield of faith helped me block the wicked fiery darts hurled at my purpose, and the sword of the Spirit – God's Word – became my weapon in the dark.

It was like God surrounded me with a force field I couldn't see but could feel. And then He showed me something deeper in a vision: everyone is born with angels assigned to their life and calling. I didn't just have one – I had many. Warring angels. Guardian angels. Ministering angels. And many more…and their very presence revealed something profound: the weight of my destiny. I wasn't fighting alone. Heaven was backing me up.

It was the beginning of a season filled with spiritual battles—attacks on my mind, will, and emotions that tested every fiber of my faith and identity. Through prayer and trust in the power of Jesus, I found strength in knowing the battle was not mine alone, but the Lord's, and He would fight for me.

I hadn't been trained in spiritual warfare, but now I was living it. Not in theory, but in trembling prayer and sleepless nights. Still, I knew this: if the enemy was fighting me this hard, it meant the promise must be near.

And I would not let go of what God promised.

REVELATIONS AND CONFIRMATIONS

"Be not afraid nor dismayed because of this great multitude, for the
battle is not yours, but God's....You will not have to fight this battle.
Take up your positions; stand firm and see the deliverance the Lord will
give you."
(2 Chronicles 20:15, 17, *NIV*)

The enemy had tried to break me in the night, but heaven had already scheduled a rebuttal.

The very next day, I attended a church service at Rod Parsley's World Harvest Church in Columbus. The sanctuary hummed with worship—lights dimmed, voices raised, people pressing in. I sat in the crowd, still shaken but hungry for clarity. My heart was raw, my spirit tender.

That's when an older Bahamian woman, regal in posture, her eyes kind but discerning, sat beside me, as if divinely assigned. She didn't speak at first. She just observed. Then as if prompted by heaven, she began to write words on a piece of paper. I looked over at her and wondered what she was doing but turned my attention to the service. After ten minutes, she handed me the folded slip of paper—precise words from God.

I opened it cautiously, unsure of what I would find. Then my eyes widened as I read the words that only could have come to the heart of the Lord.

"God is about to move you to a major Christian television network."

"You will walk in favor, and financial change is coming."

"Stay humble. Stay obedient. The Lord is pleased with you....."

She knew nothing about me. Nothing of my desires of soaring high in television. Nothing of the war I had just survived. Nothing of the dreams I had written the night before.

Yet God knew.

That paper was more than a prophecy. It was a lifeline. A confirmation. A spiritual seal that said, You are not abandoned. You are not alone.

I thanked her and tucked the paper into my Bible. And into my heart.

When God speaks, it silences every voice of fear, doubt, and delay. That moment—simple, quiet, holy—realigned my steps.

It was time to prepare for the move.

NEW DOORS: IN THE COMPANY OF LEGENDS: FROM MICHAEL JACKSON TO A-LIST ACTORS

"Your gift will make room for you and bring you before great men."
(Proverbs 18:16, NKJV)

The winds began to shift.

Not all at once, but gradually—like a sunrise that starts with a hush and ends in brilliance. Opportunities that once felt distant began to emerge with surprising clarity. The prophetic word was unfolding, not in some far-off dream, but in my own city, in my own life.

I transitioned from CTN to a local video production company, where my first assignment felt almost surreal: contribute to a promotional project connected to none other than Michael Jackson.

The King of Pop. The legend.

I had the rare privilege of sitting in our production room, scrolling through hundreds of hours of unseen footage of Michael. It felt as if the curtains had been pulled back and God had given me a front-row seat into sacred moments few had ever witnessed. I approached the assignment with the care of an undercover agent – tasked not just with editing, but with safeguarding his vulnerability.

Then the moment arrived. He was in Detroit on a special mission, and the very video I had helped to create would be played before an audience of thousands – setting the stage before he took the spotlight.

When I finally met him, it wasn't with cameras flashing or crowds screaming. It was quiet. Personal. Human. The night before, I had anointed a small teddy bear with oil, praying over it.

"Lord, let this be more than a project. Let it be a moment of purpose only You can orchestrate."

He stood there, soft-spoken and gentle, his eyes holding both brilliance and sorrow. I stepped forward with the teddy bear, looked into his eyes, and said simply:

"Jesus loves you."

His response was just as soft, just as striking:

"God loves you too."

That exchange—less than ten seconds—reminded me that my calling wasn't about lights, fame or rubbing shoulders with the influential. It was about bringing light into desperate places. Even in rooms with icons, I was still an ambassador of something greater.

PERILOUS TIMES: MY FIRST ROLE ON STAGE

The next divine door swung open not in a newsroom or a studio—but on a stage.

I was cast in the gospel stage play *Perilous Times*, a production by T.J. Hemphill, that traveled across cities and hearts, bringing messages of redemption, hope, and spiritual awakening to packed theaters. Sharing the spotlight with beloved icons—Vickie Winans, Tommy Ford, and Tiny Lister. Each performance felt more like ministry than entertainment.

I was entrusted with multiple roles, but none more sacred than Mary in the resurrection of Lazarus. I stood beneath hot stage lights, wrapped in robes of biblical fabric, but my soul felt vulnerable in the best way. As the music swelled and Lazarus came forth, I wept tears—not because it was in the script, but because something inside me was rising too.

This wasn't pretend.

This was storytelling that healed.

Backstage, camaraderie blossomed. We prayed before performances, shared testimonies in the green room, and watched as entire audiences were moved night after night. The laughter, the tears, the standing ovations—each one a reminder that God was using creativity to break chains.

After the curtain closed on that season, I shifted again—this time to serve as a rehearsal coordinator for the Boys and Girls Choir of Detroit, founded by John and Thalia Boyd. Every Saturday morning, I reported to the historic Christ Church in the heart of downtown Detroit.

The voices of children lifted toward heaven as I helped manage order, encourage discipline, and keep rehearsals on track. The Boyd family didn't just build choirs—they built legacies.

Today, their children, like Victory Boyd, are carrying the torch in the music industry with excellence and integrity.

Each moment—from stage to sanctuary—was part of God's symphony for my life. Different instruments, same Composer.

HOPE FOR A FAMILY SOME DAY

Career doors were opening. Prophetic words were unfolding. Purpose was gaining traction.

Still, a quiet ache lingered beneath the momentum.

In rare moments of solitude—between editing sessions, casting calls, and production meetings—I would envision a simple scene: a husband who adored me, children laughing in the background, holiday traditions unfolding in a home filled with warmth, music, and prayer. Not perfection—just presence. Covenant. Belonging.

It wasn't a fantasy. It was a desire rooted in God's design.

Still, for me, it was also wrapped in fear.

My heart bore the scars of instability. My father's four marriages had left emotional residue—shadows that whispered, "Nothing lasts." My mother's unpredictable love had taught me to build walls, not homes.

So, I feared marriage. Feared choosing wrong. Feared being invisible in my own story.

Yet even in those moments of hesitation, I clung to hope. I journaled prayers. I sowed seeds of love into others. I chose not to idolize the promise but to steward the longing

And I trusted that God, in His timing, would bring someone who saw me, honored me, and walked beside me in purpose.

Until then, I leaned into the now.

Destiny was calling. And God was writing a love story far bigger than romance. He was writing the story of restoration.

THE GARAGE SALE AND THE MOVE TO CBN

It began with license plates.

Everywhere I turned—at traffic lights, in parking lots, on the freeway—I saw them: Virginia.

Like breadcrumbs scattered by the hand of God, each one whispered, "You're being called."

I couldn't ignore it.

So, I started moving in faith.

I updated my résumé. Gathered my best demo reels. I began reaching out to television networks in Virginia, not knowing exactly what I was applying for—still fully believing that something holy was waiting on the other side of obedience.

At home, I took a large white poster board and taped it to my bedroom wall. I wrote down my heart's prayers in a bold black marker:

"God, grant me the talent to produce life-changing dramatic documentaries."

What I didn't realize then was that this single sentence would become a blueprint... for what God would soon unfold through a major Christian network.

First, I needed to take a step.

With limited savings and a deep trust in divine provision, I held a garage sale. Clothes, books, jewelry, household items—all laid out in my front yard like an altar of surrender. By the week's end, I had earned just over $1,000.

Enough to buy what I needed after I settled into my new place.

One afternoon, I overheard my father on the phone. His voice was low, but I caught the words:

"Yeah, it's bittersweet... she's moving to Virginia."

That moment sealed it.

Not just my decision—but the knowing.

This was it.

CHAPTER 20:

DIVINE GUIDANCE TO CBN:
THE 700 CLUB

"**A**lthough your journey has been long and marked by intense battles aimed to crush your destiny, take heart—it is a sign that what you carry is far greater than you can imagine. Stay bold, confident, and steadfast in the God who promises to complete the work He began in you. Your battles will not be in vain, for the greatness of God within you will be unveiled for the world to see. Keep your eyes on God's power and majesty."

- Michelle B. Wilson, author, *In Search of a Mother's Love.*

I had never heard of the Christian Broadcasting Network (CBN) or *The 700 Club* before, but as I searched for media jobs, I came across a listing for a producer and reporter position that involved traveling the world. It was exactly what I had prayed for—a job that combined my faith with storytelling.

Without hesitation, I submitted my application, video reels, and résumé, trusting God with the outcome. I didn't realize then this step of faith would change my life forever.

THE CALL THAT MOVED
THE PROPHETIC VISION FORWARD

A month later, my phone rang. Debbie White, the features department manager at *The 700 Club*, introduced herself. Her voice carried warmth as she said,

"I have a tape of your work in my hands, and I like what I see."

After asking a series of questions, she asked me the million-dollar question: "Do you enjoy traveling?"

I didn't hold back my enthusiasm. "I love to travel so much I'd become a flight attendant."

She chuckled, impressed by my excitement. By the end of our conversation, she invited me to CBN for an in-person interview.

Within two weeks, I boarded a half-empty plane to Virginia Beach, seated near the window. As I gazed out above the clouds, tears streamed down my face. I whispered a prayer of thanksgiving, knowing this moment would change my life forever.

As the plane touched down, I silently prayed, "God, give me a sign this job is truly mine."

As I settled into my room, at the Founder's Inn hotel, nestled on the CBN campus, I could feel the weight of God's promises coming to fruition.

The next morning, I stepped into the SHB (Studio Headquarters Building), where *The 700 Club* was taped. I met with the features manager and producers, and conversations flowed naturally, as if I'd known them for years. Their kindness and the electric atmosphere confirmed I was in the right place.

Then a defining moment happened. The executive producer of *The 700 Club* passed by, glanced at me, and casually asked the manager, "Well, when does she start?"

My heart leaped—this was the confirmation I had prayed for.

Later, in the manager's office, I poured out my heart, sharing how prophetic words and divine nudges had led me here. She listened intently before saying,

"Many others, more experienced than you, applied for this job."

Undeterred, I boldly replied with a Detroit boldness,

"You know as well as I do that this job is mine."

She seemed surprised by my confidence and smiled, promising to let me know by Friday.

By Wednesday morning, I was back in Detroit, replaying every detail of my visit. This was such a God-ordained move I couldn't imagine any other outcome.

DR. MYLES MUNROE'S PROPHECY UNFOLDS

"I know your deeds. See, I have placed an open door that no one can shut before you. I know you have little strength, yet you have kept my word and have not denied my name."
(Revelation 3:8, *NIV*)

Later that day, the manager called me.

"Well, you know the job is yours!"

I could barely contain my joy as I thanked her for the incredible opportunity. As we discussed the logistics of my move, I could feel the weight of God's promise coming to pass. I had taken a leap of faith and trusted God, and now I was on my way to a new adventure with CBN, one of the largest Christian television networks in the world. This was the door He had prepared for me all along.

FOUR SIGNIFICANT MOMENTS BEFORE MY MOVE

Before officially stepping into my role at CBN, four key moments marked my transition – a lesson in family, faith, ministry, and divine covering for the path ahead.

MY MOTHER'S THIRD VISIT:
A WINDOW INTO HER WORLD

Before I left Detroit, my biological mother paid a brief visit, hoping to rekindle her relationship with my father. It was a bittersweet reminder of how much had changed. Her lifestyle and hardened demeanor revealed the depth of her inner battles and choices to walk a path apart from God. While I had found peace in my faith, she continued to wrestle with God and a spirit of narcissism that blinded her to her own faults.

During her stay, Angel Mother stopped by to say hello. Ever gracious, she had nothing but kindness to offer, yet my mother refused to come out of the room to greet her.

The tension was undeniable. Though I longed for reconciliation, I knew some wounds took longer to heal. By the time my mother left – borrowing several pieces of my clothing I never saw again – it was a bittersweet farewell. Even so, I trusted God had something greater in store for me as I stepped into the future.

THE MISSED ALTAR CALL

God knew my desire to be totally free from the weights I carried since childhood and had prepared a way of escape for me to break free and soar into my new journey, unencumbered by the past. A friend invited me to Abyssinia Christ Centered Church, founded by Dr. Iona Locke, where Evangelist Wanda Davis -Turner was preaching.

As she ministered, I felt a stirring in my spirit like never before. A deep, buried cry from within me—one that had been buried since childhood—was rising to the surface. I clutched my stomach, as I felt a physical movement, confused by the overwhelming urge to run to the altar.

The evangelist called people who needed healing and deliverance to the altar for prayer. My heart was pounding, and everything in me wanted to respond, yet the enemy planted fear in my mind.

Paralyzed by fear and the opinion of man, I remained frozen in my seat.

As the service ended, the evangelist walked down the aisle past me. Our eyes met briefly; I felt she knew I had missed my moment. I longed to reach out to her, hoping a touch from this mighty woman of God would somehow bring me the deliverance I desperately needed.

Yet, it was too late.

I've often wondered how my life might have been different had I stepped forward that day. At the same time, I recognized through the intense struggles I faced afterward, I came to know God in a deeply intimate way. Precious moments of knowing God that can only come through the fires and trials of life. His grace carried me through unimaginable battles, reminding me of Paul's words: "My grace is sufficient for you, for my power is made perfect in weakness" (2 Corinthians 12:9).

Though I missed the altar call, God's faithfulness never wavered.

THE STAGE, THE MANTLE, AND THE PROPHETIC DREAM THAT MARKED THE END AND THE BEGINNING

Before my move, God gave me a vivid dream to reveal a glimpse of my future. I walked onto a stage before a large audience. As I gazed into the crowd, I saw familiar faces, and a deep knowing settled within me: God was calling me to preach His Word.

What struck me most was how I looked in the dream. Despite time having passed, God had preserved me. It was a Sarah anointing, a supernatural preservation of beauty and strength for His purpose.

When I shared the dream with my father, his response was unexpected. Instead of focusing on the significance of the calling, he asked,

"Where was I in the audience? Did you see me."

His question puzzled me as I responded: "Daddy, I didn't see you. I dont know where you were."

Later, I realized that moment may have confirmed something in his heart—that his time on earth was ending soon. My father never spoke of his health issues, and perhaps the dream was a gentle reminder of the legacy he would leave behind.

Although I did not discern what was in my father's heart – I pondered the revelation of what God showed me. Yet, I was afraid to embrace the ministry calling fully, clinging to my dreams in television. Still, the dream lingered in my heart, a seed planted by God that would one day bear fruit.

PRAYER COVERING BEFORE MY MOVE TO VIRGINIA

Soon, my father gathered close friends and prayer warriors to pray over me. The house was filled with food, laughter, conversation, and the warmth of shared faith, marking a moment of transformation. As I sat in my father's coveted Eames chair, I felt as though I was being anointed for my new journey, empowered to walk boldly into the next chapter of my life. With hands lifted, they poured blessings into my spirit, ensuring this transition was bathed in prayer every step of the way.

Among the prayers, was the one my father often spoke over me:

'May the Lord bless you and keep you; may the Lord make His face shine upon you and be gracious to you; may the Lord lift up His countenance upon you and give you peace' (Numbers 6:24-26).

These words would follow me into every new season of my journey.

Two months later, as the Allied team of moving professionals arrived at my home, there was a finality to seeing my belongings being packed up. I watched as movers carefully loaded my belongings onto the moving truck.

Standing at the threshold of my new beginnings, I felt an overwhelming sense of peace. Like, Queen Esther, the golden scepter had been extended, and I was stepping into the path of what God had already orchestrated.

It was a sweatless victory. The door to CBN was open, and I was ready to walk through it.

CHAPTER 21:

THE DOOR OF DESTINY: MY JOURNEY BEGINS AT CBN

"Take delight in the Lord, and He will give you the desires of your heart."
(Psalms 37:4, *NIV*)

The Atlantic wind carried something sacred that fall—salt, promise, and a whisper of new beginnings. I arrived in Virginia Beach two months early, a quiet prelude to the next great unfolding. The coastline stretched like a welcome mat from heaven, the surf's lullaby reminding me that God was already here, waiting.

This season of tender transformation came clothed in quiet nights and whispered prayers. Each evening, I knelt at the edge of my bed as if it were an altar, the carpet brushing my knees, my heart laid bare.

"Dear Lord, anoint me to produce life-changing stories that bring You glory. I've never produced at this level before. I need Your help. I trust You to lead me every step of the way. In Jesus' name, amen."

My excitement and nerves were a whirlwind of emotions. Questions raced through my mind:

Could I fulfill my assignments?

What would it be like to interview people across different corners of the world?

Would I find my place at CBN, and would people accept me?

I didn't want to fail God, CBN, my boss, family or myself. The weight of the assignment felt heavy, yet I knew God had prepared me for such a time as this.

DIVINE PLACEMENT: NOT JUST A JOB, A CALLING

I chose December 7th - Pearl Harbor Day - as my first official day at CBN, so I'd always remember it as the day God gave me a fresh start.

I moved through the early days at CBN like someone walking through an answered prayer—eyes wide, heart tender, spirit alert. There was a lightness in my step, as if joy had taken up residence in my bones. I felt it when I passed through the corridors, when I poured over scripts, when I sat at my desk humming quietly to myself.

It was as if God Himself had wrapped my new season in a ribbon of redemption.

I had my own modest cubicle, stocked with a tape deck and stacks of past stories produced by fellow producers.

My first task?

Watch and familiarize myself with the stories aired on *The 700 Club* to understand their production process. I had no idea God had arranged for my path at CBN to further heal my soul.

The stories, ranging from miraculous healings to profound salvations and deliverances, touched the deepest parts of me. As I watched, silent tears streamed down my face. I tried to hide them, but I couldn't deny what was happening – God was using these stories to heal my own heart. His tangible presence enveloped me like a warm, comforting blanket—reminiscent of the moments in my college dorm room when I first fell in love with God.

I carried a radiant joy in this new season, as if I were gliding on air, basking in the exhilaration of a fresh start unlike anything I had felt in years. My eyes sparkled with anticipation, filled with hope for all God was about to accomplish through my life.

Thanks to Angel Mother's timeless advice on haircare, my hair had grown full and free flowing like a symbol of God's glory, cascading past the middle of my back.

I was a trim size six and people at CBN often complimented my poise, my quiet grace. I smiled, grateful, but I never let those words settle too deep. I hadn't come to be seen for my outer appearance. I had come to reflect God's glory through the stories I would tell.

One producer, Kristi Watts—a vibrant presence and rising voice at the network—affectionately called me "Black Barbie." It was playful, even endearing, but to me, I was simply Michelle: a woman on assignment, carrying heaven's weight in fragile hands.

I didn't see myself as impressive. I saw myself as sent.

Every day I walked into that building, I carried a silent fire in my spirit. Not ambition—but obedience. I wasn't just there to produce television. I was there to carry healing, to thread light into the lives of strangers, and to prove that a broken girl from Detroit could be rebuilt into a vessel of glory.

BREAKING GROUND: MY FIRST CBN ASSIGNMENT

Then it came—my first real assignment. Not a practice reel. Not a trial run.

A story.

A chance to write, shape, and birth something that would be seen by millions.

It was a Word of Knowledge segment—those miraculous moments when a host on *The 700 Club* speaks a divine revelation over the airwaves, calling out a sickness or condition God is healing in real time. My job was to post-produce a story of a man named David Connery, who had suffered painful mouth sores during a getaway in Virginia Beach.

As he watched *The 700 Club*, in the studio audience, Gordon Robertson gave a Word of Knowledge about God healing someone suffering from mouth ulcers.

David heard it. Believed it. Claimed it. And within moments, the pain vanished...and so did the ulcers.

As I pieced together David's testimony, I didn't just write—it felt like I was sculpting a miracle. Every frame. Every soundbite. Every beat of music I wanted the viewer to feel what I felt when I first heard his story: awe, faith, and the quiet thrill that heaven still speaks.

When the piece aired, the response was instant. Viewers called in, emailed, and commented—affirming the story's impact. Yet for me, the greatest reward wasn't public reaction. It was private remembrance.

I thought back to my Detroit bedroom and the poster board taped to my wall. I had written it like a declaration:

"Lord, use my gifts to bring You glory."

Now, here I was—walking out that prayer. Not just a woman with dreams, but a woman walking in destiny.

I wasn't just producing Christian television.

I was proclaiming resurrection stories through screens.

I wasn't just a storyteller.

I was a media evangelist.

ON-CAMERA, ON ASSIGNMENT, ON PURPOSE

Then came a new challenge—my first assignment on camera.

The story: The Grand Illumination. A beloved holiday tradition at CBN's Founder's Inn hotel where Christmas lights, music, and laughter awaken the city's spirit, signaling the start of the season.

I arrived at the event just before dusk, the sky painted in watercolor shades of lavender and blue. There was a chill in the air—crisp but magical—as families gathered, bundled in scarves and mittens, their breath visible as they sipped cider and laughed under bright lights.

To personalize the segment, I featured the Rodriguez family from my church. I followed them as they strolled through the festive crowd, their eyes wide with delight. I captured their children's excitement as they were mesmerized by the giant-sized gingerbread house, face-painting and other festivities.

I even sampled a chocolate Yule log on camera—its rich sweetness melting into a lighthearted moment that made the story feel warm.

And then, the moment arrived.

Pat Robertson walked onto the grand stage, surrounded by bright-eyed children. He read the Christmas story with the reverence of a grandfather reading to his own grandchildren. And as his hand flicked the switch, thousands of lights exploded into brilliance—illuminating the entire CBN campus in a breathtaking burst of white and gold. The trees glittered like stars illuminating a winter wonderland. The crowd gasped and so did I.

The next day, the feature story aired. And not long after, I was told Pat Robertson had seen my work.

"Who is she?" he asked. "I want to see her more on camera."

Those words washed over me like a gentle wave—humbling, affirming, holy.

God had placed me here. Not just behind the scenes, but in front of the lens.

I continued to pray every morning before work, still that same girl on her knees, still whispering,

"Lord, lead me. Anoint me for the assignment."

And after each finished story, I picked up the phone to call my father—the one who never stopped believing in me. His pride echoed through the line, steady and full. His joy became my fuel.

WORLD TRAVEL: A HEALING ASSIGNMENT IN NICARAGUA

My first year at CBN unfolded like pages from a journal only heaven could have written. I traveled across the U.S. and beyond, documenting miracles, interviewing people whose lives were being transformed by God's hand, and seeing His Spirit move in places I had never imagined.

One of the most unforgettable trips was to Nicaragua. My first international trip.

The air was thick with heat and dust as we stepped off the plane—sunlight bathing the mountains in gold. I was there to cover a historic trip: Pat Robertson's visit to the country and the work of the Flying Hospital, CBN's state-of-the-art medical aircraft bringing free surgical care to underserved people.

Inside the aircraft, doctors moved with precision—performing cleft palate surgeries, gynecological operations, and life-changing procedures that families had once only dreamed of. It wasn't just medicine. It was ministry in motion.

I interviewed patients before and after their surgeries. Many walked in with their bodies burdened by pain and shame. Yet thanks to CBN partners who give generously to the mission of Operation Blessing, they left restored in body, and in many cases, reborn in spirit. Several gave their lives to Christ right there as nurses and volunteers prayed over them.

I watched as Pat Robertson met with the President of Nicaragua, hosted press events, and offered hope to a nation longing for more. Being part of that trip reminded me I wasn't just a journalist—I was an eyewitness to God's power.

And then there was the church service.

Tucked in the heart of one of the poorest neighborhoods I'd ever seen, a small sanctuary with barefoot worshippers. The floor was dirt. The doors were bedsheets. Yet when they lifted their voices, it was as if heaven stood to take notice.

The drums, handmade, echoed through the humble sanctuary, their rhythms stirring the soul. Tambourines shook with joy, while guitar players strummed with a fire that could only come from heaven. As I stood there, listening to a language I had never spoken, it was as if I understood everything. And in one unbroken flow, we all joined in, singing, "Hallelujah" – giving God the highest praise.

The worship singers, anointed and unashamed, drew every heart into a realm where no sorrow could remain – only awe for the God who gave everything…His son Jesus. And the people, many with nothing but the clothes on their backs, worshipped like they were millionaires, completely free, their burdens as they praised God.

And in that moment, I understood a holy paradox:

They had nothing.

Yet they had everything.

Their laughter, their praise, their love for one another—it pierced me. It redefined wealth. And I knew I had seen something rare, something eternal. Not a story to be told, but a truth to be carried.

When we flew back home, the sun disappeared behind the clouds, but a light remained in my spirit. Nicaragua had shown me what cameras couldn't capture—faith that lives not in abundance, but in surrender to a God that gave His all…Jesus.

SEEING MYSELF IN HER STORY:
THE ROBIN GILES INTERVIEW

"The Lord is close to the broken hearted and saves those crushed in spirit."
(Psalm 34:18, *NIV*)

Each story I produced at CBN brought a tangible anointing of God to transform lives.

Robin Giles' testimony was one of the latter.

Her story arrived at my desk like a mirror held up to my own childhood wounds. Robin had been raised in an abusive home, her young spirit fractured by a mother's anger and absence. At just twelve years old, she ran away, eventually entering foster care, carrying years of rejection in her fragile life.

I traveled to Brooklyn Tabernacle in New York to meet her. The church was under construction—its unfinished beams and echoing halls seemed to reverberate Robin's own story: a structure being rebuilt, beauty rising from brokenness.

As I interviewed Pastor Jim Cymbala, who had walked alongside her in her healing, he spoke not just as a pastor but as a father-figure who had watched resurrection unfold in real time. His eyes softened as he shared how Robin had blossomed—no longer a wounded runaway, but a radiant worshiper.

When I sat down with Robin, her presence was gentle but strong. She didn't mask the pain. She didn't sugarcoat it. She told the truth.

"I felt I had a right to be angry," she confessed. "But the Lord changed my life... and brought healing into my heart."

And then she sang.

Her low alto voice, a balm. Her lyrics, a lifeline.

It was her song she led with the Brooklyn Tabernacle choir, "It's Amazing"—a tender anthem of grace that carried the weight of every tear she had shed, every trauma she had surrendered. As the camera captured her in various locations, it was as if her words, her melody - her voice was rising like incense from the ashes.

Editing the story, I felt her pain. Yet, I also felt her freedom.

And I realized—a part of my heart was healing, too.

It wasn't just her story on screen. It was mine, too. Her courage to forgive gave me permission to release wounds I hadn't fully named. Her resilience reminded me that God wastes nothing. Every tear, every bruise, every unanswered prayer—they were all being woven into something glorious.

Robin's testimony aired multiple times, touching countless lives.

Still perhaps its greatest impact was what it did to me.

It reminded me that stories don't just inform—they transform. And in producing hers, I was being further molded into who God had called me to be—not just a producer, but a vessel. A witness. A carrier of healing.

CHAPTER 22:

WHEN MY MOTHER SAW ME ON *THE 700 CLUB*: HOW HEAVEN TURNED MY STORIES INTO REDEMPTION

"There is a time for everything, and a season for every activity under the heavens."
(Ecclesiastes 3:1, *NIV*)

On March 9, 2000, I was assigned a story that would profoundly impact me both professionally and spiritually. It was the story of Tom and Marilyn Rose, a modern-day testament to faith, resilience, and restoration. The Roses had endured unspeakable tragedy – a drunk driver caused a crash that killed their two children. Tom's battle with congestive heart failure compounded their suffering, yet their faith never wavered.

I carefully prepared for the interview, selecting a gray tweed Ellen Tracy suit with a cranberry turtleneck, my auburn-highlighted hair framing my face. My red lipstick added a final touch, though my overly plucked eyebrows hinted at a woman still finding her way in professional settings.

During our conversation, Tom's word resonated deeply:

"We cannot quantify God's love based on our circumstances. It cannot be weighed against the loss of a loved one, a business, a home, or even our health. The only way to gauge it is through Scripture:

'For God so loved the world that He gave His only Son, Jesus'"

At his lowest point, Tom longed for heaven – and during a church service, God miraculously healed his heart, sparing him from a desperately needed transplant.

Tom and Marilyn turned their pain into purpose through Waymaker Ministries and their book, *Valley of Decision*. Their story aired during the Thanksgiving holiday and was rebroadcast several times. Little did I know, this story would set the stage for a divine appointment in my own life.

GOD'S DIVINE PLAN: A CALL FROM MOTHER

A few days after the story aired, my phone rang. I was sitting at my desk working on my assignments when I answered. To my surprise, it was my mother.

"Hi, Darlin', this is Mom," she said as if no time had passed.

I hadn't heard from her in years, and the call stirred a complex mix of emotions.

"I saw you on television, and you looked beautiful. Send Mom that suit!"

"You saw me in the Tom and Marilyn Rose story I just produced?" I responded.

"Yes, and you looked beautiful," she exclaimed.

Too stunned, I never asked how she came across the program. Had she been watching *The 700 Club* from the beginning and seen me in the story? Or was she just flipping through the channels and stumbled upon it mid-broadcast? Either way, I knew it was divinely orchestrated for God's greater purpose. My mother now knew where I worked – and she found out in the most supernatural way.

A flood of emotions hit me. Her words, unexpected yet significant, reopened old wounds. She mentioned a new business venture, a coffee shop featuring her pastries and sandwiches. I listened, yet my heart wrestled with past disappointments.

As we talked, I felt led to speak over her, reminding her of her worth in God's eyes.

"I want you to know you are loved, and you are valued more than you realize. God has a purpose for you, just trust Him."

She listened and was receptive to my words of life over her destiny. Though my emotions were conflicted, I realized this conversation wasn't about me. It was about God beginning a work of healing in both our lives.

SEEING GOD'S PLAN FROM A NEW PERSPECTIVE

"It is in the crucible of our fiercest battles; we are stripped of our defenses. In that refining moment, we are compelled to lay down our need to be right and abandon the prison of self-pity. Only then can we see the truth from God's vantage point – a perspective that reveals the real enemy at work, not the person who hurt us, but the adversary who seeks to steal, kill and destroy. From this place of clarity, brokenness is transformed into healing, bitterness into forgiveness, and pain into restoration."

- Michelle B. Wilson, author, *In Search of a Mother's Love.*

After the call, God spoke clearly to my heart:

"You keep saying, 'Your mother left you,' however, she didn't leave you; you were removed from her care. On that day, you lost your mother, yet she lost four children. Have you ever considered your mother has also suffered?"

The realization hit me like a flood.

For years, I had seen her as the source of my pain, but now I saw her through a different lens – not as a woman who abandoned me, but as one who had suffered her own profound loss. God revealed that while He had allowed the separation for my good, my mother never stopped loving us. She simply couldn't care for us as she once did due to circumstances beyond her control.

For years, she had been haunted by the loss of her four children, just as I had been deeply wounded by the absence of a mother.

Then, God asked me a question that pierced my soul:

"What the devil did to your family – to steal, kill, and destroy – was not my best for your lives. What are you going to do about it?"

God's revelation left me shaken. For the first time, I recognized I had authority in God. I was immediately thrust into being a victor instead of a victim. I was awakened to know I could partner with God to destroy generational curses and usher in generational blessings of healing and blessings with God's help.

Suddenly, everything that had seemed so confusing and painful began to make sense. I saw, with perfect clarity, the true nature of the enemy that had been tearing my family apart.

And then, in a moment I will never forget, as if wrapping me in a blanket of peace, the Lord spoke again. God's voice wasn't audible - it came as a still, small voice—a quiet, inner witness, a knowing I had come to recognize through years of building a relationship with Him and becoming familiar with His voice through the Word of God. It was in the quietness of my spirit that He asked:

"What if I told you I allowed your mother to give birth to the very one I would use to bring healing and deliverance to her life? Would you do it for Me?"

Without hesitation, I said, "Yes, Lord."

How could I refuse the God who had created the universe, the One I had come to know intimately and trust so deeply? The God who had already started the journey of redeeming my story was now inviting me to join Him in fulfilling one of the greatest acts of love for which I had been born—to play a role in His ultimate plan to transform my mother's life for His glory.

God asked me to stand in the gap for my mother and pray for her deliverance and salvation. Without realizing it, I had been prepared for this sacred task, equipped with every grace to help her find healing.

With God's words ringing, I knew my life would never be the same. I no longer saw my mother as the enemy but as a soul in need of healing and redemption. Though I couldn't foresee the journey ahead, I felt compelled to walk obediently. God had entrusted me with a divine purpose: "to let our shared story be rewritten through love, forgiveness and ultimately redemption."

It was time to release my anger and bitterness, allowing compassion and mercy to take their place. As God's words sank in, I felt my heart expand with a newfound empathy and understanding. I realized forgiveness was not just something I could offer my mother—it was a gift I desperately needed for myself. In releasing her, I was freeing my own heart from the chains of resentment and walking in the authority of God I never knew I had.

PARTNERING WITH GOD TO HEAL
MY MOTHER'S HEART AND SOUL

That night, I fell to my knees and poured out my tears, asking God to heal my mother's heart and bring her to salvation in Him. As I prayed, anger and hatred lifted from my spirit, replaced by compassion and mercy. I knew this was the beginning of a long journey, yet I felt peace knowing I was walking in obedience to God's plan.

God was writing a new chapter of healing and restoration, one that would take years to unfold. Through this divine appointment, He wasn't just transforming her life—He was transforming mine.

And yet, even as He worked in the hidden places of my heart, He continued to lead me in the visible ones too. My assignments at *The 700 Club*, became more than work – they became guided steps in a bigger story of trust, timing and transformation.

A MINISTRY OF COMPASSION: PRODUCING
STORIES WITH GRACE, NOT JUDGMENT

Each story I produced at CBN deeply resonated with me, not because I had walked the exact same path, but because my own journey of pain and rejection gave me an understanding of their struggles. It was as though, through their stories, God was giving me more healing and restoration for my own heart.

One of the hallmarks of my career as a producer has been the ability to connect deeply with those whose stories I've told. My journey uniquely equipped me to produce stories, not with judgment, but with compassion, creating a safe space for others to share their pain and God's redemptive work in their lives.

Time and again, story subjects told me,

"You made me feel comfortable. You're so down to earth."

Their words affirmed I was not arrogant but relatable. Being a producer wasn't about titles or accolades - it was about answering a divine calling: stepping into people's lives with empathy, humility, and understanding. My role wasn't just to capture testimonies but to honor their journeys and glorify God's work in them.

Each project began with building rapport through calls, praying for the Holy Spirit's guidance, and crafting thoughtful questions. I visualized each story through a shot list designed to draw out the heart of their journey, aiming not to sensationalize but to reveal emotional truths that reflected God's redemption.

I believed nothing in life is wasted—not a tear, not a moment of suffering, or a single rejection. Each becomes part of a greater story, where God's glory is revealed through our willingness to trust Him with our pain and to use our experience to help others. It became my mission to share profound lessons of human resilience and the transformative power of God's love with every story I produced.

NINE IS ENOUGH: THE ROBBINS' ADOPTION STORY

Brian and Anita Robbins' decision to adopt seven Russian siblings reflected my own experience of being placed in a loving home while still carrying scars of rejection.

The Robbins, already parents to two biological sons, felt called to adopt. Their journey led them to an orphanage in Russia, where seven siblings, orphaned by tragedy, waited for a chance at a new life. The grim conditions of the orphanage—peeling paint, grime-covered windows, and an atmosphere of neglect—were a painful reminder of the children's traumatic past.

With immense faith and determination, the Robbins navigated the yearlong adoption process and returned home with their seven new children. Their arrival in America was a moment of hope and joy, with the children pressing their faces to the plane windows, shouting, "America, America!" It was a beautiful symbol of the fresh start they had been given.

Filming at their home, I saw how trauma lingers even in safe environments. Anita shared how she often found food hidden in the children's rooms—leftovers from a time when food had been scarce. Brian reassured them, reminding them they no longer needed to hide or fear.

One child, Noah, resisted calling them Mom and Dad – until one day he finally did. It was a breakthrough that underscored the transformative power of patience and unconditional love. That moment mirrored my own delayed acceptance of love after my mother was gone.

As a producer, I constantly listen to the Holy Spirit for creative ways to bring a story's heart to life. During the long hours of filming with the Robbins family, God gave me the idea to ask each child to share their Christian names and words of thanksgiving. Tears filled Anita's eyes as little hands clasped hers, and in that moment, the weight of their gratitude filled the room, powerful enough to touch hearts around the world

Their story deeply resonated with me. Watching the Robbins children navigate their new lives brought back memories of my own journey—from a children's home to living with Angel Mother and my father. Even in a loving environment, the wounds of the past don't simply disappear; they require time, care, and God's healing.

As the Robbins shared their story, their message was clear: every child, no matter their age, deserves a chance at love and belonging. Their faith-driven commitment to adoption inspired countless viewers when their story aired on *The 700 Club*.

A STORY OF REDEMPTION:
THE EMMANUEL DEMETRI STORY

*"My frame was not hidden from you when I was made in the secret
place and woven together in the depths of the earth. Your eyes saw my
unformed body; all the days ordained for me were written in your book
before one of them came to be."*
(Psalm 139:15-16, *NIV*)

Another powerful story was that of Emmanuel Demetri, a man whose
life began in darkness and was transformed by God's mercy and grace. My
production team and I drove to Raleigh North Carolina, to meet Demetri. I
was eager to capture his story as a testament to the power of faith and God's
ability to renew any life.

When we arrived, he welcomed me like an old friend—gentle, smiling,
radiant in a way that only someone rescued from darkness can be. We stood
near one of the places he once called home—though home, for him, had
meant cold concrete and hidden corners.

"This was it," Demetri said, eyes softening as he looked over the space. "I'd
come here to get high, to sleep. It felt safe. No one bothered me. Free rent."

His words were both revealing and heartbreaking. Born of a jailhouse
fling and taken from his mother at birth, Demetri was never cradled in
belonging. Instead, he was passed from one foster home to another like
an unwanted package, renamed "Antonio Demetrius Betts" at age three
by adoptive parents who didn't know how to love him. The abuse was
suffocating. The rejection was deep.

"I never had anyone rock me to sleep," he told me. "Never heard the
words, 'I love you,' not once."

By the time he reached adulthood, the streets felt more like home than
any house ever had. He searched for connection in shelters, clubs, strangers'
arms—anywhere that offered a glimmer of acceptance. He reunited briefly

with his birth mother, only to lose her to cancer weeks later. The wound reopened. The loneliness escalated.

On stage, he became "Diva CoCo Brown"—glamorous, loud, beloved in the drag scene. Yet behind the sparkle and applause, his soul stayed hollow. His view of God, tainted by his experiences, left him questioning God's existence.

"If there was a God out there, He must be cruel and heartless," Demetri confessed.

On the brink of despair, he walked to a lake, ready to end his life. There, much like Saul's transformation on the road to Damascus, Demetri encountered God.

"I looked up," he said, pointing to a grove of trees beside the water. "And the sky cracked open."

He dropped to his knees, trembling, undone by a love that wrapped around him like light.

"Thank you, Jesus," he wept—though he didn't fully know who Jesus was.

I stood there as he spoke, and I could feel it—that same glory hovering in the air. The place had become sacred.

From that moment on, everything changed.

Demetri traded stiletto heels for gospel tracks, rave lights for revival tents. He shared his testimony through music and ministered in the very clubs that once hosted his performances. Five albums. Two books. A ministry called New Chance International.

And one unforgettable story aired on *The 700 Club*.

As I watched the hosts introduce the piece with, "Michelle Wilson brings you this report," I felt the swell of God's promises fulfilled. Words spoken over my life about my name echoing through the airwaves were coming true—through this man's redemption.

Demetri, who had married, passed away in 2017 at just 44 years old. But he left behind a spiritual inheritance that continues to breathe. His life reminds me:

No pain is wasted when placed in God's hands.

A NOTE TO HEAVEN

If I could say one more thing to you, Demetri, I'd say this:

You finished well.
You poured it all out.
You taught us how to dance in our scars and praise in the places we once wept.
You showed us what redemption looks like with flesh and flaws and fire.

And I believe, with all my heart, I'll see you again standing in glory, singing
louder than ever, free in every way.
Until then, I'll keep telling your story.
Because this wasn't just a feature.
It was a calling. A covenant. A sound that still echoes.

OLYMPIC GOLD NEXTDOOR:
THE LATASHA COLANDER STORY

*"Whether you turn to the right or the left, your ears will hear a voice
behind you, saying, 'This is the way; walk in it."*
(Isaiah 30:21, *NIV*)

There are moments in life that shimmer with divine alignment—when purpose and preparation collide with destiny. Interviewing Olympic gold medalist LaTasha Colander was one of those moments. It was something being up close to a gold medalist that stirred in me a deeper resolve to keep fighting for my dreams and trusting God for the impossible.

We met on a sunlit morning as she stepped onto the track at her alma mater, UNC at Chapel Hill—the same kind of track where she had trained to become one of the fastest women in the world. Every stride she took carried not only muscle memory but spiritual significance. Her victory in the 4x400-meter relay at the Sydney Olympics wasn't just an athletic triumph—it was the visible fruit of years of internal battles, setbacks, and quiet endurance.

I watched her and other Olympic stars like Marion Jones stretch on the track – warming up their muscles, preparing for their practice runs. Their breathing was intentional, their form precise. Every moment, every breath, was calculated. A silhouette of grace and power against the open sky.

There was something deeper at work. LaTasha's story pulsed with perseverance. Not just the kind that pushes you through a finish line—but the kind that whispers, "Keep going," when life gives you no applause.

She spoke of her journey with clarity and conviction, offering up a powerful testimony of how faith had been the lane she never left—even when the hurdles came fast and hard. LaTasha wasn't just running for gold. She was running for glory.

And as she shared her story, I realized: this wasn't just about medals. It was about mission.

Every time I saw her in news articles or television interviews about her LC Treasures Within Foundation – which inspires youth through education, sports and spirituality - I smiled proudly. I was grateful that once again, God had given me an up-close view of what it looks like to persevere and succeed.

A DREAM FULFILLED ACROSS NATIONS

Not long after, I found myself boarding planes and crossing borders— managing production teams, re-enacting story scenes with actors, interviewing, and carrying a calling, and a heart open to whatever God wanted to show me. My work with *The 700 Club* and Operation Blessing became a passport to miracles.

From the jagged ridges of the Andes in Peru to the bustling streets of Puebla, Mexico, I walked among people whose lives had been cracked open by natural disasters, hunger, and hopelessness—only to be mended again by the hands of God through His people.

We filmed the delivery of medical supplies, clean water systems, mobile clinics, and disaster relief—all ordinary tools in extraordinary moments. Yet it wasn't the aid alone that moved me. It was the faces. The children chasing hope in earthquake zones. The grandmothers who hugged my neck in thanks. The fathers who wept when given a business to steward to help provide for their families.

With every video recording, with every interview, with every dusty prayer whispered on location—I was being transformed.

This wasn't just reporting.

It was worship.

It was calling.

It was communion with the suffering and the saved.

HOPE AMIDST TRAGEGY: STORIES OF 9/11

"When you pass through the waters, I will be with you, and through the rivers, they shall not overwhelm you; when you walk through the fire, you shall not be burned; and the flame shall not consume you."
(Isaiah 43:2, *ESV*)

As I continued to produce deeply impactful stories, God was reminding me that media the platform was never about me. It was about the people whose stories I had been entrusted to tell. Humility meant shifting the spotlight away from myself and onto those who had walked through fire and still stood. God was preparing my heart - not for the stage, but for the sacred assignment of honoring others through their pain, their courage, and their truth. I didn't know it then, but learning to steward other people's stories with compassion and reverence would soon prepare me to do the same for someone else – someone whose journey would become the most personal and profound I would ever tell.

Yes, just as I was learning to carry the weight of other's personal redemption, God was about to entrust me with stories born out of national tragedy – stories that would literally shake the world.

September 11, 2001, began like any other morning.

I was at home preparing for a routine workday, and as I turned on the television, the screen flashed. I rubbed my eyes in disbelief, as if seeing more clearly might somehow erase the nightmare playing out on the screen before me.

The news anchor's voice trembled. Smoke poured from the North Tower. Seconds later—another explosion. Another plane. The South Tower.

The images seared themselves into my memory: jagged steel twisted into fire, ash raining like snow over lower Manhattan, people running, praying, gasping, leaping.

Then came the Pentagon.

The nation held its breath as nearly 3,000 lives were lost in a single day. In the features department, we stood still for a moment—then moved fast. We weren't just reporters now. We were witnesses to the unthinkable, tasked with offering hope in the face of horror

My assignment: to find stories of faith in the rubble. To search for God's fingerprint in the ashes.

THE HEART OF COMPASSION: THE TONEA STEWART STORY

My first 9/11 assignment was on my desk.

My location - Montgomery, Alabama, to interview a woman known to millions for her powerful roles in *Mississippi Burning* and *A Time to Kill* opened her home and her heart.

Dr. Tonea Stewart wasn't just an actress. She was a spiritual mother to many—and on that day, she was grieving a personal loss. Her close friend, Ada Mason, had been inside the Pentagon when the plane hit. Ada was gone.

Yet grief didn't stop Tonea. It deepened her.

She stepped in—without fanfare, without hesitation—to raise Ada's children.

She called it a privilege.

I called it Christ in flesh.

Sitting across from her in that quiet living room, I saw no trace of self-pity. Only grace.

She spoke softly, but every word carried weight.

"We must open our hearts," she said, "and make room for those who've lost everything."

Her life preached louder than any sermon. Her love—fierce, humble, unshaken—lingered long after the interview ended.

It was an honor to meet someone so selfless.

SCRIPTURE IN THE MIDST OF RUBBLE:
THE DOLORES PARLATO STORY

Then came my Pentagon assignment. The crew and I drove four hours to Arlington to reach our destination.

We stood on a hill overlooking the blackened breach—an open wound in the side of our nation's fortress. The air was solemn. Silence stretched like a veil over makeshift memorials: flowers, flags, handwritten notes. Some knelt. Some clung to strangers. Others just stared.

I whispered a prayer into the stillness, while also thanking God for those who had been miraculously spared.

As the camera men were filming the devastation I realized that no high-end Sony or Panasonic camera lens could convey what our eyes were seeing: the blackened scar along the side of the Pentagon, the twisted metal and blown-out windows, the silent ache that hung in the air like smoke. The frame could catch rubble, but not the weight of the lives lost.

Afterward, we met Delores Parlato—a U.S. Navy Chief Photographer's Mate, who narrowly avoided death that day. She was supposed to be there. Yet in a twist of divine orchestration, she had been reassigned to Fort Worth, Texas, just days before the attack.

Her house was modest. A single-story home wrapped in quiet strength. An American flag flown proudly from the porch. Verses of scripture adorned her front windows like armor.

Inside, she spoke of darkness—but only to exalt the Light.

"As I walked the halls of the Pentagon afterward, all I could say was, 'The Lord is here. He is with me.'"

She had printed banners with scripture and posted them in the very place where fear had taken hold. Her declaration was not political. It was eternal.

"This place belongs to God," she said firmly.

"And even in evil's shadow, Satan is defeated."

Delores didn't offer clichés. She offered clarity.

"Stop wondering how you'll die," she said soberly.

"Start asking where you're going when you do. No one is promised tomorrow."

Her words struck deep. They were not meant to frighten—they were meant to awaken.

In times of such tragedy, it's natural to question: "Why does God allow tragedy to happen?"

Scripture reminds us that, "The thief comes only to steal and kill and destroy; I have come that they may have life and have it to the full," (John 10:10).

We live in a fallen world where the enemy seeks to bring destruction; God offers hope and abundant life through Jesus. He grants humanity free will allowing choices that can lead to devastating consequences. Yet, through Jesus, God redeems the world from sin, offering hope to all who believe. One day, there will be no more sorrow or pain: until then, our hope rests in Jesus, the Light in the midst of darkness.

CHAPTER 23:

A FATHER'S LEGACY: REDEMPTION, LOSS, AND GOD'S FAITHFULNESS

"Therefore, confess your sins to one another and pray that you may be healed.
The prayer of the righteous person has great power as it is working."
(James 5:16, *ESV*)

After the national tragedy of 9/11, I began to witness a shift – not just in our country, but in my father. His health was declining, and his spirit, once so independent and steady, had softened. My father was a man of quiet strength and profound creativity. Having survived parental abandonment, never truly knowing his father, and being raised by his grandmother – along with enduring racism and broken relationships - he built a life of purpose through his many talents: photography, painting, sculpture, powerful lectures on Black history, and a successful photography business.

Once he came home, he never spoke of his remarkable achievements—capturing icons and historic moments in Detroit. He laid his camera down and poured his passion into the kitchen, where he cooked with the same quiet artistry that once framed the world through his lens.

Once a week, he made his famous oyster stew or grilled thick pork chops, always with a heaping side of fresh vegetables. "Why eat the intestines of the pig when you can eat the best parts like the chops?" he'd say, shaking his head at the thought of chitlins.

He loved Chinese food and would fire up his wok, whipping up shrimp fried rice or beef stir fry swimming in bok choy. My favorite part was when he swirled olive oil into the giant salad bowl, seasoning it with garlic salt and pepper—simple, perfect dressing for beefsteak tomatoes, cucumbers, scallions, and lettuce. Daddy adored fresh vegetables and often spent hours at the Eastern Market, buying produce straight from local farmers.

"Here, Michelle. Come try this." He'd appear in my bedroom doorway with a tray of food like a royal chef, presenting his latest creation with a proud smile. I was his happy taste tester—his princess—and marveled at how he could bring flavors to life.

When he wasn't serving up culinary masterpieces, he was in his library, lost in thick volumes on African history—especially race, religion, and truth. "They never taught us real history," he'd say, handing me books like *They Came Before Columbus*. "Don't let anyone tell you our story started with slavery. We came from kings and queens, scholars and scientists, architects and builders of gold-rich empires." I listened, intrigued, as he showed me other books that revealed our origins, "The first woman came from Africa," he said, "and she is referred to as Nana Buluku, a revered figure in West Africa tradition." I marveled at his knowledge–and even more so at his deep love and pride in our African heritage.

And when the kitchen quieted and the books were closed, he retreated to his darkroom, where he reviewed rolls of his latest photographic project or gently swished photo paper through a chemical bath to reveal a beautiful portrait he had captured with his camera.

As his youngest child, born decades after my siblings, I became a source of joy and pride for him in his later years. In essence, my father poured the best of himself into me-wanting to give me everything he never had; while also hoping I would carry on the Wilson legacy of creativity and innovation.

DADDY'S REDEDICATION TO JESUS

He was larger than life, yet things were shifting. I became a quiet witness to both his unraveling health – and, unexpectedly, to his spiritual rebirth. When Daddy and Angel Mother visited me at CBN, what was meant to be a routine trip became a divine appointment. At that time, he had long stopped saying the name of Jesus. Years of injustice, personal disillusionment, and the sting of racial inequity had hardened his heart. He sought answers through Afrocentric teachings and Egyptology, distancing himself from the Christian faith he once held.

Through observing my work—traveling the world and producing stories showcasing God's transformative power—something in him began to soften. He couldn't deny the hand of God on my life and gradually reopened his heart to his faith, saying the name of Jesus again.

The turning point came during an impromptu birthday dinner at the Swan Terrace restaurant inside CBN's Founder's Inn, held in honor of my colleague Janet's mother. Her father, Apostle Zin White, a powerful prophetic deliverance minister, began speaking to my father with a gentle authority, inquiring about his relationship with God, and lovingly urging him to reconcile with the Lord.

In that sacred moment, my father's heart broke open. Tears streamed down his face as he repented of his sins and rededicated his life to Christ. The commanding tangible presence of God filled the room so strongly it felt as though heaven had paused to rejoice. For years, I had prayed for this moment, wondering if I would ever see it come to pass. Witnessing his miraculous transformation was a profound reminder of God's faithfulness.

GENERATIONAL WOUNDS AND
UNEXPECTED STRENGTH

Over time, Daddy shared fragments of his life with me, and I learned we shared a painful connection: neither of us had been raised by our mothers; a generational curse on both sides of my family. His life was shaped by hardship – never knowing his parents and facing the prejudices of being a dark-skinned man during segregation. He once revealed the pain of a teacher telling him he could never achieve his ambitions because of the color of his skin.

Despite these challenges, he rose above it all, creating a successful life. He could have easily attained millionaire status with his talent and favor. Yet, like many, he had struggles that held him back including complicated relationships with women echoing Proverbs 6:26, which warns of the pitfalls of unchecked desires. Yet, it didn't erase his resilience or brilliance.

Throughout my life, I observed a striking dichotomy in my father. One part of him was pioneering and innovative-a man who could accomplish anything he set his mind to. However, the other part carried a quiet brokenness, perhaps rooted in childhood wounds and unspoken trauma he never dared to share. Yet the effects were visible, haunting him in subtle yet undeniable ways, shaping the decisions he made-especially in matters of intimacy and relationships.

Known affectionately as "Professor," he was just 21 credit hours shy of his doctorate. Though he didn't finish it, his legacy lived on through the students he mentored and the art he created.

Daddy loved to sing. Sometimes, I would catch him humming around the house, and one day, we sang together - "Everything Must Change" by George Benson. He began with a deep tenor voice that was captivating and controlled, and I joined in as we harmonized and sang the words:

"Everything must change. Nothing stays the same.
The young become the old, and mysteries unfold."

Our voices harmonized as if they were dancing together. It was a special moment of connection, one I still treasure.

THE WILL: THE LAST CHAPTER BEGINS

*"Surely the Lord Jehovah will do nothing except reveal His secret unto
His servants, the Prophets."*
(Amos 3:7, *ASV*)

I used my vacation to fly home to Detroit. As the plane descended, a quiet foreboding settled over me. I knew this trip would be different. Daddy met me at the airport and handed me a freshly updated will. His house, his possessions – would go to me. His face bore the weight of unspoken thoughts, and though I didn't want to discuss his impending death, he insisted.

"Death is a natural part of life," he said calmly as if trying to prepare me.

"I went to a trust attorney and made sure that once I pass, you will be taken care of," he explained.

The thought of not having my safety net, my only true support system, left me anxious and unsure about the future. How would life look without the steadfast presence of the one person I could always count on?

THE WEDDING: OUR FINAL DANCE

Before I began working at CBN, my father, a prophetic dreamer, shared a vision of a wedding which he initially thought might be mine. Years later, in October 2002, our family gathered for my cousin Simone's wedding. She looked stunning in her wedding gown next to her groom. As one of her bridesmaids I wore a velvet yellow dress. At the reception, I danced with my father, cherishing what I didn't know would be our final dance. His health had visibly declined; the vibrancy once in his eyes was now replaced with fatigue, yet he held a quiet hope, as if willing the strength to make it through just one more celebration with his daughter.

True to form, despite his fatigue, he took out his Canon camera and gathered the family together, determined to capture every moment, sealing what would be our last time together as a family – with him. After I said my goodbyes to everyone and gave my father and Angel Mother a hug, I flew home to Virginia.

THE COMA: SACRED GOODBYES

Just weeks later, I got the call. My father had suffered a brain stem stroke, a heart attack, and slipped into a diabetic coma. Miraculously, he was still alive.

Thanks to CBN's support, I rushed back to Michigan to be by his side. The plane ride felt like an eternity as I silently prayed and prepared myself, knowing I would soon face one of the most difficult moments of my life.

When I arrived at the hospital and entered the waiting room, I heard some family members say, "Michelle's here. He'll probably wake up now for her." It was a familiar undertone by this point in my life – the way people acknowledged the special favor my father wrapped me in. It wasn't something I had asked for—it was simply the life I lived.

I maintained my focus, greeted everyone briefly and walked straight into his room with a maturity and boldness that felt divinely orchestrated. I was immediately struck deeply by the sight of him, once vibrant, now in a coma on life support.

As I gently squeezed his hand, a tear slipped down his cheek. It was as if he was saying, "You've made it. You're here." It felt like he was imprisoned in a body that had betrayed him—that once was full of life now rendered silent and motionless, frozen in time.

As I stood there staring at him, every fiber of my being was focused on doing whatever I could to keep him alive, to hold onto him for just one more day. The thought of losing him was unbearable. I was believing God for a miraculous recovery; my mind was fixed on the possibility of my Father waking from that coma and living once again.

I prayed the most anointed prayer of faith, believing God for a miracle. I even prayed over and anointed cloth, hoping-trusting-that as I placed it beneath his pillowcase, just as Peter's shadow brought healing in the Bible, God would look favorably upon my muster seed of faith and grant me my request.

There is something about the human psyche and the spirit within us that fights to hold on to the ones we love. Even when the signs are clear that the end is near, we cling to hope even when we witness their suffering. The thought of living without them—the unknown reality of a life where they no longer exist—is too painful even to comprehend.

CLEANSING THE HOME: A SPIRITUAL ASSIGNMENT

The next day, the Holy Spirit entrusted me with a task I had read about but had never participated in myself: a spiritual house cleansing. My instructions were clear—cleanse our family home, by removing anything contrary to God's Word. Although I didn't understand the fullness of what God was asking me to do, I was obedient.

Following the Holy Spirit's guidance, I returned to the home, and over the next hour, I prayed in the Holy Spirit as I removed each object—whether a book about other gods, statues of idols, and trinkets representing Egyptian deities. For some items, the Holy Spirit instructed me to burn them, symbolizing the destruction of anything that could bring a spiritual hindrance or curse. I placed other items in trash bags and threw them away in the dumpster. As I prayed, I knew warring angels were assisting me in the spiritual realm. This was a battle beyond the physical, and as I continued to pray, I felt a heavy weight lift. I saw in the spirit, the blood of Jesus covering the walls of the house, sealing it as a clean sanctuary where God's presence could dwell.

God let me know that I was obedient to cleanse my father's house of idols – just as Hezekiah and Josiah did.

> *"He removed the high places, smashed the sacred stones and*
> *cut down the Asherah poles."*
> (2 Kings 18:4, NIV)

> *"He purified the temple… and threw out all the idols*
> *that were offensive to God."*
> (2 Chronicles 34:3–7, NLT)

What I did was a prophetic act of deliverance. As I removed idols from the house, the Lord removed idols from my father's soul as he lay in a coma.

I sealed my father's salvation — not because I had the power, but because I partnered with the Spirit of God in obedience.

As I walked out of our home having completed the assignment, God whispered in my spirit:

"As you were obedient in cleansing this home, I was doing another layer of cleansing in your father's heart."

The house cleansing was not just physical — it was a prophetic courtroom decree that broke generational curses and secured my father's eternal life.

His journey had been marked by disappointment and a search for identity that led him away from Christ. He began filling our home with objects and books that revolted against the knowledge of the most high God, Jesus. While I never saw him pray to those idols, their presence in the home created an altar of worship to false deities that conflicted with God's Word. Yet, even in his disillusionment, God's grace prevailed.

God was leaving no stone unturned in my father's life. This act wasn't just symbolic. It was spiritual warfare. His rededication was real, but this cleansing was deeper—God was removing every foothold the enemy had tried to hold on to.

It was a powerful reminder that salvation is a starting point, yet sanctification is an ongoing process. God was preparing him for eternity, removing anything that could jeopardize his spiritual freedom. It was as if God was saying, "This is My temple, and I will not share it with anything or anyone else."

The Holy Spirit then prompted me to play the Book of John, narrated by James Earl Jones, in his ears as he lay in the coma. I asked the

nurses to make sure it remained on continuous play, trusting God to work even in his stillness.

While the book of John played in my father's ears, Heaven played the sound of mercy over my father's spirit.

God wasn't just cleansing our home but also my father's soul as he lay in a coma. His journey had been marked by disappointment and a search for identity that led him away from Christ. He began filling our home with objects and books that revolted against the knowledge of the most high God, Jesus. While I never saw him pray to those idols, their presence in the home created an altar of worship to false deities that conflicted with God's Word. Yet, even in his disillusionment, God's grace prevailed.

God was leaving no stone unturned in my father's life. This act wasn't just symbolic. It was spiritual warfare. His rededication was real, but this cleansing was deeper—God was removing every foothold the enemy had tried to hold on to.

It was a powerful reminder that salvation is a starting point, yet sanctification is an ongoing process. God was preparing him for eternity, removing anything that could jeopardize his spiritual freedom. It was as if God was saying, "This is My temple, and I will not share it with anything or anyone else."

The Holy Spirit then prompted me to play the Book of John, narrated by James Earl Jones, in his ears as he lay in the coma. I asked the nurses to make sure it remained on continuous play, trusting God to work even in his stillness.

THE FINAL MOMENT

On December 4th, 2002, at 3 a.m., I awoke from a deep, uneasy sleep. At 8 a.m. I received a call from the hospital asking me to come. As I drove, I was filled with faith I'd hear news of improvement. When I arrived, I sat in the waiting room with great expectancy my father would be moved out of ICU into a regular room for recovery. After 20 minutes, the doctor came in, sat next to me, and confirmed that at 3 a.m., my father's vitals began to drop. He had suffered a series of four code blue heart attacks and had died. Unable to process what I had heard; I went into journalism mode and asked the doctor how he coped with caring for patients who died. His response was a blur as my anxious thoughts drifted to how I would walk out the rest of my life without my father.

Seeing his lifeless body in the hospital bed was the hardest moment of my life. His vibrant personality and essence were gone. It was in that moment, as I gazed at him, the truth became unmistakably clear: we are made of dust, and to dust we will all return. This life is but a vapor, and one day we must all meet our Creator and give an account for our lives. The essence of who we are—the person we truly are—is the spirit dwelling within this fragile, temporary vessel. My father's body, once so full of life, now was an empty shell, a vehicle that had served its purpose. It was then I cried like I had never cried before, yet I felt peace knowing I had played my part in sealing his eternity with Jesus.

DADDY'S CELEBRATION OF LIFE

As I prepared the details for Daddy's celebration of life - writing his obituary, meeting with funeral directors - I felt exhausted in my body yet strong in my spirit. I must have lost 20 pounds, had barely eaten, my focus solely on honoring my father one final time.

At his funeral, many gathered - students, friends, and family - to pay their respects. I was able to speak knowing the body in the casket was no longer him, especially without his signature mustache he had worn all his life. I shared the wisdom he had imparted to me over the years: the value of perseverance, humility, entrepreneurship, and adding beauty to the world through the gifts God gave us.

Afterward, one of his friends approached me and said, "Your Father was so proud of you. He always believed you could spin gold from straw." Another friend told me, "You did everything your father wanted you to do. You got your education, just like he always wanted."

Though life without him felt incomplete, I clung to the memories and the faith that God was now my ultimate Father. The world felt different without him as if forever shifted out of place, and I wasn't sure if life would ever feel right again. Yet despite the ache in my heart, I resolved to keep moving forward, holding onto the legacy he left me and God's purpose for my life.

THE LOST INHERITANCE:
GAINING AN EVEN GREATER ONE

My thoughts now turned to the family home my father left me in his trust. I worked hard, spending thousands, to restore it, making improvements, transforming it into a rental income property. However, there were unforeseen challenges. A family member remained in the house for an extended period, which made it difficult for me to occupy it or rent it out to help cover expenses. As time passed and the bills mounted, I was unable to keep the home, and it was lost to foreclosure.

This was a difficult and painful experience, yet it taught me valuable lessons about forgiveness and letting go and trusting God. I had to come to a place of peace, choosing to forgive and release the burden to God. God would later tell me He had a greater inheritance in store – one that would be entrusted to me in His perfect timing.

A CLOSER WALK WITH GOD:
FINDING THE ULTIMATE FATHER IN GOD

Yet, despite these incredible losses, God was writing an even greater story in my life. He began to stir something new in me. For the first time, I found myself in a new and unfamiliar place where I had to rely on God in a way I had never done before. My earthly Father's presence had allowed me to lean on his provision, but with him now gone, I had to discover what it truly meant for God to be my Father.

Scripture says, "A father to the fatherless, a defender of widows, is God in his holy dwelling" (Psalm 68:5).

This truth became more than words to me; it became my lifeline. God graciously revealed Himself as the ultimate Father, teaching me no matter what happened in life, He would support, provide, and care for me in ways far greater than my earthly father ever could.

That realization drew me to press into God more deeply than ever, praying more, seeking His presence and provision in a way that transformed my understanding of His love and care. It was as if I stood at the edge of a diving board, looking down into the deep waters of faith, ready to jump and trusting God would catch me. And He did!

DADDY HEARD EVERYTHING:
THE RON WINANS'S INTERVIEW

Even before my father passed, I had always wondered if he could hear me. While he was in a coma for two weeks, I prayed the prayer of faith, anointed him with oil, and believed God to raise him up in perfect health. He squeezed my hand whenever I entered his room, or a tear rolled down his cheek. These were signs he knew I was there with him and that he loved me, even though he couldn't express it verbally.

In their cold, sterile, matter-of-fact manner, the doctors continually reminded me not to get my hopes up, insisting it was just a reflex. Yet deep down, I believed it was something more—that he could hear me and was responding.

God, who cares about everything we're concerned about, knew the weight that lingered in my heart over this matter, and He was about to confirm what I had always believed.

Months later, while co-producing a story for *The 700 Club* on Ron Winans's miraculous recovery, I would finally find the answer to the question that had plagued me. After Ron's interview, I asked him if he could hear people speaking while he was in his coma in the hospital room. Ron confirmed he had heard every prayer, every word. At that moment, God reassured me my Father had listened to my prayers, every conversation spoken around him and especially heard every word from the book of John. It was the answer my heart needed, a final gift from God.

CHAPTER 24:

EMBRACING THE DIVINE CALL

"And I heard the voice of the Lord saying, 'Whom shall I send, and who
will go for us?' Then I said, 'Here I am! Send me."
Isaiah 6:8, *ESV*)

SPIRITUAL SEEDS FOR A NEW SEASON

Although I attended church regularly, God opened an unexpected door for me to experience more of Him and the gifts of the Spirit. A local prophetic deliverance ministry introduced me to the gifts of healing, deliverance, prayer, and prophecy in action. This opportunity deepened my understanding of how the Spirit moves and God's desire to touch lives in extraordinary ways.

For two years, I felt privileged to serve in this space—learning, growing, and participating in transformative events. I preached my first message, "The Coat of Purity," at a tent meeting in South Carolina, connecting Joseph's coat of favor to God's call for purity in our lives. I also contributed financially to back-to-school giveaways, helping children in need prepare for a fresh start. These experiences planted spiritual seeds that would take root and bloom in future seasons of my journey.

In time, however, God began leading me into a new season and personally anointing me for the ministry He had prepared for me. This shift was confirmed by prophetic words from strangers—people who knew nothing of my private prayers but echoed what I had already sensed deep within: it was time to move on. I left with a wealth of experience and greater prophetic clarity.

USING MY GIFTS FOR GOD: WALKING IN MY MINISTRY CALLING

The CBN Prayer Center became a spiritual refuge – a place where voices from around the world called in desperate, seeking hope, prayer, and encouragement. God had placed a longing in my heart to pray with more intensity. One day, God whispered to me to go to the prayer center.

It was there I first met Diane Stevenson. Her peaceful demeanor stood out like a beacon amid the hum of prayers. When I asked if she would pray with me, she smiled warmly and agreed. That single moment marked the beginning of a spiritual journey that transformed my life.

Over the next several months, Diane and I began meeting in the SHB chapel on Saturdays, where the very architecture seemed to echo God's presence. Its dome-like structure was supported by columns with Bibles at their bases, reminding all who entered God's Word is the foundation of life. The central wooden cross that hung from the ceiling and statues of angels symbolized God's presence, holiness, and protection for His people.

One morning, Diane directed me to walk and pray around the chapel as she played the piano. As I opened my heart in prayer, she began to prophesy, unveiling God's plans for me – plans so vast they felt beyond my comprehension. She wasn't merely praying; she was helping me step into the greater ministry God had ordained I didn't yet recognize within myself.

I'd received prophetic words before, like the time Pastor Myles Munroe declared I would reach millions through a media platform, still this was different. Diane spoke of a calling beyond cameras and interviews, one deeply connected to God's desire for me to impact others through the preached word. She awakened a dormant understanding: God had prepared me as a chosen vessel equipped for great exploits in His Kingdom.

SERVING IN MINISTRY: GOD MOVES MIGHTILY

Diane invited me to her ordination service, led by Apostle Garna Trafton, where she launched her ministry. I joined her church and soon found myself leading the choir. Our small group sang with passion, and God's presence moved among us bringing many to their knees in worship. As I led in song, I silently prayed to experience the same depth of vulnerability and surrender. I preached the word of God and accompanied Pastor Diane as she ministered in various churches in the area.

One night, God confirmed my place in this ministry through a dream: I was washing dishes and handing them to Pastor Diane, who rinsed them and put them on a dish rack. In the same dream, I stood on a large stage singing before a huge crowd of young people. I knew God was affirming my partnership with Diane and His call to minister to the next generation.

However, serving in a small church required wearing multiple hats. The workload became overwhelming, and I eventually stepped away due to overwhelming stress. Still, peace evaded me after leaving. God had chosen that ministry as a training ground for my higher calling, and despite my determination to move on, my heart knew I should have stayed. Unfortunately, for several years, I would remain without peace, unable to find the sense of belonging I once experienced in her church.

Regardless, I was thankful for every lesson, every opportunity to grow, and the reminder God was preparing me for a ministry far greater than what I ever imagined.

DISCOVERING AWARD WINNING GRACE:
MINI-MOVIES & MAJOR MIRACLES

Producing stories and traveling the world for *The 700 Club* became more than a job—it became my media ministry. It allowed me to witness first-hand the miraculous works of God in the lives of others.

Stories like:

- **Lucretia Church**, who courageously shared about being molested by a family member and giving birth to his child. She became a drug dealer and got arrested. Despite the trauma, God met her in prison, redeemed her life, and used her testimony to minister to others.

- **Almetia Mack**, who was miraculously healed after receiving a word of knowledge while watching *The 700 Club*, embraced me like family, surrounding me with unconditional love.
- **Shevika Ward-Hannah**, who lost her sight, experienced miraculous restoration after leaning on her faith and the prayers of her family.
- **Tony Spears**, who lived a homosexual lifestyle for years, was completely set free after an encounter with God that transformed his life and allowed him to walk in the purpose God intended for him.
- **Ty Adams**, who shared her journey from sexual immorality to spiritual freedom, reminded me of the depths of God's redeeming love.
- **Ann Lesley-Smith**, who fell from wealth and societal prominence to despair, shared how Christ's redemption restored her life.
- **Bishop D.K. Jones**, miraculously healed from a brain aneurysm, exemplified a father's heart and the power of God's healing hand.
- **Jada Collins**, an *Ebony* fashion fair model, recommitted her life to Christ after leaving a relationship that conflicted with her Christian values. As part of her story, I learned to walk the runway with her, which became an unexpected and memorable part of visual storytelling.
- **Stella Reaves**, through giving her last $20 and becoming a faithful monthly partner with CBN, she was able to secure a high-paying job, live in her dream home, and even inspire her daughter, Jackie to give – introducing the concept of generational giving to CBN's fundraising stories.
- **Sherry Jones**, who endured the loss of her husband and a cancer diagnosis, displayed remarkable faith as she declared, "Though He slay me, yet will I serve Him" – a testimony of trust that deeply resonated with my spirit.

Through producing, I noticed a common thread in many of the stories we aired on *The 700 Club*: they often centered around individuals who had fallen into drug addiction or sexually destructive behavior mostly due to childhood wounds and trauma. I realized that if, by the grace of God, you could keep those doors from opening in your life, you were already ahead of the enemy's strategy to derail your purpose and block the abundant life God intends.

Yet no matter how dark the path, every story shared one unshakable truth: God can redeem any life—no matter how far someone has strayed. You truly can go from the pit to the palace of His mercy and grace, if you dare to trust Him and put Him first. As a producer handpicked by God, I had the privilege of witnessing these miracles unfold firsthand. It wasn't just storytelling. It was sacred ground.

DEVELOPING INTO A MOVIE PRODUCER, "MURDER, FORGIVENESS & REDEMPTION": THE BERT BAKER AND JAMES LEGGETTE STORY

And now, God was about to open up doors for me to use my storytelling skills to create exceptional, award-worthy reenactments. I wasn't just producing stories anymore - I was beginning to move like a movie director and producer, bringing narratives to life with more vision, depth, and prophetic insight and it was exhilarating.

One powerful testimony involved Bert Baker and James Leggette, whose lives were intertwined by tragedy. James, in a jealous rage, killed his wife – Bert's sister. Bert harbored hatred for years even plotting to kill James.

I vividly remember meeting James, asking him to relive the day he killed his wife. As he recounted the events, the same rage that had overtaken him in that moment flickered across his face. It was unsettling to witness, but it reminded me of the depths of pain and transformation God had worked in his life. I hired actors and recreated the scene of that fateful day in a trailer home, like the one where the tragedy had occurred. The camera crew and editors worked with me to create scenes so vivid and compelling they felt like a movie scene.

Overtime, God softened Bert's heart, leading him to forgive James. When the two men met after James's release from prison, they embraced and later ministered together in prisons, sharing their story of redemption, and healing. Producing this story was both challenging and rewarding earning me a Telly Award. The story's impact was undeniable, and it remains one of the most powerful examples of the transformative power of forgiveness I have ever produced.

THE INNER BATTLE BREWING

"The seeds of destruction the enemy sows into our lives often begin as a faint whisper—barely noticeable yet insidious in its intent. These echoes drift into the soil of our hearts planting lies so subtly we walk forward unaware. For a time, life continues as usual, the ground appearing undisturbed. Beneath the surface, those seeds stretch their roots deep, intertwining with our thoughts, our identity, our very sense of self. And soon what was hidden grows into a tangled harvest so vast it can no longer be ignored. The roots, now thick and unyielding, give voice to the fears and struggles you've tried to bury. Now so inseparable from the fabric of who you are. Yet deep within, a spark of truth remains which cannot be extinguished – a quiet knowing that THIS does not define you. The challenge lies in finding the courage to grasp the unseen hand of God, uproot the deception, and uncover the true you—the masterpiece God originally intended"

- Michelle B. Wilson, author, *In Search of a Mother's Love.*

Soon, I was given another opportunity to use my on-camera talents to create a memorable holiday story with interior designer Moll Anderson in her exquisite home.

Moll gave me the warmth and welcome I needed to break out of my shell.

After rehearsing the script and fine-tuning the camera settings and lighting on our multi-camera set up, we were ready.

Action!

As the cameras rolled, Moll showed me how to create festive decorations for the Christmas holidays, including cranberry spritzers topped with pomegranate and stunning table décor as a showstopper for any family gathering. My favorite moment was when she taught me to make chocolate-covered Oreo Christmas balls. We both delightfully sampled them on camera, sharing laughter and lighthearted joy in a way that brought warmth to the story.

Each production like this, which pushed me out of my comfort zone, felt like an incredible accomplishment. What no one knew was I was still overcoming deep insecurities—wondering if I was good enough—while also battling great bouts of anxiety and fears I never spoke of yet had learned to live with.

After our taping, Moll said something that stayed with me: "Why aren't you on television more? You could have your own show. You've got it all— the looks, the personality. Why don't you go for it?" Moments like Moll Anderson encouraging me to pursue on-camera opportunities stirred something in me but doubts still whispered I wasn't enough.

I carried the weight of brokenness everywhere I went, feeling like an incomplete canvas. Yet, I knew God was creating a masterpiece—each stroke healing me, teaching me, and strengthening my faith.

ANOINTED FROM MY MOTHER'S WOMB: A DELIVERER HIDDEN AMONG YOU

From afar, people admired my confident exterior, but up close, they sensed the brokenness I tried desperately to hide—silent battles that echoed louder than words.

Rejection was a recurring theme. I felt it in the stares, the undertones, the whispers just loud enough for me to hear. I was labeled as different, someone who didn't fit the mold. Like the young girl on the school bus—sitting alone, called "weird"—I often prayed, "God, when will my breakthrough come?" Though His answer wasn't immediate, I felt strength rise within me, a grace that carried me.

Still, God anchored me through prophetic words at ministry meetings. One stood out: "What you've gone through would have broken most people. God is keeping you." That reminder reassured me that He saw me and would redeem my pain for His glory. In time, He would make all things perfect. My trials were not wasted—they were shaping my character, teaching forgiveness, and forming the testimony that would one day speak for itself. Amid accusations, I never retaliated. I remained silent, listening to God's still, small voice, trusting Him to fight for me.

The life of a prophet is lonely, often misunderstood, and forged through fire. Yet I came to understand that nothing would be wasted. Every trial, every tear, every act of surrender would be used for His glory.

Whether in school, my family, or my job, I often found myself the target of misunderstanding, rejection, or judgment. Many couldn't see past the pain to perceive the purpose. But God did. He saw the treasure hidden beneath the trauma, the oil pressed from my process, and the calling wrapped in my contradictions.

Just like God used the least likely to do the greatest exploits in Scripture, I, too, fell into the category of those He described as "the foolish things of the world to confound the wise." I was a prophet, a minister, a hidden gift in the midst—yet most could only see the brokenness…

We often overlook the very ones God sends as deliverers because they don't fit our definition of what anointed looks like. Yet God doesn't choose based on appearances—He chooses based on assignment – based on the heart. The accusations spoken against me were seeds of discord, the kind God despises— just like when Miriam spoke against Moses and was struck with leprosy (Numbers 12:1–10). Yet instead of lashing out, I asked God to extend mercy. They were blind to who I truly was and to who God had called me to be.

In prayer, God revealed why the warfare was so intense: I was chosen— called as a prophetess, ordained from my mother's womb to speak to nations. The wilderness was preparation, a lonely path reserved for prophets. I was being chiseled into a vessel for His glory. No one knew the weight I carried. No one saw how God was fighting for me as I kept my heart pure.

Just as Jesus was driven into the wilderness before His ministry began, I too was being refined. "Very truly I tell you, whoever believes in me will do the works I have been doing, and they will do even greater things than these…" (John 14:12). God was cultivating something deep within me—lessons only learned through the fire.

Along this journey, God sent people to remind me He was orchestrating a greater plan—like Bonnie, who nicknamed me "Josephina." Her words echoed Joseph's story: betrayed yet elevated to a position that saved many. In the same way, God was preparing me to steward unimaginable opportunities for healing and deliverance. When Bonnie would greet me in the CBN hallways, calling out "Hi, Josephina," it was more than a nickname—it was a prophetic reminder to stay focused on the bigger picture.

Then there was Matt, whose dry humor never failed to make me laugh. His jokes gave me permission to release parts of myself long hidden beneath sorrow. We shared light moments—talking about stories we produced, walking the campus, even mimicking Michael Jackson's dance moves until we couldn't breathe from laughter.

Michael, a multi-talented artist and trusted friend, amazed me with his gifts. He once drew a penciled portrait of me that I proudly framed. We especially enjoyed each other's company during office parties—his presence always a highlight.

Occasionally, I'd pass through the offices of Marcia and Jo-Ann, cherishing the rare moments of connection that reminded me I was part of the CBN family.

Then came Sandra—a rare and treasured gift from God. She noticed me during chapel, where employees gathered to pray. She introduced herself, as if heaven had whispered, "Be a friend to her." And she listened. Sandra didn't see my brokenness; she saw me through eyes of grace. She called forth the beauty God had planted deep within me—beauty long buried beneath pain but never forgotten by God. Encouragement became the language of our friendship, spoken with ease and soaked in grace.

Her gifts were never random—they were prophetic. For my birthday, she once gave me beautifully decorated jars of flavored honey. "Michelle," she said, "this is to remind you that God is bringing sweetness to your future." Just as honey in Scripture represents abundance and the promised land, her gift spoke of joy replacing sorrow.

I looked forward to those gifts—silent affirmations that God still had a plan. During holidays, when loneliness weighed heavy, Sandra opened her home and folded me into her family. The warmth of their laughter, shared meals, and simple joy flowed through me like living water. Her friendship was more than kindness—it was healing. It reminded me that even in isolation, God sends people to anchor and sustain us. Ours became exactly that: a lifeline, divinely timed and gently held. One that needed no explanation.

CARRYING GOD'S HEALING ATMOSPHERE AS A PRODUCER: THE ATEBA CROCKER STORY

And yet, the crushing I endured produced oil – an anointing that enabled me to tell stories with a fragrance of deliverance. It blanketed every environment I entered, allowing those I interviewed to receive a deeper measure of healing in their souls. Perhaps that was why I was always given the weighty testimonies because God knew I would understand and honor their journeys in ways that brought a deeper depth of healing.

Like the Ateba Crocker story.

As a child, Ateba was molested, and later turned to the escort industry as a way of providing for her son. She remained there for two years longer than most, revealing the depth of her anguish.

During our interview, Ateba described the moment she cried out to God at a church altar: "Make me like Lazarus - I want to feel alive again."

With desperation she pleaded for God to call her out of the tomb of her past and strip away the grave clothes of shame and bondage that had clung to her for far too long. As she spoke, the Holy Spirit filled the room so powerfully that we paused filming. The crew and I wept alongside her, overwhelmed by the weight of God's presence. It was clear God was doing yet another layer of cleansing and healing in her heart – a testament to His relentless love and redemptive grace.

Ateba later married and become a university professor, serving as a living testimony to God's ability to redeem even the most broken past and rewrite it with purpose and grace.

FROM WORSHIP TO WARFARE: MY BAHAMIAN FAMILY

One day, as I browsed the bookshelves at work, a bold green cover caught my eye: Breaking the Chains – From Worship to Warfare by Bahamian prophetic minister Mattie Nottage. The title and image of her wearing army fatigues resonated deeply with me. It was a visual reminder that life is a spiritual battle; yet one God ordained for me to win. By now, I had started going to counseling and attended countless deliverance meetings seeking healing from the hurts of my past that lingered.

I contacted Prophetess Mattie and discovered she was preaching at a church in Maryland. I drove to the service, where she prayed with me and invited me to visit her and her husband, Apostle Edison, at their church, Believers Faith Outreach Ministries International in Nassau, Bahamas. Every visit was marked by grand hospitality, deep teaching, and a smorgasbord of the best Bahamian dishes - peas and rice, cracked conch, grouper, johnnycakes, guava duff, and much more.

Their church services were electrifying, filled with prophetic precision and a tangible anointing that brought healing and deliverance to desperate souls. The intense times of prayer felt so powerful; it seemed as though any mountain could be moved. I kept returning whenever I had a break, drawn to the tangible presence of God and the genuine love of the congregation.

I came to realize spiritual deliverance is often a process. God was still at work, perfecting me layer by layer - chipping away at the hurts and pains that had bound me for so long. One of the most important elements God loves is as we draw closer to Him, we learn to trust and lean on Him. My Bahamian family became instrumental in my journey of healing and unbeknownst to me God would use them to confirm the very assignment for which I had been birthed. Until then, His infinite wisdom and love, kept me strong as I trusted Him to bring me to my breakthrough.

FROM PROPHECY TO FULFILLMENT: A FULL-CIRCLE MOMENT WITH DR. MYLES MUNROE IN THE BAHAMAS

The prophetic word I received in college – that media would be my pulpit to reach millions for Christ – had always echoed in my heart. So, when I learned I'd soon come face to face with the very one who spoke it, I was overwhelmed with joy. My next assignment: filming powerful stories in the Bahamas with Victor Oladokun and Holly Flood to co-produce stories for *The 700 Club* and *CBN's Turning Point*, a program reaching viewers in Africa and the Caribbean.

One of our assignments took us to Clifton Heritage National Park in Nassau, where we filmed the ruins of a former slave village and the "Pirate Steps" – pathways believed to have been traveled by enslaved Africans as they disembarked from ships. Walking through the site stirred memories of my father's lessons about our ancestors' resilience.

One of the most profound moments of the trip was visiting Dr. Myles Munroe at his home. I was surprised to find despite his global influence, he still lived in the same modest house where he and his wife Ruth had started their ministry - his resources clearly devoted to advancing God's Kingdom rather than personal gain.

As the crew prepared for his interview with Victor, I showed him the book he had signed when I first interviewed him for my college radio show. In it, he had prophesied television would become my pulpit, and I would reach millions for Christ. Now, as a producer traveling the world to share stories of faith, I told him how that prophecy had come true. He smiled and said, "At least I know I am a real prophet."

Listening to him speak, with such wisdom about life, leadership, and faith left an indelible mark. Tragically, years later, on November 9, 2014, Dr. Munroe, his wife Ruth, and several others lost their lives in a plane crash. Despite his untimely death, his teachings, books, and ministry continue to impact the world.

GOD'S TRANSFORMATIVE POWER: PRODUCING 700 CLUB TESTIMONIES FROM PROPHETESS MATTIE NOTTAGE'S MINISTRY

While in Nassau, I had the privilege of capturing stories that were brimming with both suffering and salvation at the Nottage's' church.

One was Melissa Nottage, daughter of Apostle Edison and Prophetess Mattie Nottage. At just eight years old, she was molested by her piano teacher—a wound that led her down a dark path of rebellion and gang life. The loss of close friends to senseless violence became her breaking point. It was there, at the edge of despair, that she turned to God. Today, as she plays the piano, she leads worship with an anointing that breaks chains, her talented gift of music dripping with the oil of someone who's been through the fire and come out refined. We filmed her interview on a sun-warmed beach where waves whispered grace and beauty wrapped around brokenness like a covering. It was a living picture of Isaiah 61: beauty for ashes.

Another story unfolded through Johnathan Ash, who rose from poverty to become the top drug dealer in San Salvador by age fifteen. Survival had once demanded it. But after his cousin's arrest, he accepted an invitation to church—and encountered the One who rewrites stories. Today, Johnathan is a thriving businessman, a loving husband and father, and a vessel of ministry. His life is a walking sermon, a vivid reminder that no pit is too deep for God to reach.

Then there was Dinah Knowles. We stood together outside a crumbling house where her forty-year crack cocaine addiction had once ruled her life. "The smell," she said through tears, "I remember it so clearly." Though the air held no trace of it for me, I understood—some battles leave residue only survivors can sense. Her now aged father, a pastor who had interceded for decades, stood beside her that day, his eyes reflecting the joy of a prodigal returned. It was a moment soaked in the sweetness of answered prayer. I was so overjoyed he lived long enough to see his prayers answered for his daughter.

Filming reenactments with passionate members of the congregation brought these stories to life with cinematic depth. There was rawness, reverence, and a holy fire among them. These weren't just testimonies for broadcast—they were altars, each one testifying to the miracle-working power of a God who still heals, delivers, and restores.

THE GOOD SAMARITAN'S CHARGE: THE BEGINNING OF A DIVINE MISSION OF HEALING

"But a Samaritan, as he traveled, came where the man was, and when he saw him, he took pity on him. He went to him and bandaged his wounds, pouring oil and wine. Then he put the man on his donkey, brought him to an inn, and cared for him."
(Luke 10:33-37, *NIV*)

Most years, my birthday came and went without fanfare. However, this year was different. I chose to celebrate in the Bahamas with my Bahamian family, unaware that heaven had choreographed something deeper. It was conference week at Prophetess Mattie Nottage's church—a divine intersection of nations, voices, and heavenly agendas.

One evening, after a powerful sermon, a minister from Africa looked at me and asked, "Are you married?" My flesh nearly responded with a sarcastic retort, but something deeper held me still. "I see a ring on your finger," he said, then called me forward. What followed was a flood of prophecy—God's heart unveiled over my future husband and destiny. As he laid hands on me, I fell beneath the weight of glory. My body hit the floor, but my spirit soared, searching the skies for what had just been released.

The next day, another evangelist preached on the parable of the Good Samaritan. She painted the scene: a broken man left for dead, religious leaders who walked past, and the unexpected stranger who dared to stop and bind his wounds. Before she closed, she stepped down, pointed at me, and declared: "You are that Good Samaritan. God will use you as a Moses to your family and to millions around the world."

Her words pierced my soul. In that moment, I knew. The assignment I had long sensed but never named had found its voice. I thought this season would be about marriage, building a family, and stepping into rest. Instead, God was asking me to pick up a different mantle—one soaked in oil, weeping with intercession, and weighted with love.

Like the Samaritan who crossed cultural and emotional boundaries, and like Moses who stood before Pharaoh to free his people, I was being called to extend healing to someone who had wounded me deeply—my own mother.

This was not a duty born of guilt. It was a divine mission birthed in mercy. God was sending me to bandage old wounds, to carry her to safety—not in the flesh, but in the Spirit. I was the vessel He had chosen. And though I felt small, the call was clear.

My mother, too, was deeply loved by God—so loved that heaven had orchestrated every detour to bring her to this moment. Her freedom was drawing near. And now, in the mystery of grace, He was sending her youngest child, her only daughter, to help midwife her deliverance.

God had seen it all from the beginning. And now, in the fullness of time, the assignment was unfolding—not through revenge, but through redemption. I would carry the oil and wine. I would become her "Good Samaritan."

CHAPTER 25:

A DAUGHTER'S CALL TO CARE

*"For I was hungry, and you fed me. I was thirsty, and you gave me
a drink. I was a stranger, and you invited me into your home. I was
naked, and you gave me clothing. I was sick, and you cared for me. I
was in prison, and you visited me. 'I tell you the truth, when you did it
to one of the least of these, my brothers and sisters, you were doing it to
Me!"*
(Matthew 25:35-40, NLT)

Soon after returning from the Bahamas, I knew the next thing I needed to
do was find my mother who was living in Memphis. My cousin Belvia
and I drove around the city listening to the still small voice of the Holy
Spirit who led us straight to the transitional home she was now living in. She
proudly introduced me to her friends: "This is my daughter, and she works
for *The 700 Club.*"

We went grocery shopping with my cousin, who walked beside us, her
steady presence a silent balm to the emotional current swirling between us.

"Buy me some cigarettes?" she asked, almost casually, as if testing the
waters.

I stopped in my tracks and turned toward her. "No," I said gently but firmly. "I can't buy you anything that harms your health."

She paused, looking up at me with eyes that had once held the entire sky. "When you were little, I made sure you had everything. The best dresses, the prettiest bows. I never told you no." Her voice softened, hoping to sway me.

I stood firm.

Years of burned bridges had left her largely alone. Even my two older brothers, who lived just across town, had long grown weary of her volatility. Still, I had glimpses of who she used to be—who she could be again.

A few days after I returned home, the phone rang. A social worker explained she'd been placed in a new transitional shelter, her rent temporarily covered. Vulnerable. Alone. My heart cracked a little, but I thanked God for His unseen protection, for mercy that blankets even the most frayed souls.

I sat quietly that night, asking God what this meant. How far would this road go? I had no map—only a whisper that told me to stay open. To stay ready.

The answer came sooner than expected.

A month later, a nurse from Memphis called. My mother had been hospitalized and couldn't be discharged until she had a place to go. Her voice was clinical but heavy with implication: As her daughter, wasn't it my responsibility to take her in?

I hesitated. Not out of resentment, but out of fear—of what it might cost, of what might be required of me. I asked the nurse to give me thirty days. I needed time to investigate. To pray.

Thirty minutes later, the phone rang again. "My husband and I will buy her a Greyhound bus ticket," the nurse offered, kindness now blooming where bureaucracy had been. "We can send her anywhere you want her to go."

I closed my eyes, and without missing a beat—as if the Holy Spirit Himself had nudged my tongue—I said, "Send her to Virginia." I had twenty-four hours to prepare for a stranger who gave birth to me.

THE LEPER'S CRY: HOPE IN THE
MIDST OF BROKENNESS

July marked a quiet turning, a divine pivot written not in ink but in the invisible script of obedience. When I said yes to taking in my mother, I wasn't just opening a door—I was stepping into holy ground.

The warnings came swiftly, laced in logic: "She'll derail your life. She doesn't deserve this. She abandoned you—how can you forget that? She will be nothing but a distraction." Their voices echoed what my wounds still whispered. Yet, how could I pour meals into the hands of strangers, comfort the homeless on city sidewalks, and turn away from the woman who had birthed me? She was one of them. And I was one of the wounded.

So, I said, "Yes." Not to her, but to God. A trembling yes, but a yes, nonetheless.

And as I did, the Holy Spirit began to reveal something deeper. My mother and I were not just connected by blood—we shared something more elusive and haunting: the wound of rejection. The kind that doesn't just bruise—it brands. Like lepers of old, we had both walked through life marked, cast out, misunderstood. Their cry, "Unclean! Unclean!" was not so different from the silence cries of our hearts we had both learned to live with.

She bore the visible signs—burned bridges, closed doors, a reputation that shadowed her. I bore the hidden kind. Emotional scars, pressed deep beneath my smile. We were kindred lepers, wandering in different deserts, but crying the same unseen prayer: "Don't leave me alone. Please understand me."

God gave me eyes to see her not as an offender, but as a survivor. Not as a villain, but as a woman with wounds so deep they distorted her reflection. I began to see her pain as a mirror of mine—twisted in different ways but birthed from the same ache.

It wasn't her I was fighting. It was the spirit of rejection itself—a generational, strategic assignment sent to fracture what God had knit. I stopped blaming her and began hating the enemy who'd tried to write our story in ruins.

I thought of the ten lepers who cried out to Jesus for healing. Only one returned to thank Him. Yet all were made clean. That gave me hope. If He could touch their skin, couldn't He touch our souls?

Like Job, I chose to believe in restoration even when I was still sitting in ashes. That our story would not end in exile, but in embrace.

God whispered it over me like rain: "You are not disqualified. You are not forgotten. In Me, you are chosen. Set apart. Called."

And so was she.

THE GREYHOUND BUS, A PURSE, AND THE COUNTDOWN TO REDEMPTION

As I waited for her arrival, I was a mixture of anxiety and hesitant hope. The Greyhound bus station in Norfolk was quiet at 3 a.m., except for the occasional shuffle of footsteps and the whisper of diesel engines cooling in the dark. I waited beneath the dull yellow glow of the terminal lights, clutching the paper I'd been advised to prepare—a list of house rules.

No smoking inside. Clean up after yourself. Attend church on Sundays.

It felt strange to draft expectations for a woman who once bathed me in bubbles and tucked me in with her sweet lullabies. Stranger still to ask her to sign them. Still, this wasn't nostalgia—it was necessity. I wasn't receiving a mother. I was welcoming a soul, both familiar and foreign, into the fragile peace of my home.

When the bus finally came to a halt, she stepped off with the regal air of someone who'd never been displaced—her back straight, chin lifted, her only baggage a modest purse, the clothes on her back, and a smile on her face. I embraced her. Her body felt smaller than I remembered, as though life had deprived her.

"Hi, Darlin'. Mama is here."

"Hi. How was your bus ride? You hungry?" I asked gently.

"It was just fine. Yes, I want some pancakes," she said. "Blueberry."

I took her to the nearby IHOP, where she sat across from me, scanning the menu like a woman who had been here before and yet hadn't tasted rest in years. After the waiter took her order, I slid the paper across the table.

"These are just a few rules," I said. "Things that will help us live peacefully together."

She read them without flinching, then looked up with a curious glint in her eye. "I'm glad you did this. We're gonna have so much fun," she said, and smiled. It was a moment of unexpected grace—brief, but tender. We both signed. I sighed relief.

When her pancakes arrived, the scent of warm syrup and butter filled the booth. I reached for a bite, lighthearted.

"No," she said sharply, pulling her plate closer.

It was such a small refusal, but it landed with weight. Not because I wanted pancakes, but because it revealed something deeper. A closed spirit. A guarded heart. I thought to myself, "What have I gotten myself into?" I swallowed my disappointment, folded my napkin, and smiled. I made small talk while she ate, each bite a silent statement that she was still in control.

When we got home, I took her to her room, that I made sure felt like home for her. I went to my bedroom and afterward, we collapsed into sleep. No grand conversations. No tender mother-daughter reminiscing. Just quiet exhaustion wrapped in new unfamiliar walls.

And just as Angel Mother had once blessed me with a large bag of new clothes the day after I entered her tender care at seven years old, I now followed in her footsteps – doing the same for my mother. The next morning, I took Mother shopping. She needed everything—new clothes, undergarments, toiletries. I loaded the cart while she picked out the items she needed. To outsiders, it might have looked like a generous act of a devoted daughter. Yet internally, I knew this wasn't just provision. It was reintroduction. Rebuilding.

She still saw me as the six-year-old who used to trail her heels in admiration. But I no longer saw her as "Mom." She had become something different now—a woman in need of grace, a soul God was chasing, and I was the vessel God had chosen to help Him.

MEDICAL INTERVENTION: DIVINE
OBEDIENCE EXTENDS MOTHER'S LIFE

August drifted in with something more than heat: tension, transition, testing. Her birthday approached, not with celebration, but with a warning wrapped in chest pain.

It began with her hand pressed just beneath her collarbone, a wince she tried to mask. "It's probably just a passing pain," she muttered, brushing it off like it was nothing. Yet I saw it, the shortness of breath, the weariness in her eyes that no amount of sleep could erase.

I drove her to the emergency room. They ran tests, wheeled her away, spoke in foreign medical terms. Then came the news: a blockage. A stent was needed. Immediately.

Dr. Mark East—a young African-American man with the kind eyes of someone who had learned to make peace with urgency—performed the procedure. And as I sat alone in that sterile waiting room, the Lord's voice came not with thunder, but with clarity that split through my fear.

"I used you to save her life. I added years to her days to do the deeper work—repentance, salvation. Your obedience spared her."

The revelation rippled through me like a lightning bolt. My yes to God—shaky and uncertain—had become the hinge upon which her life now turned. What I thought was an inconvenient act of caregiving was divine intervention. A rescue mission clothed in the ordinary.

In Memphis, she had fallen through the cracks. Her years of smoking, of ignoring symptoms, of living as if tomorrow was always guaranteed, had taken their toll. In Virginia, under my roof, God was orchestrating something different. Not just survival—but redemption.

And deep down, I believed that if He had preserved her body, He would also reach her soul.

I had seen too many transformations to doubt it—former drug addicts weeping at altars, hardened men and women reborn in prison chapels. I had produced those stories, pieced together for broadcast. Now, the miracle sat at my kitchen table, sipping coffee and talking about her next business venture or delicious dish she would cook.

And maybe—just maybe—God was healing something in me too. Not as loudly. Not as quickly. Still, just as surely.

SHOWING LOVE IN THE KITCHEN: FIVE-STAR CHEF

The kitchen became her place of true comfort.

When she moved in, I was a trim size 6 who only ate one meal a day. Now I was eating breakfast, lunch and dinner and soon gained twenty pounds. Every day, after I came home from work, I'd jokingly announce, "I'm bringing home the bacon!" She'd chuckle and point to the stove, where something delicious was waiting.

"Isn't it nice," she'd say, "that you can have a home cooked meal when you come home?"

Her food wasn't just good—it was soul-warming. Pot roasts with smothered gravy and vegetables, golden-brown fried chicken paired with creamy mashed potatoes, collard greens with cornbread, pinto beans with smoked turkey, tender baby beef ribs with meat so tender it fell off the bones, fried fish with perfectly crisp edges, macaroni and cheese so rich and creamy it could rival top chefs, her signature potato salad, and her pineapple coconut cream fluffy cake—every dish was a masterpiece.

"Baby," she'd say, dusting flour from her hands, "a woman should always have a cake in the house. You never know who might come through that door needing something sweet." I'd nod, in agreement.

One of her signature creations that she named "Bobbie Jean's Fruited Cream Biscuits"—was my favorite. Buttery layers filled with cinnamon apples or ripe strawberries, drizzled with her secret glaze that tasted like something from heaven. I was her official taste-tester, though my hips quickly protested the honor.

Her meals became our bridge. Every dish a thread weaving us together. In the clatter of utensils and the aroma of simmering broth, our strained history softened. We didn't talk much about the past, but we passed the peas, the cornbread, the cake. And that was its own kind of communion.

One plate at a time, God was rebuilding something only He could.

TENSIONS RISING

Despite the fragrance of delicious meals she cooked, a quiet war settled into the corners of our home. Something unspoken lived between us, and it was heavy. Every look she gave me felt layered—love tangled with loss, pride shadowed by regret.

She stared at me, as if studying a life she couldn't touch. I was her reflection and her reminder—of time lost, chances missed, and the unfamiliar territory of a daughter who had grown strong in the wilderness without her.

She clung to noise. The television stayed on constantly, even through the night. Westerns, soap operas, reruns of old shows filled the space of her thoughts. I realized the sound wasn't entertainment. It was her escape. Denial turned up to volume ten, drowning out the past and the uncomfortable truths that silence might dare to speak.

Navigating our dynamic felt like being caught in the relentless ebb and flow of a tsunami – a collision of past and present pain, where the weight of her regrets and choices crashed into the burden I carried from her absence. The force of it was overwhelming, an emotional wreckage neither of us knew how to repair. And yet, amid the chaos, I clung to the only hope I had – God, the only one capable of bringing healing to what seemed impossible.

We argued almost daily. Any suggestion I made was unwelcomed. Once, I suggested she look toward the water and boats while walking for a video I wanted to record of our journey. She responded angrily, "Listen, I know about television. I used to film commercials as a model before you were born. You don't need to tell me what to do!"

Her words hit hard. I wasn't six-years old anymore. I wasn't kneeling at her feet in admiration. I had become a woman. And not just any woman—a daughter called to be her kinsman redeemer in the winter of her life.

Like Ruth caring for Naomi, I was pouring out of my harvest into her famine. And yet, she resented the roles reversed.

Her anger puzzled me, pierced me. Still, in prayer, God gently lifted the veil. "She isn't angry at you. She's afraid. She sees in you the freedom she forfeited. And that fear feels like failure."

Yet I knew, she wasn't the enemy. The enemy was rejection. The enemy was shame. The enemy was the shadow that haunted our lineage and dared us to carry its name.

I held onto God like a woman caught in a riptide, praying He'd calm the waves we couldn't.

DON'T BE HOLY SPIRIT JUNIOR!

My mother and I fussed so much it became clear we needed outside help to navigate the fragile relationship we were trying to rebuild. There was so much pain and frustration beneath the surface—hers from years of untold struggles and secrets, and mine from the lost years that left us with no true mother-daughter connection. So, one day, I suggested a solution.

"I think we should try counseling," I offered one evening.

She hesitated. Sighed. Then, slowly nodded.

Our first session felt like navigating a field of landmines. The counselor's office was softly lit, filled with chairs and boxes of tissue. My mother sat with her arms folded, gaze cool but compliant. When asked what bothered her most, she didn't hesitate.

"She fusses with me too much," she said. "Always correcting. Always arguing. It wears on me."

I listened, stunned not by her words but by the truth in them. I had argued with her—often. Not out of rebellion, but out of exhaustion. I was giving everything—my time, my income, my energy, my prayers—and still, the relationship felt lopsided, like trying to build a bridge with only one set of tools.

The counselor gently looked my way. "Try not to argue. Choose prayer over protest. Let the Lord lead."

I nodded, swallowing pride and resentment like bitter medicine.

After just three sessions, the counselor pulled me aside. Her voice was kind, but clear.

"I can't continue with your mother. She doesn't believe I know more than she does."

And just like that, we were done.

She never went back, but I did. I needed the space. The strategy. The strength. I learned how to let go of needing to fix every word she misspoke, every wound she denied.

One afternoon, in the quiet of my room, the Lord whispered to me with such clarity it stilled my soul:

"You don't have to be Holy Spirit Junior."

The words landed with a powerful softness, sinking gently into the soil of my heart.

"You're not called to correct every error. You're called to be a sanctuary. Just provide her stability, and I will do the rest."

That truth became a turning point. I wasn't her judge. I wasn't her counselor. I was her daughter—recommissioned as a vessel of mercy. A conduit of divine compassion, through whom God's healing love gently flowed into her life.

No longer trying to mold her into someone she was never meant to be—I began offering peace instead of pressure. Presence instead of perfection.

And in doing so, I found peace for myself, too.

2008 BARAK OBAMA, POLITICS, AND A REKINDLED CONNECTION

The year 2008 unfolded into something hopeful. Across the nation, people held their breath as history hovered nearby. And in our small corner of the world, something quietly historic was happening, too: my mother and I were finding a fragile rhythm.

We didn't always speak the same emotional language, but when the news came on, we spoke politics fluently.

Night after night, she sat riveted by the debates, her eyes alive in a way I hadn't seen in months. She dissected campaign strategies and state polls with the same precision she used to dice onions and season meat. She wasn't just watching—she was invested. Barack Obama's campaign stirred something in her: remembrance, possibility, and a sense of being seen.

"You need to run for office one day," she said once, glancing over her glasses as if declaring prophecy.

I laughed it off, but her words hung in the air, golden and rare. She didn't often offer verbal praise. Love came through meals, not compliments. Yet every so often, it broke through—unexpected, like water to a parched soul.

"If I had to do it all over again," she confessed quietly one afternoon, "I'd do it like you. No rushing into marriage or babies. I'd live first. Travel. Be free."

I nodded slowly, unsure what to make of the statement. She had lived much of her life on her own terms, often apart from her children, chasing independence like it was oxygen. I didn't always understand her longing or her regret. Nevertheless, I listened.

For me, the dream had always been simple—a godly husband, children, a home filled with laughter and worship. Yet here I was, caring for the mother who once vanished from my life, now returned like a question with no easy answer. And in that strange divine plot twist, my dreams were paused, my heart stretched.

Still, we found connection in this shared moment. Just like when I was eighteen and had voted for the first time after our eleven-year separation, now we stood side by side once more, casting our ballots together in an election that stirred the soul of a nation.

It wasn't just about politics. It was about proximity. It was about presence. It was about knowing we could still witness history together—even after all that time apart.

MOM'S FRONT-ROW SEAT ON CBN'S
DANCING WITH THE STARS

When she wasn't stirring pots or watching political debates, my mother sank into the familiar glow of her favorite television shows—*Jeopardy, One Life to Live*, and *Dancing with the Stars*. She adored the elegance, the rhythm, the drama. The dancers moved like they belonged to the music, and somehow, watching them made her feel part of it all. She would laugh with childlike glee, often calling me into her room as the dancers twirled endlessly across the screen. "Come here Michelle - watch him wiggle his hips!" she'd say, slapping her leg and cackling, as if their rhythm stirred a memory of her own moves on the dance floor.

So, when CBN announced our Christmas party theme that year would be Dancing with the Stars, I said yes without hesitation.

Harrison, my dear friend and co-worker, invited me to be his dance partner. For three months, we rehearsed after hours in quiet hallways and empty studios, twirling and laughing as we tried to perfect our rumba. I was particularly obsessed with nailing one move—the open hip twist into fan position. It was fluid, expressive, free. Every time we practiced it, I felt like I was dancing out of something old and into something new.

I kept it all a secret from my mother.

On the night of the party, I helped her get dressed—a red blouse and black pants that brought out the glow in her complexion. She sat in the front row, unaware of the surprise about to unfold. The ballroom shimmered with holiday lights, laughter, and the expectancy of celebration. My heart thumped beneath my sequined red dress, matching red sequin heels and a burlesque-style headdress adorned with peacock feathers. Harrison looked handsome in his black tuxedo with matching red accents. I had chosen it intentionally—a little boldness for a woman who had lived too long in the shadows.

As the music began, Harrison and I took our places. Before the routine, a video played across the screen with a dedication: To my mother. Her hand flew to her mouth in surprise.

As the music played, Harrison and I launched into our routine in front of hundreds of eager faces. We remembered every step - until we got to my favorite move, the open hip twist to fan position, which didn't go as planned. We skipped it entirely, and though I was disappointed the joy of the moment remained undiminished. Harrison later confessed that he'd spotted Pat and Gordon Robertson watching and panicked. I totally understood and we both laughed.

Afterward, I presented my mother with a rose—a small gesture that said everything we never found the words for. She beamed as she clutched it, as if that flower represented a hope for a brighter future between us.

In that brief, glittering moment, we weren't just mother and daughter trying to mend what time had unraveled. We were two women, sitting side by side in the audience of each other's stories—learning to clap, to cheer, and to dance again.

CHAPTER 26:

A DAUGHTER'S JOURNEY OF HEALING OLD WOUNDS AND HONORING SACRED PROMISES

"Gracious words are a honeycomb, sweet to the soul and healing to the bones."
(Proverbs 16:24, NIV)

Before my mother came to live with me, I was answering God's nudge toward ministry—pursuing my Master of Divinity at Regent University with a quiet sense of purpose. I had finally begun the climb, steady and hopeful, completing a few foundational courses that felt like the laying of sacred stone.

By the middle of 2009, the winds shifted. The emotional weight of caregiving for my mother—once absent, now ever-present—grew heavy. Arguments flared over house rules. Our rhythms collided. The house that was supposed to be a sanctuary began to shake under the pressure of two wounded souls trying to cohabitate peace.

Eventually, she moved out, retreating to temporary housing when the tension became too thick to breathe through. I brought her meals. She returned when her money ran out and rent was overdue. It became a pattern – one she seemed to make intentional – spending her checks on endless products advertised on television. It was as if, with every package, she was protesting the weight of responsibility itself.

"Anyone that pays rent is a fool," she'd often exclaimed.

And though she never contributed financially to the household needs, I never expected her to. That was never the arrangement. I was just grateful God had blessed me with a great salary – enough to take care of us both. She didn't have to carry the burden. She only had to be.

Even in the mess, God was moving. I had grown familiar with His voice—sometimes gentle, sometimes repetitive, always purposeful. And in that season, He taught me: words spoken in obedience can realign destinies.

THE HOLY SPIRIT SPEAKS:
"YOU WERE A GOOD MOTHER"

One day, as my mother stepped into the bathroom, the Holy Spirit spoke clearly:

"When she comes out, tell her she was a good mother."

I froze. I knew His voice—but I didn't know if I could say those words. They felt dishonest. She had left us. Wounded us. Failed us.

Still, the Spirit pressed in. "Remind her of who she once was."

And suddenly, I remembered. The little things. The love she poured into us before the darkness dimmed her light—before life and trauma and possibly depression pulled her under.

When she passed by, I obeyed.

"You were a good mother," I gently said.

She stopped, stunned. Tears spilled from her eyes as if the words themselves cracked something open inside.

"I'm sorry," she wept. "I didn't mean to leave my children."

Stunned by her words and the raw tenderness of her vulnerability, I leaned in and whispered, "It's okay."

In that moment, I saw how words, when guided by the Holy Spirit, could unlock healing. Words carry weight, and they can either bring life or death - and new life was given to my mother. She had believed lies about herself for years, but those five words shattered them.

Forgiving oneself is often the hardest challenge, and my mother was no exception. That day marked the beginning of her repentance, a step toward accepting God's love.

THE PERFECT MOTHER'S DAY CARD: CHOOSING LOVE OVER RESENTMENT

Mother's Day came like it always did—with dread. The card aisle mocked me, full of messages I couldn't relate to. "You were always there. You gave everything for me."

I would stare at those words, wishing they were true. Then one day, God spoke gently, "Why don't you choose a card that will heal her heart—even if it doesn't reflect your history?"

He reminded me, "You're not validating her past. You're sowing into her healing."

So, I picked the most beautiful card I could find. Not just one—for her, but several. One from me and one for each of my brothers, just in case they didn't remember.

When I gave them to her—along with flowers and her favorite perfume— she was overjoyed. Not just from sentiment, but from longing. I could see it in her eyes. She wanted her sons to hand her cards too. She wanted all her children nearby.

I kept praying for that day—for reconciliation, for full-circle healing. Still, I knew my job was to love her faithfully, even if I walked alone in that obedience. And God, in His kindness, gave me grace to do it.

DREAMS, BUSINESS, AND BISCUITS: A DAUGHTER'S DETERMINATION

Years earlier, God told me, "Help your mother with her business ideas."

At the time, I didn't even know where she was. Now, here she sat on the porch, cigarette in hand, talking about her biscuit business like it was gospel. She dreamed big: Denny's restaurants and national contracts.

The problem was, she didn't trust anyone. Not even me.

"Mother," I pleaded, "Let me help you. These biscuits could seal your legacy and bless generations."

She barely looked up. "I've got it handled. You do your business, and I'll do mine. I've already talked to my lawyers."

Walls. Always walls.

God reminded me: You're not doing this for recognition. You're doing this out of obedience.

THE $2,000,000 BANK OFFER TO FUND MOTHER'S BUSINESS IDEA

Mother secured a meeting at a credit union for a business loan. She had a rare gift with words and a confidence that could sway anyone. I worked tirelessly on her proposal, adding photos I had captured with my camera of her perfectly baked biscuits that could have graced a Southern comfort magazine for the final touch.

That morning, we walked in dressed for destiny—her in bold red, me in quiet black. Watching her transform into her business persona was inspiring. Her confidence was undeniable.

She took the lead. "Hello, I'm Bobbie LaMaster. This is my daughter Michelle. She works for *The 700 Club*."

She spoke with ease, listing achievements I couldn't verify, but her confidence was magnetic.

"I have a cooking business," she continued confidently. "I've catered for the mayor in Memphis and other political offices."

After ten minutes of reviewing the documents, the loan officer smiled. "Your proposal looks great. With a co-signer, we can approve the full two million."

We walked out victorious, but the celebration was short. There was no co-signer. Another door, cracked open, then quietly closed.

THE DENNY'S OPPORTUNITY: A DREAM DEFERRED

Still determined, we secured an opportunity to send samples of my mother's delicious food products to Denny's corporate office.

We baked all night—until my old college mixer broke at 3 a.m. We raced to Walmart in frustration, buying the only one available - a $300 replacement I couldn't afford. At 8 a.m., I shipped the package overnight via FedEx—another $500 gone - but hope was riding on those biscuits.

Unfortunately, she never followed up. She wouldn't let me either.

Her trust issues won again.

And still… I knew God was watching my heart. I had obeyed. That was enough.

While her biscuits never made it into Denny's, I believed God had a greater plan for both of us. He taught me success isn't always measured by the outcome but by the heart of obedience and the lessons learned along the way.

STANDING FIRM IN RIGHTEOUSNESS: WHEN INTEGRITY IS TESTED

Not long after, I met a Christian businessman at my church who owned several popular chain restaurants. He invited me to meet with him to discuss my business ideas. He offered me access to his restaurant, free meals, and a studio space. It felt like a breakthrough.

However, I chose to prioritize helping my mother launch her business first, knowing she had fewer years left to pursue her dreams. I introduced her to the businessman, and he seemed genuinely enthusiastic about her biscuit ideas.

Later, in a one-on-one meeting, his intentions became clear when he propositioned me. I was shocked. In that moment, I recalled the words spoken to me years earlier: "Men will only want you for one thing." It was disheartening to see those words reflected in someone who claimed to be a man of faith.

I walked away - not from an opportunity, but from a situation that never truly aligned with my values. For me, achieving success that required compromising my integrity, wasn't worth it.

Then came the second test.

My doctor—married, a professed Christian—made inappropriate advances during a routine visit. His words were laced with desire, veiled in spiritual flattery. "You're driving me crazy," he said.

I left that office and never returned.

God whispered again: "My favor doesn't require compromise."

I never got the business deal. My mother never saw her biscuits in Denny's. Yet I stood tall in righteousness. I stayed faithful when it cost me. I loved when it hurt. I obeyed when it didn't make sense.

And I believe that is the kind of success that heaven applauds.

CHAPTER 27:

SAYING GOODBYE TO AN ANGEL

"Precious in the sight of the Lord is the death of His faithful servants."
(Psalm 116:15, *NIV*)

THE LAST VISIT IN A FADING ROOM

The year 2010 carried a quiet ache long before the grief arrived.

Angel Mother—my spiritual anchor, my comforter, the woman who took me in and laid the foundation of my faith—was nearing the end of her journey.

By then, her memory had begun to fade, and the thought of visiting her – of witnessing the quiet erosion of the woman I once knew – was both heartbreaking and daunting. This cruel disease was slowly stealing pieces of her, and I wasn't sure if I was ready to see it.

In 2009, I made the trip to Indiana with my cousin. Having her beside me felt like God's kindness. I was returning to the sacred wellspring of my formation—grateful, anxious, and afraid this might be my final chance to look into the eyes of someone special who provided me a haven of unconditional love to rest in.

When we arrived at the home, she was now living in with her family members, I wasn't sure what to expect.

I entered her room slowly. She sat in stillness, fragile and quiet, her eyes distant. I crouched gently at her side, whispering, "It's me, Missy."

She tilted her head, eyes soft, smile kind.

"Who are you?" she asked. "You're so beautiful."

The name she once used like a song no longer registered in her mind. And yet, her voice carried no fear—just a kind of reverence, as if she sensed I was someone who had once mattered deeply.

My cousin and I spent the day loving her in the simple ways that still made sense. We took her to the grocery store, watched her eyes light up as she selected things she liked. It wasn't recognition that made that day holy. It was the sacred echo of love that needed no introduction.

Even if she didn't remember me, I remembered everything.

THE CALL THAT MARKED THE END ON EARTH AND THE BEGINNING OF ETERNITY WITH JESUS

Time passed. I returned home. Life settled back into its strange new flow of caregiving, ministry, and unanswered questions. And then, the phone rang.

It was January 7, 2010.

Angel Mother was gone.

She had finished her race. Quietly, faithfully, gracefully—just as she had lived.

I sat in silence, staring at the wall, letting the finality wash over me. Her body had grown frail, her memory had betrayed her, but her spirit had never dimmed. She was finally back with Jesus - the savior she had come to know so intimately.

He was no stranger to her. She often told me of the moment when she was born, when death tried to claim her, how God's hands was on her life. And by his mercy she lived to fulfill a divine plan which was to touch many - including me. She never feared death, and I can only imagine the peace that filled her soul as she stepped into heaven, finally home, finally at rest.

There was peace in that thought, yet also an ache—the kind that lingers in the finality of death and quiet beauty of what once was.

LITTLE ROCK MEMORIAL SERVICE

On January 15th, we gathered at Little Rock Baptist Church—the place where Angel Mother had once stood tall and steady, teaching and serving without needing spotlight or recognition.

I walked into that sanctuary and felt her everywhere. Her prayers, her presence, her legacy still alive As I approached the casket, something holy settled over me. She looked beautiful – serene – as if heaven itself had placed its seal upon this moment, her reward shimmering quietly for all to witness.

Pre-selected people shared stories of how she changed their lives. Some cried. Others laughed softly at old memories.

Many were shocked to discover for the first time that she wasn't our biological mother. They had assumed—naturally, rightfully—that love like that could only come from blood. Yet Angel Mother's love was never bound by biology. It was higher, deeper. Divine.

As the casket closed and the service continued, tears welled up in my eyes, but gratitude rose to meet them. I wasn't weeping for what was lost—I was honoring all that had been given. She had taught me obedience in the quiet moments, courage in the hard ones, and faith when nothing else made sense.

UNSPOKEN EULOGIES: HEAVEN HEARD
WHAT WE COULDN'T SAY

Though my brother and I were not listed as speakers on the program, I didn't need a platform to declare what she had done for me. Of course, I wanted to express how deeply she influenced my journey with God, but my heart was already full of gratitude for the memories she left me.

She had led me to Jesus.

She had taught me to pray for my biological mother steering my heart of hatred toward forgiveness and love.

She had given me faith that held steady in valleys and bowed low in triumph.

That was her sermon, living and breathing in me.

Every prayer I whispered, every time I forgave, every moment I walked in obedience—it all spoke of her.

Angel Mother didn't live a life without pain. She bore scars—wounds that could have turned to bitterness. Yet instead of building walls, she built bridges.

God entrusted her with something rare: two broken children, needing more than shelter. Needing soul repair. She gave it freely.

She wasn't just a caregiver. She was a spiritual midwife—ushering in the rebirth of faith and healing.

Ours was no ordinary bond. It was stitched together by worship songs, whispered prayers, and late-night talks about God. She didn't just care for my soul—she stewarded my destiny.

A LEGACY OF LOVE THAT TOOK ROOT

Angel Mother's love was never passive - it was active, intentional, and unwavering. She didn't just speak about faith; she lived it. Whether through styling hair for her customers, sharing her favorite scripture - Romans 10:9-10 - or offering encouragement, she infused every moment with divine purpose.

I could still see us sitting together on her bed, watching Christian television featuring powerful preaching, anointed singing, and biblically relevant topics. Immersing ourselves in those programs was our shared bond, our secret place - a connection that nurtured our hearts and drew us closer to each other and to God.

The foundation of the faith she instilled in me would later guide me through my life's calling. As I reflected on her life, I realized something profound – she had unknowingly prepared me to walk out my greatest test of love.

Angel Mother had raised children who were not her own, giving of herself in ways that defied logic and explanation. Without realizing it at the time, I was walking in her footsteps. When my biological mother returned into my life - broken and in need of love and a second chance – I embraced her. Not because it was easy. Not because it was deserved. Because obedience required it.

I had extended to my mother the same grace that had been given to me. I had loved her in a way that was unconventional, inconvenient, and costly.

Outside of leading me to salvation in Jesus, I now see this was Angel Mother's greatest lesson - the seed she had unknowingly planted in my heart.

The love she poured into me had not only begun healing my wounds but had also equipped me to become a vessel of love, bringing healing to someone else – my biological mother.

HER LEGACY LIVES IN ME

Many admired Angel Mother. Many were drawn to the light she carried. Yet few ever truly embraced what mattered most to her – the quiet, unwavering faith that shaped every part of her life in the end. Somehow, by God's grace, I did. And I carry it still – not as a trophy, but as a torch.

A living legacy. A spiritual inheritance.

Not just for me – but I pray, for anyone with eyes to see and a heart ready to receive it.

Wherever God sends me…

Whatever I build in His name ..

Whomever I reach…

Her fingerprints will be on it.

Angel Mother's legacy isn't buried beneath the soil of Detroit. It lives in every word I speak, every hand I hold, every soul I help guide back to the Father.

Her love shaped my calling. Her faith unlocked my destiny.

I'll never forget how she faithfully read her large, leather-bound, Scofield study Bible—marked up, prayed through, and worn soft with time. Seeing her keep it near, as her lifeline cultivated my love for the word of God.

I like to think that in heaven, she's got one of the biggest mansions not because she was rich or famous or a world renown evangelist – she was simply obedient and to God that means everything. I can see her dancing in the presence of the One she served so selflessly. And every so often, I believe she leans over heaven's balcony and smiles when she sees me walking out the very faith she taught me.

Rest well, Angel Mother.

Your legacy lives in me.

And through me… it lives on.

CHAPTER 28:

GOING HIGHER: FAITH IN THE SPOTLIGHT - PRODUCING STORIES OF INFLUENCE AND IMPACT

"There is no greater honor than to steward the vulnerabilities of humanity, to hold space for the raw, unfiltered pain of another soul – to stand in the sacred place where a soul is stripped bare, and all that remains is truth. In our deepest struggles, beyond the masks we wear, the colors of our skin, and the beliefs that divide us, we are all reaching for the same unspoken thing – to be seen without judgment, to be loved without condition, and to know our existence has weight in this world."

— Michelle B. Wilson, author, *In Search of a Mother's Love.*

CBN: THE ARK THAT CARRIED ME

After Angel Mother's memorial, the winds in my life shifted again—gentle at first, yet laced with destiny. I used to think CBN would be a two-and-a-half-year stop—an ark where I'd wait for the flood of uncertainty to pass before launching into my next venture in journalism in New York, but God had a different plan. As some co-workers began looking for other jobs God clearly spoke to me: "No one can close the doors I have ordained to be open. I have you here for a reason."

God was teaching me steadfastness, resilience, and complete trust in Him. CBN was my Noah's Ark – a place of refuge and just as the ark carried both the beauty of a fresh start and the stench of the past, my journey held both blessings and challenges. It also carried legacy, worship, and promise. Within its walls, God stripped away pride, built humility, and refined obedience.

And so, beneath the weight of countless stories, God began to sow something new. My role at CBN quietly expanded, and I was called into deeper waters – on-camera interviews, faith-driven celebrity profiles, and disaster coverage that placed me in the center of both brokenness and beauty.

FAITH IN HOLLYWOOD: THE KEVIN SORBO STORY

From the genesis of my CBN career, God had equipped me with a natural gift for asking meaningful questions, drawing out compelling answers, stirring dormant emotions, and engaging in creative, fun interactions with story subjects. One such opportunity came when I was chosen to interview Kevin Sorbo, renowned for his role in *Hercules* and the faith-based film *God's Not Dead*.

The road to Kevin Sorbo's home curved through the hills, each bend revealing more of California's vast beauty. When we arrived, the air was welcoming, and his home - perched on the hillside - overlooked the ocean, with palms swaying gently in the distance. It didn't feel like an interview—it felt like a divine appointment.

Kevin met us at the door, easygoing and kind, and gave us full access to his home—no ego, just open space and trust.

I wanted to open Kevin's story with something fun that would capture his spirit right away. And what better way than to challenge him in the very thing he was best known for – his strength in a friendly game of arm wrestling. After all, this was Hercules himself!

Our elbows locked; hands braced. The camera rolled. After 10 seconds of showing off his strength he finally conceded and with a playful grin, he let me win. We burst out in laughter as I declared victory,

"And I win. Whoo Hoo."

His fun, generous spirit made the experience unforgettable.

The interview unfolded in his cozy library, surrounded by natural light peering through floor-to-ceiling windows. The atmosphere was warm and intimate, making our conversation feel more like a heartfelt exchange than a formal Q&A. Kevin opened about his incredible journey of faith—one that was tested after a routine chiropractor visit led to three strokes, nearly ending his career and his life. He should have died. Hollywood nearly forgot him. Yet God remembered. This difficult season drew him closer to God and deepened his relationship with his fiancée, now his wife, Sam.

He spoke of his wife, the woman who stayed, who prayed, who pulled him back from the edge of despair. Their love stood like an oak—weathered but unbroken. His voice steadied when he spoke of making faith-based films—not for applause, but out of calling. Hollywood didn't need more glitter. It needed glory.

I walked away changed. Not because I met Hercules, but because I met a man who walked through fire and came out with greater purpose, and faith in God.

DUCK DYNASTY'S MISS KAY ROBERTSON: A WOMAN OF IMMOVABLE FAITH

One day, I was given the surprise of a lifetime – to interview Miss Kay Robertson from the hit show, *Duck Dynasty*. This was a major opportunity, as the show was already drawing millions of viewers each week. I had never watched a single episode. Instead of being nervous, I quickly caught up on its themes-watching hours of footage to familiarize myself with the family and formulate compelling questions. After watching the show, I could see why they were so popular. I found myself laughing along with them in every episode and cherished the unity I saw especially in the end when they all gathered at the table to eat Miss Kay's mouthwatering southern food. I looked forward to sitting down with Miss Kay, the glue that held them together, to find out what made this family so special.

The sun had barely risen over Louisiana's swamplands when we arrived at the Robertson estate. Their property stretched across vast open land, perfect for hunting and fishing, with their home nestled at its heart.

Miss Kay Robertson, the matriarch, greeted the crew and I with good ole' southern hospitality.

"You're so beautiful," she said, taking my hand as though I had come home.

Her home was cozy, filled with worn-in furniture, wild duck feathers, and pictures of legacy. After meeting Phil, her husband, he stepped away to give us space to talk. The crew quickly set up their three cameras and lighting. Once everything was in place, the cameras rolled, capturing what would become a monumental interview.

Miss Kay and I sat across from each other at her kitchen countertop —just two women, decades apart, bound by something deeper than story: faith that clung through fire.

She spoke of the hard years, of praying for Phil when his heart was stone. Her voice cracked when recounting their anniversary—how their son Jase said, "My mom dared to stay with a hard marriage and stand by that commitment. She's my first courageous person." Tears streamed down her face, and I instinctively paused, allowing the moment to settle. I compassionately reached out and held her hands.

In that moment, I didn't need a script. Empathy came naturally.

Afterward, Miss Kay invited me to her kitchen, where she showed me how to make her famous macaroni and cheese, and duck wraps. And it was soo delicious. I kept going back for seconds and we all started laughing. I was so happy squirrel stew wasn't on the menu, but I probably would have bravely tried it if offered.

Her kindness extended beyond the camera, as she gave me her phone number to stay in touch, as if to say, "You're family now."

And I believed her.

Our moment of connection resonated deeply, earning praise from my peers and CBN leadership for the empathy I displayed on-camera.

The finished piece aired multiple times on *The 700 Club* and was well received, as a testament to her powerful story and God's grace in her life.

Before this moment on camera, I had always felt uncomfortable-but this time was different. It was as if God was whispering to me, "That beautiful personality I gave you-childlike, full of innocence, humility, and light-that's exactly how I made you. And that's what draws people to you. There was an authenticity about me that was pure that was rare and inviting and what the world needed. I saw it clearly in the way I was received-not just by Miss Kay, but also by the viewers. In that moment, I knew with certainty: I was created for television and the world was looking for what I had to offer. I was no longer in hiding.

STANDING TALL: COACH VIVIAN STRINGER'S JOURNEY THROUGH ADVERSITY TO VICTORY

Miss Kay's interview left me feeling deeply affirmed. Yet, in this line of work, no two stories are ever the same. The next assignment would lead me into the world of women's basketball. Coach C. Vivian Stringer of Rutgers – a legend in women's basketball had a story of resilience and leadership that was both compelling and inspiring.

Although I wasn't an avid women's basketball fan, I looked forward to meeting Coach Stringer who lived a life forged in the fire on and off the court. As the head coach at Rutgers University, she achieved historic milestones, leading her teams to two Final Fours and earning recognition as one of the most accomplished coaches in NCAA history. Yet, what set her apart wasn't just her success on the court—it was her faith in the face of profound personal challenges as revealed in her book, *Standing Tall.*

Inside her home a warmth radiated—not just from her heart but from all the pictures of her family lining her walls.

Once the interview began, she shared how her faith in God carried her through life's toughest battles, including the impossible task of balancing the relentless demands of coaching with the heartbreak of caring for her daughter, Janine. A single medical mistake – one moment of human error – forever altered the course of her daughter's life leaving her permanently disabled – unable to walk or speak. I could feel the weight of that anguish – the silent unanswered questions, the what-ifs that must have haunted her every milestone, every victory, every quiet moment in between.

Then came her husband's sudden death.

Yet she kept coaching. Kept leading. Kept praying.

During the end of her interview, one moment stood out as she reflected on how she navigated an impossible decision early in her career. Her voice trembled with emotion as she said, "At the end of the day, it's the faith and relationship you can have with the Lord, that will get you through life's tough battles."

After the interview, we followed Coach Stringer to the Rutgers gym, the hallowed ground where she built her legacy. Standing amidst the banners and trophies, I saw a woman who had overcome adversity and used it as a steppingstone to inspire generations. Her story was a testament to perseverance, faith, and the power of leaning on God's strength.

JOLINDA WADE: SAVED BY GRACE – A MOTHER'S ROAD FROM THE STREETS TO THE SANCTUARY

Flying to Chicago to produce Jolinda Wade's story was deeply personal, as it mirrored so much of my own journey. Like my mother, she was a mother who had faced immense brokenness yet was redeemed by God's grace. Her testimony wasn't just a story of redemption—it was a living reminder of God's ability to rewrite even the most shattered lives for His glory as she shares in her book *Divine Grace Behind the Walls*.

The interview took place in her beautiful home in Chicago, Illinois, a gift from her son, NBA star Dwyane Wade. The house stood as a testament to his love and gratitude for a mother who, despite her struggles, never stopped loving him. When she gave birth to her only son, she believed God told her to name him 'Blessing,' never realizing the profound gift he would become to her later in life.

Yet before there were blessings, there was brokenness.

The day unfolded when her daughter took me to the very drug house where her mother once struggled with addiction. With tears in her eyes, she described the deplorable environment her mother often lived in for days. She recalled the countless times she begged Jolinda to leave, only to be met with refusal. Standing outside that place, I felt an unshakable connection to her pain—I knew that same desperate longing to rescue a mother from the grip of destruction. I, too, had prayed that God would not let my mother die in her sins.

Jolinda spoke of prison, of losing her children, of losing herself. Yet it was there, behind bars, where she received the letter from her son Dwyane that became her resurrection: "You say I'm your hero. You are my hero." Those words breathed new life into her weary soul. Encouraged by her son's love, Jolinda gave her life to Christ and allowed God to transform her from the inside out.

After her release, Jolinda walked in the strength of her newfound faith, experiencing the joy of watching her son lead Marquette University to the Final Four. For a mother who had once seen her son only through the glass of a prison visitation room, this moment was nothing short of miraculous.

Jolinda's story culminated in triumph as she took me to the $2-million church Dwyane purchased for her, where she now pastors and leads outreaches to bring hope and healing to her community.

Producing this story wasn't just about honoring Jolinda's journey—it was a way to bring hope to other families in need of God's healing touch. Jolinda's strength, and faith reminded me behind every story of success, there is often a mother's love—broken, yet redeemed, and ultimately restored by God.

HURRICANE KATRINA - WHEN THE WATERS RECEDE: SURVIVING DISASTER AND REBUILDING HOPE

When I wasn't producing celebrity stories, I found myself on the frontlines of natural disasters - capturing both the heartbreak and strength of those affected. From interviewing families who survived Hurricane Katrina in Louisiana to covering Operation Blessing outreaches in various places around the US including Minot, North Dakota, during their historic flood in 2011, each experience left an indelible mark on me.

In Minot, I stood atop the rubble of a once beautiful home, now nothing more than splintered wood and scattered debris. As I surveyed the wreckage, I thought of how many lives had been displaced in an instant. It was humbling to witness how volunteers worked tirelessly alongside Operation Blessing, rebuilding not just homes, but the shattered souls of those who lost everything.

Hurricane Katrina was no different. As our crew and I drove through eerily deserted streets, houses bore spray-painted numbers on their doors – grim reminders of how many had been saved …and how many had perished. Walking besides survivors as they pointed to the water lines inside their homes,

I listened to them relive the horror of watching their world disappear in the flood. Their grief became my own.

I didn't just want to report on these disasters—I wanted to immerse myself in the stories of those who had endured them, to feel their losses as if they were my own. Yet nothing could have prepared me for what happened next – the day I became an unintentional storm chaser.

UNEXPECTED DETOUR: REPORTING IN THE EYE OF AN F5 TORNADO

I had flow to Oklahoma to produce a story on Crystal McVea, a schoolteacher who chronicled her near-death experience in her book, *Waking Up in Heaven*. I've always loved producing Heaven stories because they offer a sacred glimpse beyond the veil – where people describe being wrapped in radiant glory, perfect peace, indescribable colors, and the overwhelming love of God's glory that erases all pain and fears. So, I was eager to hear Crystal's story - especially her account of what she experienced after she died and had lived to come back and tell us about.

Yet before we could meet Crystal, God had prepared an unexpected detour – one we would never forget.

As our plane prepared to land, our camera operators received an urgent call from a storm-chaser friend: an F5 tornado was forming - and it was heading straight for Moore, Oklahoma.

We hadn't planned to cover a storm, but we were going to be in its path.

Once we landed, the crew—Gus, Hunter, and I—made a bold decision: we were going to cover this storm for CBN News. As we drove, we playfully gave ourselves storm-chaser nicknames: Gus became "Gust," Hunter was "Chase," and I was "Storm." We had no idea how fitting those names would become.

When we arrived in Moore, the devastation was apocalyptic.

- Dead animals lay strewn across the roads.
- Power lines dangled dangerously overhead and on the ground.
- Entire neighborhoods had been reduced to rubble.

I called my mother to let her know what we were about to do. Concern and excitement filled her voice, but she reassured me God was with us.

IN THE AFTERMATH: FINDING GOD AMID RUINS

Stepping into the wreckage, I instinctively shifted from producer to reporter. Survivors recounted their narrow escapes, the loved ones they lost, and the sheer terror of facing the storm head-on.

Among the scattered remains of homes, a mud-soaked baby doll caught my eye. It was a haunting image – a painful reminder of the children whose lives had been forever altered in an instant.

The F5 tornado ripped through Moore at 210 miles per hour, claiming 24 lives and leaving hundreds injured. Yet, amid the devastation, I witnessed something just as powerful as the storm itself: the strength of the human spirit.

Neighbors became family.

Strangers became heroes.

Hands that had never met before worked side by side to rebuild lives.

During a break, we knocked on a stranger's door to ask if we could use the restroom. Without hesitation, she welcomed us in. In another era, I might not have been granted that same kindness simply because of the color of my skin. Amid this natural disaster - that small act of kindness moved me deeply. Even in the face of unimaginable loss, humanity prevailed.

FAITH IN ACTION: OPERATION BLESSING RESPONDS

Within hours, Operation Blessing was there. Not for coverage, but for comfort. Volunteers wept beside homeowners. They rebuilt more than houses—they rebuilt humanity.

It amazes me to think that when Pat Robertson launched Operation Blessing in 1978, God had already planned moments like this—moments where His love would shine through disaster, loss, and heartbreak.

My time in Moore, Oklahoma, was not just about covering a story.

It was about witnessing the power of faith, and hope.

Because even after storms…

Even after headlines fade…

Even after the waters recede…

God still remains.

And I'm still telling stories that carry His name.

CHAPTER 29:

MY PROPHETIC JOURNEY THROUGH PURPOSE-DRIVEN STORYTELLING: REACHING 1 MILLION VIEWS

"The Lord will fulfill His purpose for me; your steadfast love, O Lord, endures forever. Do not forsake the work of your hands."
(Psalm 138:8, *ESV*)

MY SEASON OF GROWTH AND REVELATION: THE ORRIN PULLINGS STORY

The first story I produced that garnered 1 million hits in one week after it aired on *The 700 Club* was the miraculous healing story of Bishop Orrin Pullings. After suffering a massive hemorrhagic stroke caused by a ruptured brain aneurysm, Bishop Pullings' extraordinary recovery became a testimony of faith and prayer. His wife, Dr. Medina, and their congregation stood by his side, believing God to do the impossible even when doctors gave a grim outlook.

God healed him completely and their church family united in a powerful celebration dressed in white as a symbol of renewal and triumph through faith.

Seeing how God used that story to impact millions filled me with overwhelming gratitude. During this time, I began visiting the Pullings' church, United Nations Church International in Richmond and eventually made it my church home.

While there, God used Dr. Medina to affirm and stir up the gifts He had placed inside me. On one occasion, she called me to the altar in front of the congregation and declared, "This is a mighty woman of God." Her acknowledgment was overwhelming and rare, solidifying the mantle God had given me to carry in ministry.

Though after two years, God began to steer me in a new direction, the mentorship, love, and affirmation I received left an indelible mark on my life. It was a season of divine preparation for what lay ahead.

FROM THE PRODUCER'S DESK TO THE PRAYER CHAIR: 700 CLUB INTERACTIVE SHOW

Though I was always comfortable behind the scenes and preferred staying out of the spotlight, God spoke powerfully to my spirit during prayer: "It's time to get out of Lo-debar. What I've given you is a forefront ministry. I've entrusted you to carry my glory - and with that comes visibility. You have been chosen from your mother's womb." In the Bible, Lo-debar was a barren place where Mephibosheth lived in hiding, but spiritually, it also represents a mindset that keeps you from stepping fully into your calling. God was breaking that off my life and preparing me for greater purpose.

One of the ways He did that was by opening the door for me to join *The 700 Club Interactive* show - a seat that required me to filter through viewer request and lead prayer live on the air. Though it took me out of my comfort zone it was a step of obedience and a clear sign that God was shifting me from the background to the forefront.

It was humbling to pray alongside Gordon Robertson and Terry Meeuwsen trusting God to work miracles in the lives of the viewers.

In this new role, Gordon, became a spiritual father to me. His words of encouragement often came at just the right time. Once, in passing, he looked at me and said, "Stay with it." Those three words carried more weight than I realized at the time. Although it seemed I was always fighting for belonging, Gordon's encouragement pushed me to trust God and lean into the assignments He had for me. It reminded me God's plans were far greater than my fears. Through this season, I learned to embrace the unknown, knowing He was leading me every step of the way.

SOUL-WINNING PRODUCING IN FLORIDA

God continued to stretch my reach. Jacksonville, Florida became a familiar stop—home to Spoken Word Ministries, led by Pastor Kimberly Daniels. Her church didn't hold back. Testimonies of deliverance from gang life, addiction, and prison poured from the pulpit —undeniable, unfiltered, raw.

Pastor Kim treated our crew like family, often praying for us before we filmed, declaring that the anointing on those stories would break chains. And it did. Souls came into the Kingdom by the thousands. These weren't just TV segments—they were weapons of war. Seeds of deliverance. Altars through the airwaves.

THE MOVIE BREAKTHROUGH: A PROPHECY FULFILLED - THE JOHN SMITH STORY

Certain stories carry an unmistakable sense of divine purpose. For me, John Smith's story was one of those. A teenage boy falls through ice, is declared clinically dead, and comes back to life through the cry of a praying mother could only be explained by God's amazing intervention.

Filming their story, I felt it in my bones—this wasn't just a testimony. It was prophecy. As I stood with Joyce Smith in her kitchen, I told her, "Your story will be a movie." I hadn't planned the words. Yet they rang with heaven's certainty.

Not long after, as their segment aired on various Christian platforms, DeVon Franklin caught the interview and highlighted clips of my produced story. From that spark came the film *Breakthrough*, which garnered over $40 million and reached countless lives.

When I found out my *700 Club* story was featured on the DVD as bonus content, I smiled. Not for accolades. Instead for the intimacy of a God who lets us co-labor with Him in ways we could never imagine. My fingerprints were on a miracle. Only God could have done that.

A WELCOMED REPRIEVE

During a season of rest and reflection following Breakthrough, my mother temporarily moved in with my oldest brother in Memphis, giving me a much-needed break from caregiving.

When she returned five months later, I encouraged her to pursue her goals. She enrolled in culinary arts and online courses, tapping into her creativity and love for learning. Her sharp insights often surprised her classmates—and me.

"Barack Obama wasn't the first Black president," she'd say. "Jefferson, Lincoln, and Harding had African ancestry too."

These moments filled me with awe. We had become a team—united in purpose, navigating both challenges and blessings.

FROM A LOST INHERITANCE TO INHERITING THE NATIONS

Taking walks around the neighborhood became my time to pray and release stress. One day, I passed a construction crew renovating condos. A worker shared, "We're fixing these up for a woman whose father left them to her."

His words pierced me. My thoughts turned to the home in Michigan my father had intended to leave me. I couldn't help but wonder how life might have been different—how much easier things could have felt if I had secured that inheritance.

Before I could sink further into those debilitating thoughts, the Holy Spirit interrupted:

"When will you stop focusing on the lost inheritance when I have given you the nations to inherit?"

I stopped mid-step, stunned. In that moment, I repented. God was calling me to release what was lost and step into what was promised. He was calling me to rise above the mindset of lack and embrace the greater inheritance—not just a house, but souls, nations, and destiny.

As I walked home, I was overwhelmed with God's unending love for me.

LIGHTS, CAMERA, ACTION: MOTHER'S 700 CLUB ACTING DEBUT

My mother had always dreamed of being an actress. Yet, life hadn't made room for that dream. One day, in a rare moment of honesty, she told me:

"See, you were smart. I didn't have anyone to guide me."

Though life had taken her in a different direction, God had not forgotten the dreams.

"Want to act in one of my *700 Club* stories?" I asked.

She lit up. It was as if time rewound, letting her step into a part of herself that had been buried but not dead.

In 2013, I cast my mother in her first acting role for *The 700 Club*. She played a terrified bank teller in the reenactment of *The Dana Bryant Story*—a woman whose life of addiction and crime led her to prison, where she found redemption.

CBN's talented scenic department created a realistic bank setting, and my mother brought her character to life with such authenticity I couldn't have been prouder. After the story aired, she joked, "Well, I guess I've been robbed on national television!"

Her second acting role came the following year in *The Mary Pappas' Story*, in which she played a compassionate nurse caring for a woman diagnosed with cancer seven times—a woman who refused to let disease steal her faith.

Her most significant role came in 2015 when she portrayed a nurse in *The Bishop Orin Pullings' Story*. My mother was part of a pivotal scene, pushing the actor portraying Bishop Pullings in a wheelchair as he left the hospital fully healed from a hemorrhagic stroke.

Watching my mother's performance and seeing how God anointed it to reach millions filled me with overwhelming gratitude.

God's fingerprints were all over that season. Stories like Demetrius Guyton's—an infant burned with acid by a relative for life insurance—were entrusted to me. He forgave his mother when he met her years later. His story reached over a million views in two weeks.

I was producing stories that changed lives. More than that, I was watching God redeem the years—for my viewers, my mother, and for me.

CHAPTER 30:

PRAYERS ANSWERED, BONDS RESTORED: A SEASON OF SWEETNESS AND DISCOVERY

"Let us not grow weary in doing good, for at the proper time we will
reap a harvest if we do not give up."
(Galatians 6:9, *NIV*)

THE WHITE HOUSE, HOLY LAND, HOLY COMMUNION, DISNEY FIREWORKS

Our house no longer echoed with sharp tones or silence; instead, there was laughter, long talks, and the quiet hum of unity. God was healing what years of strain had fractured. We were finally able to create cherished memories together—moments I had prayed for but never imagined could be this fulfilling.

We made plans to go on a trip together. One of our first trips was to Washington, D.C., where we stayed at the stunning Hilton Hotel, where the glass walls of our room offered a breathtaking view of the city skyline shimmering in the morning light off the Potomac.

My mother, a lifelong lover of politics, stood in awe before the White House gates.

"I never thought I'd see this," she whispered.

"See how God blesses us?" I said, framing her smile in my camera.

The following year, we had our first plane ride together when we traveled to Orlando, Florida, to visit TBN's Holy Land Experience. Walking through the biblical recreations felt as though we had stepped back in time. The streets of Jerusalem, the Garden Tomb, and the breathtaking depiction of the Messiah walking among visitors were so vivid they seemed to bring the Word of God to life before our eyes.

We experienced holy communion together where an actor portraying Jesus led participants through the communion ceremony in a room adorned with a table set with ornate goblets. When they offered to pray for us, my mother received prayer which deeply touched my heart. I witnessed God opening her heart to greater closeness, fellowship and trust with Him.

Afterward, we attended the *Behold the Lamb* theatrical production, a 75-minute play depicting the crucifixion and resurrection of Jesus. It was during this trip I saw my mother in a new light—her heart softened, and her spirit filled with awe. She smiled more than I'd ever seen before, and I knew God was answering every prayer to restore our bond we had longed for.

The next day, we visited Disney World. Her first time. Since walking long distances was a challenge, I pushed her in a wheelchair, which became our "golden ticket." I jokingly told her she was "the golden girl" because we moved to the front of every line for every ride. We both wore Mickey Mouse ears, laughing and posing for photos. Watching my mother release her cares and become childlike was unforgettable. By the end of the day, we sampled food from around the world as we were treated to the famous Disney fireworks. The bright, colorful bursts of light illuminated the night sky, symbolizing the hope and joy I had only dreamed of experiencing with my mother.

As the vibrant lights danced in the sky, I felt an overwhelming sense of gratitude—not just for the beauty of the fireworks but for the beauty of this season. This was more than a vacation; it reflected God's ability to redeem, restore, and make all things new.

BORN WITH A VEIL: 30/30 BIBLE READING:
HOLY GHOST ANOINTED FISH FRY

By now, my mother and I were discovering a harmony in our relationship that had once seemed out of reach. God was not only restoring our bond but also exceeding my expectations in ways only He could orchestrate. Though she often longed for me to show her affection—asking for hugs or kisses on the forehead—she rarely initiated those gestures herself. It was as if she was waiting for something she didn't know how to give. Even in that, God was working.

One day, during a rare moment of openness, my mother shared something that caught me off guard.

"You were born special," she said.

When I pressed her to explain, she told me I was born with a veil, a spiritual sign God had placed special gifts in my life. She recounted how healing would take place instantly whenever I prayed for her.

"Come here, baby daughter," she would often say, calling me to pray and lay my hands on the part of her body that was in pain. Every time, the pain would leave. Seeing her recognize and encourage the gift of healing God had placed in me was deeply affirming.

During this time, I also felt God's prompting to start a Facebook Live Bible reading show. Though I initially resisted, feeling unqualified without a completed Bible degree, I eventually surrendered. The show, *30/30 Bible Reading*, encouraged viewers to read the Bible for 30 minutes over 30 days.

Every morning at 6 a.m., I anointed my hands with oil and taught as the Spirit led. Sometimes thirty minutes turned into sixty. Viewers joined from everywhere—sending testimonies, asking for prayer, sharing how God was meeting them.

Then one day, I couldn't find my anointing oil.

"Oh, that?" my mother said casually. "I used it to fry fish. Couldn't find any other oil."

I was stunned—and amused. The situation was too funny not to share, so I convinced her to join me on Facebook Live to tell the story. Holding a plate of fried fish as our prop, we recounted the tale of the "missing oil." My mother, with her natural comedic timing, added she felt so invigorated after eating the fish that she ran down the stairs to get the mail! Viewers loved it, dubbing the meal "Holy Ghost Fried Fish."

Moments like these reminded me even in the smallest, funniest interactions, God taught us to cherish each other and find joy in the journey.

For 90 days, God used me to faithfully read the Bible aloud to my Facebook community through the 30/30 Bible reading challenge. What started as simple obedience turned into a deeply intimate encounter with the Lord. I saw God move in and through me—touching hearts, releasing healing, and teaching me how to minister in the purest way. Pastor Rabbi Schneider of Discovering the Jewish Jesus graciously joined us to teach on the biblical feasts and their significance to the Christian faith, enriching the experience even more. At times, I would feel waves of heat in my body—what the Lord revealed was His healing anointing being released through the reading of His Word. People shared testimonies, expressed gratitude, and I was left in awe that God would sit with me, speak through me, and use something so simple to do, yet something so sacred.

Looking back, I now realize the Holy Spirit was leading me to mark a milestone. Reading the Bible daily - Monday through Sunday, for 90 days straight - was no small feat. It became a sacred rhythm, like preparing a fresh sermon every day, studying background and context so I could make the word plain. It was more than obedience - it was training ground, consecration, and communion.

DRESSED TO WORSHIP:
MEANINGFUL CONNECTIONS AT CHURCH

Church became our door to further healing, but first, God had to calm her spirit before she could venture back into the world. Mother had a heightened gift of discernment and often absorbed the weight of others' emotions, sensing the atmosphere of a room almost instantly. The emotional overload left her anxious, and in time, she found refuge in isolation - a quiet place where she could regain peace and control in a world that often felt chaotic.

One of my ways of encouraging my mother to attend church was dressing her in some of the fanciest outfits, making her feel like a queen. Tea-length dresses with pearl-detailed cuffs, matching shoes, hats with gentle brims. She looked like royalty.

We began attending new members class at Christian Embassy International Church, led by Pastors Tim and Rodica Lambert. After three months of classes, we stood at the front of the church holding our new member certificates. I was so proud of the milestone we had reached together.

With my encouragement, she began venturing out with loving people who embraced her like family. She joined me at women's events, movie nights, and Christmas parties. Each step outside her comfort zone felt like a leap of faith. And each time, I saw how God honored her courage.

We'd pose after service in matching outfits, and people would ask why she wore the short dresses, and I wore the long ones. "That's just our style," I'd say, smiling.

Those moments of connection were a gift, allowing us to share this special bond as mother and daughter.

During this time, I faced personal loss with the passing of my oldest brother and sister from my father's first marriage. Before their passing, God led me to guide each of them in the sinner's prayer, ensuring their salvation. Though I couldn't attend their memorials, I found peace knowing they had received the greatest gift of all: the assurance of eternal life through Jesus.

THE INTERVIEW: WRITING HER OBITUARY

Through it all, my mission with my mother remained clear: to provide her with an environment where God could continue His deeper work in her heart. I no longer asked her where she had been during her years of absence, as those questions only led to anger. Instead, I focused on creating a space of peace and understanding.

However, I began to grow concerned – when the time came for her to pass on to eternity, what kind of obituary could I write? No one knew much about her life, where she had been, or what she had done, and I knew it was my responsibility to find out the answers.

One day, I approached the topic uniquely, as if I were interviewing her about her life, gently drawing out her story piece by piece. I sat next to her on the couch and asked, "Mother, what was your father's name?" She responded, "His name was James Gray."

I asked more—about Detroit, Aunt Bessie, her teenage years. Thirty minutes passed. Then she looked over, smiled slyly. "You're writing my obituary, aren't you?"

I laughed. She wasn't wrong. I was gathering the fragments of a life that no one had fully known. I wanted to honor her, not just with flowers and tears, but with truth. With legacy.

GIFTS OF GOD'S LOVE: YOU ARE MY LEGACY

By God's grace, the anger I once felt was replaced with a love for my mother that was deeper and more selfless than I had ever known. I no longer saw her as a burden but as a blessing. She became someone I fought for—not just spiritually, but in practical, tangible ways.

Every time I shopped, I found myself thinking, What would make her happy? What would bring her joy? I made sure to keep her favorite perfume, Red Door, always on hand, ready to gift it to her whenever she needed it. This selflessness wasn't my doing; it was God's hand, teaching me to love beyond myself.

Years ago, God placed it on my heart to help my mother bring her ideas to life. Though one venture didn't succeed, I was determined to support her dreams. She once shared her vision of creating a chicken cookbook series.

She had already envisioned everything—the recipes, the pictures, and the stories. She asked me to take photos of her dishes for the cookbook, which I was more than ready to do. I encouraged her to finish what she had started every chance I got.

She had a creative gift, still her focus often shifted. I'd walk into her room and find her engrossed in a TV show or passionately playing games on her iPad.

"Mother," I'd tease, "did you finish your cookbook?"

She'd look up with a sly smile. "No," she'd say before diving back into her game.

I tried to inspire her. "When I start my ministry, I'll need your help. You could speak to seniors, share your journey, and encourage them to keep dreaming."

Her response was classic: "I don't want to be around old folks. All they do is sit around."

I pressed, "Don't you want to leave your legacy? Something with your name on it?"

She looked at me, her eyes softening. "I've done the work I'm going to do," she said firmly. Then she added, "You're my legacy."

At the time, I didn't fully grasp the weight of her words. In retrospect, I realized she saw something I didn't.

She saw the bigger picture.

God had already written her legacy—not in a book, but in the life of her daughter.

My mother was incredibly prophetic, and I held those words—"you're my legacy"—close to my heart.

Her declaration gave me purpose. It wasn't just about fulfilling her dreams—it was about continuing her story, it was about carrying her essence, her wisdom, and her spirit forward in ways God entrusted me to do.

WHAT DID YOU DREAM? PROPHETIC ECHOES BETWEEN MOTHER AND DAUGHTER

God continued to deepen the spiritual bond between my mother and me. One morning, I asked her, as I often did, "What did you dream?" Her response left me in awe. She described word for word, the exact prayer I had whispered to God the night before. It was a divine moment that deepened my appreciation for our spiritual connection – one I was pleasantly surprised to discover.

From then on, I began to ask her every morning about her dreams and prayers, listening intently. I knew we were both true prophets of God, and her words carried wisdom and revelation. It was humbling to see how intricately

God had woven us together for His purposes. He often reminded me of His promise in Numbers 12:6:

"Listen to my words: When there is a prophet among you, I, the Lord, reveal myself to them in visions; I speak to them in dreams."

One morning, my mother looked at me seriously and said, "You better stop speeding." Surprised, I asked, "Why?" She replied, "God gave me a dream you got a speeding ticket." I laughed, insisting, "There's no way I'm getting a speeding ticket."

Three months later, as I sat in my car holding a speeding ticket, her words echoed in my mind. God had revealed His protection and guidance through her dream, reminding me of the spiritual connection we shared. This unexpected place of harmony didn't happen overnight—it was the result of years of prayer, patience, and God's grace.

FAITH AND BREAKTHROUGH IN THE PANDEMIC

When COVID-19 shut down the world, we transitioned to attending church online. Though I missed the fellowship, I prioritized protecting my mother, whose immune system was vulnerable.

In late 2021, I experienced a spiritual awakening—a hunger for God like never before. My living room became my prayer altar as I poured myself into prayer, fasting, and studying God's Word. I would set up my computer, notepad, and Bible and dive into their spirit led bible teachings, taking countless notes and spending hours praying. I also sought out trusted individuals who helped me work through deep-rooted issues from my past.

Through weeks of pouring my heart out to God in prayer, and even fasting I noticed the issues that had once caused me such anguish were losing their power over me. I felt overwhelming gratitude for this new season of freedom and breakthrough.

During this time, my mother began sharing recurring dreams about my future—vivid, hope-filled visions that gave us both a sense of expectation. These dreams, combined with the spiritual breakthroughs I experienced, became our anchor as we faced one of the most challenging seasons of our lives in 2022.

CHAPTER 31:

A JOURNEY OF SURRENDER: THE START OF OUR 21-MONTH MEDICAL JOURNEY

"I have fought the good fight, I have finished the race, I have kept the faith...."
(2 Timothy 4:7-8, *NIV*)

When COVID-19 hit, it became a divine pause. I was thankful to be able to work from home which allowed me to protect my mother and spend invaluable time with her—never realizing it was preparation for what lay ahead.

"I CAN'T BREATHE" AN EARLY MORNING CRY

It was April 2022. Dawn had not yet broken when a frantic knock shattered the silence of my slumber. I opened the door, and there she was—clutching the frame, trembling.

"I can't breathe," she gasped.

Her voice trembled, raw with fear, piercing my soul. I leapt out of bed, heart pounding, and called 911.

As I waited for the paramedics, I whispered, "It's okay... you're going to be okay. Help is on the way," I whispered, my voice both pleading and reassuring. I prayed fervently, rebuking sickness and commanding the breath of God to fill her lungs. Slowly, peace replaced panic as she calmed in my embrace.

Paramedics arrived quickly. Watching them wheel her out on the stretcher felt surreal, the sound of the wheels on the hardwood floor echoing through the silence. I followed close behind as they rushed her to the hospital, red lights reflecting off the stillness of the early morning, marking the beginning of a twenty-one-month journey neither of a us could have foreseen.

HOSPITALS, HOPE, AND A WITHERING STRENGTH

The fluorescent lights in the emergency room flickered above us, sterile and unfeeling. I sat beside her hospital bed, holding her hand, now frail and cold. I learned the rhythm of the machines – the vital signs monitor beeping steadily as blood pressure, oxygen saturation, and heart rate fluctuated on the screen. Tubes. Needles. Silence.

"Stay by my side," she whispered one night, her eyes searching mine. "You don't know what they're doing to me in here."

I smiled gently, brushing a tear from her cheek. "I'm here, Mother. I'm not leaving."

They found no cause—no diagnosis to explain her breathless nights. A week later, she came home. We dared to believe the worst was behind us.

But just months later, another knock. Another plea. Another gasp for air.

It became a cruel pattern—911 calls, hospital rooms, prayers whispered into sterile air. And then came the words that stopped time:

"Her Widowmaker artery is 100% blocked."

THE WIDOWMAKER EMERGENCY:
A RACE AGAINST TIME

I sat in the doctor's office frozen, barely breathing as the words settled into my spirit like a storm cloud. Widowmaker. The artery of death.

She turned to me weakly. "Michelle... do you think I'll make it?"

My hands held hers, trembling. "God has brought us this far. He won't leave us now. We'll trust Him to guide the surgeon's hands."

In the days that followed, prayer warriors from across the country lifted her name before Heaven's throne. Scripture became my anthem, Isaiah 53:5 a battle cry.

On the morning of the surgery, I stayed by her side as she was prepped. Hours later, Dr. Summers, a renowned cardiologist, emerged with a reassuring smile. "She's a fighter," he said. "The procedure was successful." Relief overwhelmed me as I whispered, "Thank you, God."

When I saw her in recovery, her face was flushed yet peaceful. "You did it, Mother. God brought you through," I said, kissing her forehead.

Released just in time for Christmas, I decorated the house, laughed, and cherished every moment together. Though her journey ahead was uncertain, I held on to hope, not knowing this would be one of our last peaceful seasons.

STEVE FORTNER: HONORING A BROTHER IN THE FAITH

Mother's world had grown smaller, and she often told me not to contact relatives who inquired about her well-being. Perhaps it was because she didn't trust anyone to truly love or understand her. Or maybe she feared that revising her past would only stir more questions, judgment, and pain. Isolation, it seemed became her way of protecting her peace. To avoid an argument, I complied - still this often meant we missed out on help from those who genuinely wanted to be a blessing

Still, God allowed me to confide in a few—one being Steve Fortner, a man of deep prophetic insight whom I had once produced a story on for *The 700 Club*. His life of radical giving had opened doors in the Navy and the Kingdom of God.

Before his death, he invited me to help write his love story—*My Blessed Bride*—a tribute to his wife, Darlene. When his daughter invited me to his memorial service, I was surprised when my mother agreed to join me. We made the three-hour drive in quiet companionship.

At Quantico National Cemetery, beneath the soft rustling of wind and folded flags, I felt peace. After the ceremony, we returned to the hotel, ate dinner in bed, and smiled at the simplicity of being away. "I needed this," she said.

So, did I.

LURAY CAVERNS: WHERE MY MOTHER SAW THE FACE OF JESUS

The next day, we took a detour to Luray Caverns, the largest cavern system in the U.S.

The vast chambers stretched 3.5 acres, with ceilings towering ten stories high. Each step opened before us like a cathedral carved by the hand of God. I pushed her wheelchair up winding inclines, past dripping stalactites and stone curtains that glistened like frozen waterfalls.

We stopped at one formation—majestic, radiant, holy.

"That looks like Jesus," she whispered.

I looked up—and gasped. There, etched in stone, was the unmistakable profile of His face. Peace enveloped us.

As we descended deeper into the chambers, our laughter echoed like music. "Hold on, Mother!" I teased as we rolled down a narrow path. "I will not let you fall out of this wheelchair!"

For those few hours, she wasn't sick. She was radiant. Hopeful. Whole.

"Baby," she said, "when God blesses us, I want to go to Europe. I want to sew again. All I want is a Singer serger, a new sewing machine… and a fur coat."

"You'll have it all," I smiled. "Just keep getting stronger."

STANDING IN THE GAP

2023 brought relentless hospital stays, an unending cycle of setbacks and survival. At one point, she was diagnosed with COVID and pneumonia. It felt like I was breathing in and out for her, willing my breath to become hers to help her breathe more easily.

With a CPAP mask forcing air into her body, the doctors soon realized it wasn't enough. "We need to intubate her," they told me, ushering me out of the room. My heart broke as I left, knowing the toll intubation takes and how many don't survive it. I prayed with every step.

Miraculously, within a week, and nothing short of a miracle, my mother came through. The doctors marveled at her resilience, yet I knew it was God's hand sustaining her. Every victory unraveled another thread – blood thinners led to nosebleeds, internal bleeding, and renewed breathing struggles. Her once strong heart now fought to keep going, running on faith alone.

I prayed without ceasing, anointing her body with oil, whispering life into rooms filled with beeping machines. The prayers more desperate.

Nurses and physical therapists became regular visitors to our home, offering care that was both necessary and humbling.

One day, blood poured from her nose like a faucet. I called the nurse. She protested. "I'm fine," she insisted.

But she wasn't.

And again, we went.

Seven days later, we returned home. Her body weaker. My spirit stretched thin.

Still, God never left us.

CHAPTER 32:

THE MISSING YEARS FINALLY REVEALED

"The longer we linger in the mysteries of darkness, the greater the residue of our secrets. They will always be found out, often when we least expect it, destroying the image we sought to construct. In the end, truth has a way of demanding to be seen."

— Michelle B. Wilson, author, *In Search of a Mother's Love.*

ANOTHER HOSPITAL STAY: WHEN THE TRUTH CAME TO LIGHT

We had been home for three weeks, and for once, life felt uneventful—a rare blessing we didn't take for granted. It was a time of rest, a fragile calm before another storm.

As February rolled in, our strength was tested again. One afternoon, as I was writing a script for a story I produced, I heard her urgent voice call:

"Michelle, come here! I can't breathe!"

I dropped everything and raced to her room. Her hand clutched at her chest; her face drained of color. Her eyes, wide and watery, searched mine as if pleading for life.

I knelt beside her and gripped her hand tightly. My voice shook yet didn't falter. "In the name of Jesus," I prayed, "I rebuke this spirit of infirmity. You will live and not die. Breathe, Mother—breathe the breath of God."

Slowly, her breath steadied.

Familiar paramedics arrived and worked to stabilize her. I felt grateful I'd always been home whenever she needed me.

I didn't know this would be the beginning of an unveiling – a divine reckoning that would finally bring closure to the mysteries of her life.

God was preparing to open the vault of decades-long silence.

THE CONVERSATION:
THE WORDS I WAITED YEARS TO HEAR

It happened on February 26, 2023. I walked into a dimly lit hospital room, with my overnight bag slung over my shoulder. A Christian television program played softly in the background, soothing her weariness. I kissed her on the forehead.

"One for each of my brothers and one for Royal Blue," I'd teased, referencing her beloved Russian Blue cat. She smiled with appreciation, eyes weary but warm.

The faint hum of monitors filled the silence, as I sat beside her bed, sensing a quiet weight between us. After about an hour of small talk I sensed now was the time to ask the question I had asked many times before. Maybe, just maybe she trusted me now to share her closely guarded secrets. And then I felt it – the nudge from the Holy Spirit. Ask her now.

"Mother," I began casually, "where were you all those years?"

This time, she didn't deflect.
She didn't get angry.
She simply….surrendered.

Disclaimer: As you read the following sacred exchange - divinely orchestrated by the hand of God, may you witness the rescue of a mother on the edge of eternity, drawn back by mercy before she was lost forever. May your spirit recognize the fingerprints of deliverance, grace and redemption woven through every word. And may you see the power of prayers sown in childhood – small voices crying out in faith – now blooming into the miracle of a mother's return to the grown children who never stopped needing her. Most importantly, to her creator, God, who never stopped pursuing her with His unconditional love.

At 11:44 p.m., I pressed record on my phone, heart pounding with great expectation. The air shifted. Something eternal entered the room. It was a moment I knew I needed to preserve.

Her voice, hoarse with memory, cracked open the silence. "I called my Mama," she began. "She called your daddy and told him. I think she almost had a heart attack when she heard me say, 'Hi, Mama.' She said, 'Lord Have mercy. Jesus!'"

She continued, piecing together memories with shaky breath. She told me her mother had reassured her we were safe. That Daddy had us.

I probed gently. "What did Daddy say when you first called him?"

"He couldn't believe it," she admitted. "I told him, 'Jimmy, this is Bobbie,' and gave him my number. He said, 'Where are you?' I said, 'I'll be there in a couple of days.' He said the children were fine. I knew he would take care of you."

I paused, letting the weight of her words settle. "So...you didn't contact anyone to check on us?"

"No," she replied plainly. "I figured your daddy had you. That's what I thought. I wasn't worried about Jimmy taking care of you. I knew he would."

Her candor stunned me. "What happened after we were first taken away? Were you crying?"

A pause.

"Yes," she nodded.

"Why?"

"Because I never knew a system that just comes and takes your children when they aren't being abused or battered."

Her words landed heavily. As much as I wanted to challenge her, I stayed silent, letting her tell her version uninterrupted. Like a journalist collecting pieces of the truth, I wanted the full story from her point of view. I knew God was orchestrating this divine moment.

Then, I asked about the last time I saw her before she left for good. My voice trembling. "Do you remember the day at the children's home when I was crying under the piano?"

She nodded but didn't elaborate. Her silence held more weight than words ever could.

"So, what happened that day when you came, and I couldn't be consoled? I was underneath the piano crying—and you came underneath too?"

She simply stared out into the distance, lost in thought, as if searching for answers only silence could give.

Instead of waiting patiently for her answer, I rushed ahead, unable to hold back. Years of professional interviewing skills dissolved in an instant. This wasn't a story – we were the story. And I could feel her window of vulnerability cracking open, so I pressed on, afraid that if I paused, she might retreat behind silence again.

This was too personal now – too sacred. I wasn't just asking questions. I was chasing closure for myself, and in doing so, I was also helping my mother release a weight she was never meant to carry alone. A mountainous burden, silent but suffocating, that had lingered far too long. It was time for us both to be free-truly free.

SHADOWS OF A DOUBLE LIFE

It was past midnight, February 27, when I asked what had haunted me most.

"Where did you go after you left the children's home?"

I listened more intently, not moving an inch so I wouldn't disturb this moment.

"New York," she said. "I went to visit your Uncle Billy first, and then I went to New York."

I leaned in closer. Why didn't you let anyone know?"

"I was young," she said, voice tinged with regret. "If I'd had the maturity, I would've kept my children with me." She paused. "I cut off ties. I didn't let anybody know. I was a real mystery. I changed my name."

My voice gentle. "How did you survive all those years?"

She took a breath, then began to unravel the mysteries – her life in New York, the reinvention, the secrecy, the survival. She spoke of danger cloaked as safety, of communities that both sheltered and shrouded her. The new name she carried, the ones who took her in, the loyalty it required. It was more than I ever expected – and more than I'll ever say.

I expected hardship, not a secret life surrounded by people who lived by their own rules. I asked more questions – many of which she willingly answered – but some details she didn't dare reveal. This wasn't just a story of a mother who vanished - it was the silent testimony of a woman who reinvented herself to survive. A woman who sank into the deep, suffocating waters of disappointment, and emotional turmoil, weighed down by a life she could no longer mend.

Somewhere between the brilliance of her talents and the brokenness of her dreams, she disappeared – not just from us, but from the version of herself she once believed in. And along the way, she came to believe a heartbreaking truth - that her presence, in its broken state, might do more harm than good. Her children would be better off without her. And in some mysterious way, she was right. She knew she could no longer guide our destiny in the way we deserved – so she made the ultimate sacrifice.

Like the mother of Moses, who placed her infant in a woven basket and released him into the reeds of the Nile - entrusting his future to a river she could not control in hopes of a better future- our mother, too, let us go. Not out of abandonment, but out of a desperate hope that God would carry us where she could not. That in her absence, we might find safety, stability, and the kind of life her brokenness could no longer provide.

She then wrapped herself in the persona of a woman who belonged to another world – a hidden world where names were changed, loyalties shifted, and silence became a currency. The longer she stayed away, the more her absence carved into her soul a debt she didn't know how to repay.

As she spoke, the machines monitoring her vitals beeped in rhythm – like a metronome marking time we couldn't get back. I listened, stunned – not just as her daughter, but as a storyteller conducting the most personal interview I'd ever help bring into the light. I stepped into the untold journey of a survival story she had never dared to tell – until now. It was sacred terrain of her unspoken story – one shaped not only by pain, but by the impossible choices she made to survive. As a journalist, I had finally been given the interview of a lifetime – one that just happened to belong to my mother and me.

I marveled at how through danger, deception and decades of silence – God had preserved her. And when the time was right, God brought her home – not to a city, but to her children…to a daughter. To a hospital room lined with forgiveness. To a final chapter only God could orchestrate.

THE STORY BEHIND THE STORY

She talked of her dreams. Of being an actress. Of starting over. Of the moment she decided to come back.

"I was tired," she said. "Tired of New York. I wanted to see my children."

Then I asked, "What were you thinking as you came to see us for the first time after all those years?"

"I was happy," she said.

"What were you thinking about, though?" I pressed gently.

"How would we look?" I asked.

"Mmmm-hmmm. How big will you be? I only remembered you as babies," she replied.

"And what did you think when you saw us?"

"Oh, I thought you all were the most beautiful, cutest little children," she said with a soft smile.

We talked for hours—until the sky outside the hospital window shifted from darkness to a deep indigo blue, hinting that morning was near. I laid down on the couch next to her bed, heart full of awe and quiet relief.

The missing years weren't missing anymore.

CLOSURE IN THE UNFOLDING

Listening to her, I realized this wasn't just about answers—it was about closure. About redemption. A mother and daughter finally confronting the shadows of the past and finding light in the truth. I was truly thankful she had finally bared her soul to me. Perhaps, in her way, she wanted her story told – entrusting her truth in the heart of the daughter who had sacrificed her life to care for her.

The truth had come—not as a thunder, but as a gentle wind. She hadn't vanished because she didn't love us. She vanished because life had broken her, and she didn't know how to pick up the pieces.

But God… God had gathered the shards. He carried her through the wilderness of her own wandering and brought her back.

She entrusted her story to the daughter who had kept watch.

And I had stayed—long enough to hear it.

Long enough to carry it forward.

Long enough to become her legacy.

Now it was 3 a.m., and we were exhausted. I kissed her forehead and laid down on the hospital couch next to her bed marveling at the journey we had just shared. The missing years had finally been revealed, bringing with them a quiet, peaceful finality.

"As you step into your newness, whispers of who you were echo loudly. Ghosts of old identities waging a tug-of-war with the truth of who you're becoming. It's a sacred battle, fought in silence and surrender. Though the battle is fierce, the victory belongs to those who anchor themselves in God's truth, no matter the cost."

— Michelle B. Wilson, author, *In Search of a Mother's Love.*

CHAPTER 33:

THE REFINER'S FIRE: FINDING GOD IN THE BATTLE

"The greatest treasures are often hidden, buried deep - waiting to be searched for – unearthed through fire. They're not visible to the untrained eye. They're often overlooked and discarded, deemed insignificant by those who measure value by worldly standards. Only those whose hearts beat in rhythm with God's, possesses vision that pierces through the hardest surfaces to reveal the brilliance of riches no amount of wealth could ever buy."
– Michelle B. Wilson, author, *In Search of a Mother's Love.*

THE WEIGHT OF CARE, THE GRACE TO STAND

Mother had just returned home from another hospital stay. The machines were gone, the sterile halls behind us, but the war wasn't over. Illness lingered like a shadow, pressing down on both of us. Each breath she took felt borrowed, fragile. I was relieved to have her home—but I was exhausted, too. Only God's hand had kept us standing.

Early on, there was support – prayers, visits, texts. As time passed, concern faded, and silence set in. Life must go on. And it did. That's when I learned:

there are places in this journey where only God can walk with you - especially when the road feels endless. Through it all, Proverbs 18:24 became my anchor: "There is a friend who sticks closer than a brother." When human hands failed, God never did.

People mistook my strength for not needing help. Strength isn't the absence of need – it's the quiet determination to keep going when no one else notices. I often wondered, does anyone see me? Does anyone care? And just when I thought no one did, God sent whispers of love through others - a $20 bill from a doctor, a thoughtful gesture from my supervisor, a prayer text sent from a friend. In this medical journey, I discovered that certain roads – especially the ones paved in suffering – can only be walked with God. And God walked with me.

THE GREATEST TREASURES ARE OFTEN HIDDEN

During this time, I often thought, if my mother had been wealthy, I knew offers of help would've flooded in. My mother, though flawed, had a different treasure - one not visible to the naked eye. She carried a wealth of wisdom, faith, and untapped potential, hidden beneath years of pain. Her treasures weren't material but spiritual, requiring patience and love to unearth.

James 2:5 echoed in my spirit: "Has not God chosen the poor of this world to be rich in faith?"

I saw her faith emerge in small moments—a smile during prayer, a quiet nod when I reminded her of God's promises. God gave me the honor of uncovering the treasures she carried—treasures no amount of money could buy.

And then the fire turned hotter.

Her body, once strong, began to betray her again. The swelling returned. Breaths became shallow. It felt like no matter how hard we fought, no matter how much progress we made, we were always one step away from another hospital visit.

Then came the moment that tested my strength like never before. The nephrologist said:

"Her kidneys are failing. She'll need dialysis."

Something about hearing the word dialysis spoken aloud triggered a sudden surge of anger and frustration. It hit me like a wave - tears welled in my eyes, and an invisible weight pressed hard against my chest. This wasn't supposed to be her story. Not my mother. Not like this.

I swallowed my pain, then I called a prayer line – desperate and exhausted, yet still believing God could give her new kidneys.

A man answered—not just with prayer, but prophecy.

"I see you and your mother standing on stages, ministering to crowds," he said.

His words struck deep. I remembered my mother's dreams—of us flying together, riding in limousines, preaching the Word. Dreams she'd spoken in passing, but I'd stored like treasure.

The word he shared became a beacon of hope, a reminder God was still writing our story. It wouldn't end with dialysis – it would end with destiny.

SACRED WORDS WRITTEN IN FAITH

By now, I had resumed writing the book God had told me to begin years ago - *In Search of a Mother's Love*. I hesitated because Mother wasn't ready to tell her story, and I wasn't ready to dive into the pain of my past. Not finishing it wasn't an option. Now, the book felt like an act of faith, a way of telling God, "See, Lord, I'm finishing it." It became my plea for her life—a declaration she wouldn't just survive, but one day testify of her miraculous journey.

The first half took over a decade to write. I'd start and stop – emotionally drained and paralyzed by the weight of what I'd endured. The second half, beginning with my time at CBN and our reunion, poured like oil, and was completed in just seven months. Fueled by renewed purpose, our miraculous healing journey was written with prayer and redemption.

Simultaneously, I returned to Regent University to finish my Master of Divinity. I often joined Zoom classes from emergency rooms or hospital bedsides. My classmates prayed. Professors extended grace. I was deeply grateful, and I pressed on.

I called my brothers, too—urging them to speak life over her, to offer forgiveness she could feel. Even from afar, their words helped stabilize what her body threatened to release.

SHE'S "MY BABY"

My mother endured endless days of excruciating arthritic pain - bone - deep agony that often left her gripping the handrails of her medical bed just to cope. Not to mention, the endless blood draws that felt like jagged edges going into her arms. In those moments, she lashed out at the person closest to her: me. And yet, despite her sharp words and raw frustration, the deeper love that had taken root in my heart over the years never wavered. Somehow, I understood her frustrations. I let those harsh moments pass, choosing not to carry them but to focus instead on what mattered most: helping her heal so we could one day do the work of the ministry together.

My devotion to my mother didn't go unnoticed. One day, a nurse stopped me: "Are you Bobbie LaMaster's daughter?"

"Yes," I smiled.

"You're popular," she said. "All good things. You take such good care of her."

"She's my baby," I said with passion. I wasn't just her daughter anymore—I was her caregiver, her advocate, her champion.

Then the nurse chuckled: "If that were my mother, I would've run away long ago."

I laughed. "Yes, she's feisty," I said. "But she's made it through storms many wouldn't have survived. And she can be sweet and very comical."

I'd learned to comfort my mother, smoothing away her fears in her most difficult moments. One day, I sang over her as she rested: "It is well with my soul." The words seemed to float through the room, carrying peace. Her countenance softened; her spirit lifted by the hymn's powerful reminder of God's faithfulness. For that moment, it was well.

At home, I reminded her of God's dreams for us. "Mother, we will stand on stages and share this testimony. Hold on a little longer," She'd smile faintly, her eyes flickering with hope as I held her frail hands.

THE ROYAL TREAMENT: CARRIED IN GRACE

Dialysis became routine. Three days a week. Long hours tethered to machines filtering toxins her kidneys could no longer manage. She asked me to sit with her the first time, not understanding it wasn't allowed. Yet, I understood her fear.

Even in suffering, joy found us. His name was George—her medical driver. Gentle. Soft-spoken. Full of dignity. He carried her like royalty. At under 100 pounds, she was featherlight in his arms, but to him, she was gold.

She adored him.

"I just love when George carries me," she'd say, giggling like a teenager.

We'd perfume her wrists with Red Door. Dress her in layers of color. She'd insist: "Spray me now, Michelle. Hurry!"

Week after week, I searched store racks for the warmest, thickest jogging sets in bold colors—anything to shield her from the bitter chill of the dialysis center that bit through her fragile frame.

It became our ritual—me, dressing her in layers of love; her, showing up wrapped in joy despite her suffering. In those simple moments, I felt God's love for us. Through George's arms, the scent of perfume, and laughter in pain—God was there. Comforting. Covering. Carrying.

At home, I cooked protein-rich meals, to help regain strength. Yet, her taste buds betrayed her. She'd accuse me of adding sugar and clung to her saltshaker like a lifeline. Every meal became an act of love and patience.

THE CRUCIBLE OF CARE: THE REHAB THAT TESTED AND TRANSFORMED US

In June, after another hospital stay, she was sent to rehab.

She hated that I couldn't stay overnight. Soon, she made friends—nurses admired her sass. I brought thank-you trays to the staff and gently reminded her of the advice she gave me.

"As God continues to bless you, stay humble and sweet." I reminded her of her own words.

She gave me that look—the one that said that rule only applied to me.

There were moments of hope during her rehab stay. I'll always treasure the times I surprised her and found her slowly marching in place. And like an intuitive producer, I captured the moment - recording it for the testimony we would one day share. It filled me with hope. She was fighting, and we both believed she was improving.

I appreciated any support and was especially grateful when our co-pastor, Rodica Lambert, sent me a photo of her visit with her. The Lambert's love and encouragement showed us the tangible love of God.

PASSING MANTLES: A LEGACY OF FAITH THAT TOUCHED THE WORLD

"Each interaction with a spiritual giant is a holy exchange – an invisible weaving of destinies across time. Their obedience becomes a seed in our soil of divine purpose, and their harvest, our inheritance. Through these divine connections, we glean from their wisdom and labor, carrying their mantles forward in ways unimaginable. To help build the vision of a general of the faith is to be entrusted with a sacred mantle, a flaming torch passed from one generation to the next. This is the mystery of legacy: the roots of one man's faith keep us forever entwined by covenant, calling, and Kingdom purpose."

- Michelle B. Wilson, author, *In Search of a Mother's Love.*

In June 2023, as my mother continued her rehab journey, the world bid farewell to a towering figure in Christian broadcasting – Pat Robertson. He passed away on June 8th. As the founder of the Christian Broadcasting Network and the host of the 'The 700 Club,' his visionary leadership and unwavering faith reshaped Christian television and deeply impacted my life. Pat was a spiritual father to me through his example in both faith and media.

At his Celebration of Life service, I reflected on his legacy. Pat's life had touched millions, reminding us God's plans reach far beyond what we can imagine.

Being part of the CBN legacy remains one of the greatest privileges of my life. Through the stories I produced, I witnessed God's power across the globe. From riding on a firetruck in Fort Pierce with paramedic Tommy Neiman, to learning stunt driving from Terry Cadiente, who taught me how to do a dangerous 90-degree turn and land perfectly between two orange cones.

One of the highlights of my career was producing a story for Scott Ross, featuring X-Men producer Ralph Winter at Paramount Studios—each assignment reflected CBN's creativity, mission, and excellence. I traveled to Peru and Mexico to cover stories for Operation Blessing's disaster relief outreaches and with Terry Meeuwsen to Ukraine to produce stories for Orphan's Promise and the hope they gave to orphans.

By divine providence, CBN became the bridge that reconnected me with my mother. She saw me in a CBN segment I produced and reached out. That moment became the beginning of a healing journey we both desperately needed.

I see how God tucked sacred moments into that season—like when I invited Mother to *The 700 Club* studio to meet her favorite televangelist, Joel Osteen. She smiled, took a photo with him, and left with a signed book and joy on her face.

What began as stories I produced for others became the soil for my own healing. Even the moment Pat and Gordon Robertson prayed over me in Studio 7 remains a spiritual mantle I cherish.

At 93, Pat entered his eternal reward, leaving behind a global ministry born from just $70 and a mustard seed of faith. His beloved wife, Dede - who passed the year before – stood faithfully by his side and was just as integral to the ministry's success. She also contributed through her writing – authoring two books, *My God Will Supply* and *The New You* and wrote a monthly column for *Christian Life* magazine. Together, their lives touched millions for the glory of God, and I could only imagine the celebration in heaven as they were reunited and heard, 'Well done, good and faithful servant.'

Pat's legacy now rests in the capable hands of his son, Gordon Robertson, whose quiet strength continues to carry the vision forward. Under his leadership, CBN expands its global reach through *The 700 Club, Superbook, The 700 Club Interactive*, CBN News and digital platforms designed to reach younger generations. Gordon's steadfast commitment ensures CBN's impact will continue to grow, advancing the mission to prepare the nations for the coming of Christ and establish God's Kingdom on earth.

CBN: GOD'S DIVINE PURPOSE

CBN became a place of divine safety during one of the most vulnerable seasons of my life. Every story I produced was a seed of healing—some planted for others, some planted for me. While many only saw what aired, God was doing a deeper work beneath the surface.

During those years, I wrestled with public scrutiny, private pain, and the long road to inner healing. Yet, I also learned how to fight the right battles in hardened places—against fear, shame, and spiritual opposition—not people. Through God's grace, I became a woman of intercession, shaped in the fire of trial, but rooted in tender mercies of God's love.

There were moments when the future He showed me—preaching, healing, ministering to multitudes—felt impossible to reach. Still, I held onto His promises. And with every setback, He kept reminding me: Your journey is not in vain.

My relationship with my mother became a mirror. Our shared pain became sacred ground. We forgave. We grew. We found friendship in places where there had once been distance.

In the end, it wasn't just about becoming the woman I dreamed of—but becoming the woman, He designed: whole, radiant, and full of love for those He placed in my path.

MONDAY, SEPTEMBER 11, 2023:
THE FINAL SURGERY – THE FIGHT OF OUR LIVES

Yet, just as I was stepping more fully into who God designed me to be, life reminded me that love often requires more than words – it requires sacrifice.

As summer turned to fall, my mother's health declined again. The aneurysm discovered the year before had grown by two centimeters. It could rupture at any moment. The weariness in her eyes mirrored my own, and we made the only choice we could: move forward.

By this point – after almost 17 months of hospital visits, close calls, and medical interventions – we knew the truth: any surgery could be high risk. This aneurysm procedure was no exception. We understood it could take her life. And yet, we trusted God with the outcome. Not blindly, but fully. Because what else could we do but place her in the hands of the One who had carried her- and us-this far?

I prayed fervently, calling on every ounce of faith I had left. I gathered as much prayer support as I could and was deeply moved by every petition to God on our behalf.

My car was in the shop for minor repairs, so I rented a scooter. I slung my backpack filled with my computer and work assignments over the handlebars and rode the ten-minute journey to the hospital. The wind blowing through my hair and the sense of being carefree, even if just for a moment, felt like a release from the constant tension and weight I had been carrying.

On September 5, the morning of her surgery, I prayed with her, holding her hands firmly, transferring strength. Then I went to the chapel—my war room. The dimly lit 20x20 space was lined with blue cushioned chairs and an altar at the front. It was empty. I was grateful. I answered emails and worked on assignments for my job, yet my spirit was in intercession.

"Lord, we are weary. You've brought us this far," I whispered." Keep us in your hands and bring total healing."

The chaos of the hospital faded as His presence filled the room. His strength carried me. His grace sustained me. I prayed for the surgeons' hands and my mother's fragile body to endure.

Finally, after many hours I received the call - her surgery was successful, but complications arose, leading to a second surgery six days later, on September 11th. This time, the surgeon was more confident, and God's peace surrounded me. I prayed at home, pacing my living room, believing this wasn't just about her healing—it was preparation for a spiritual inheritance yet to come.

WHEN LEGACY SPOKE:
A MOTHER'S FINAL PROPHETIC BLESSING

God was preparing my mother to pass on a profound blessing—one that echoed the weight of blessings in Scripture. These weren't just words. They carried divine authority. We see this in the lives of Abraham, Isaac, Jacob, and

Joseph's sons, Ephraim and Manasseh, where each blessing held the weight of heaven's approval and set the trajectory for those who received them.

Though I didn't fully grasp it, I knew it was the result of obedience—laying down my life so God could use me as a vessel to help redeem hers. This moment wasn't just about her receiving her blessing; it was about God writing a legacy of love and restoration.

John 15:13 echoed in my spirit: "Greater love has no one than this: to lay down one's life for one's friends." And in that moment, I was about to reap the benefits of this sacrificial obedience, a love poured out in service and faith. An inheritance greater than any earthly possession.

In the early hours of September 12, 2023, I entered her hospital room. After back-to-back aneurysm surgeries, she was miraculously still here. I knew God had preserved her for something sacred.

As I approached her bed. the sun was shining through, and yet there was a brightness that far outweighed it - a radiance not of this world. It was God's glory that hovered over us, tangible and holy. Her body looked frail, yet somehow radiant, bathed in light that fell eternal. She turned to me, her gaze piercing, her presence commanding my full attention.

"Daughter," she said. "God showed me great things about your life."

Tears ran down her face, yet her voice held calm authority. Time seemed to freeze, the world outside the room vanishing. I leaned in, pulled out my phone, and began recording knowing – I'd want to seal into eternity every word she spoke. Her voice carried the weight of heaven itself, each syllable infused with prophetic divine authority. She spoke of things only God could have revealed, my future, my calling, and the lives I would touch. These were not mere affirmations. They were divine decrees that left me in awe.

"What else did He show you, Mother?" I asked repeatedly.

She turned to me, eyes shining, and said, "He showed me your husband – and the great love the two of you will share in your marriage."

Her words warmed my heart and answered prayers I had whispered to God for years – prayers about covenant, companionship, and a love that reflects His heart.

Thirty-two video clips later, her words became a sacred treasure. Each one unveiled heaven's assignment. Her voice had become the voice of heaven, speaking destiny over me.

Her words were not just a conversation; they were a spiritual transaction. I could feel the weight of her blessing, like a mantle being passed from mother to daughter. She entrusted me with her legacy, not because of her inability to carry it, but because the choices she made led to intense warfare that had blocked her path. Her calling was now mine to fulfill. Her gaze held unshakable conviction, her tears streaming as if to say, you must carry this forward.

Then her eyes shifted to something unseen.

"I see Jesus," she whispered. "He's over there. He touched me. I see His blood."

Though I couldn't see Him, I felt His presence – holy, weighty, undeniable.

She wasn't just my mother who embraced the daughter she had once prayed to give birth to; she was a mother who now understood the magnitude of those prayers. Right then, I realized her love for me, though at times imperfect, had always been rooted in God's divine plan. She had carried wounds, but she had also carried grace, and now she passed that grace to me, a love that transcended the ordinary, a blessing that carried eternal significance.

There was finally no doubt – she loved me. Deeply. Imperfectly. Fiercely. And I loved her too.

A LOVE THAT LIVED BEYOND THE FIRE

I left her hospital room carrying her blessing. Her faith. Her calling. Her legacy.

This wasn't just the end of her story—it was the beginning of mine.

What the fire didn't destroy, it refined.

What the journey didn't erase, it sanctified.

And what my mother couldn't finish, she passed on to me—with tears, prayers, and heaven's authority.

CHAPTER 34:

A SACRED JOURNEY HOME: FINAL THREADS OF GRACE

"When you sacrifice everything—your time, energy, and very life—for a dream you are certain will unfold, only to see it interrupted, crushed, or seemingly fade away, don't let go. Hold on tighter because the seed has been planted into the soil of limitless possibilities. Though the roots may grow in a new direction, the harvest is sure. That spark, that flicker of faith, will ignite a blaze of possibility, transforming everything it touches and reshaping the world in ways you never imagined. The dream was never only yours; it belonged to the world. Whether it blossoms in your lifetime, or in generations to come, the dream will live on."

– Michelle B. Wilson, author, *In Search of a Mother's Love*.

THE UNSPOKEN GOODBYE

The air shifted before the heavens ever whispered it. There was a stillness—like something holy was preparing to pass through.

Mother returned home, frail but determined. She survived what others might not have, and I knew God was keeping her His specific plans and purposes.

Mother refused rehab despite the medical staff's urging, and I couldn't convince her otherwise. At home, her therapist continued to visit weekly. Her breathing grew more labored, requiring oxygen 24 hours a day.

One day, she called me close. Her tone was different - nostalgic, reflective, as if her life were flashing before her.

"All my girlfriends had girls. I had boys. I said to the Lord, God, please give me a baby girl to dress in ruffled dresses, white bobby socks and put bows in her hair."

She looked at me as if seeing me again for the first time. "Then you came," she whispered. "My beautiful baby girl. You were bald and you'd blow bubbles and play with your toes." Her smile revealed the joy.

"Isn't it amazing, Mother, how God gives us the desires of our hearts?" I remarked.

"Yes," she replied, her smile widening.

A few days later, her tone shifted. She called me into her room again and said something I wish I hadn't dismissed.

"Isn't it something," she said, her voice heavy with concern, "when you know your time is up?"

I should've paused. Should've held that space. But I couldn't take it in. I redirected her to the future—to hope—to the promises God had shown us.

I didn't know it was her quiet goodbye.

SUNDAY, NOVEMBER 19, 2023:
THE SALVATION PRAYER OF REPENTANCE

November 19th arrived like any other day, yet it held eternity within it.

The call came softly yet urgently, "Baby daughter, come here."

I rushed into the room. She was sitting upright in bed, her face glowing with a strange light—one that seemed to come from beyond the veil. I instinctively grabbed my phone and pressed record.

"Today," she said, "I said to the Lord, forgive me. I'm a sinner. I repent. I'm so sorry. Forgive me for all my sins."

My mother - who once could never admit she was a sinner - was now freely confessing her sins and asking God for forgiveness. And that, to me, was the unmistakable work of the Holy Spirit."

Time stilled. My knees weakened.

I had prayed for this for fifteen years.

I had begged. Fasted. Pleaded. And now, without my coaxing, she was praying—from her heart, with trembling lips and full surrender.

I whispered, "Thank You, Jesus." She had crossed over from resistance to redemption. Heaven rejoiced, and so did I.

Her health seemed to stabilize. Two follow-up appointments brought good news. Her heart doctor said, "This is the supernatural hand of God." Her aortic aneurysm surgeon agreed. "Your aneurysm is shrinking." My mother, ever gracious, replied, "Doctor, thank you so much for what you've done for me."

He stopped her. "Don't thank me. Thank God."

I believed she was on the road to recovery.

FRIDAY, DECEMBER 1, 2023: THE FINAL 9-1-1 CALL

December 1st felt like a milestone. I ran into her room just after midnight. "Mother, we made it!" I exclaimed. Yet, she didn't share my enthusiasm. Her breathing betrayed the celebration. Her chest heaved and sweat beaded her forehead.

"I can hardly breathe," she whispered.

Despite her protests, I called 911. Afterward, she struck the bed with a balled-up fist – frustrated but resigned. It was a gesture that thundered louder than words: this was her last ride…and she wasn't coming back.

At the hospital, they removed fluid from her lungs once again. Four days later, on December 5th, she was transferred to a rehab facility. This time she didn't resist. Her silence held a knowing.

SUNDAY, DECEMBER 17, 2023:
THE UNEXPECTED CALL – SHE EXPIRED!

The day began like any other morning. I planned to visit my mother later that day, still clinging to the hope of her recovery. However, at 8:38 a.m., the phone rang. On the other end, a nurse's calm, clinical voice spoke words that shattered my world.

"We went into your mother's room and found her unresponsive. We've called the EMT's."

Unresponsive? My heart dropped. I could barely process the words before another call came at 8:41 a.m.

"They did everything they could do. I'm sorry to inform you, but your mother has expired."

Expired. The word hung in the air as if I could reach into the atmosphere, snatch it, and cast it away, replacing it with something full of life and possibility.

I sat frozen trying to make sense of what I had just heard. This isn't over. God, You promised. You gave us dreams. We were supposed to minister together. How could this end before we even began?

Months earlier, God gave me a dream - EMTs working on her with little urgency. Her frailty. Their mechanical movements. I had buried that dream. It's not her time. Now, it returned, haunting and clear.

I had fasted, prayed, and believed for healing. Yet here I was, unprepared to face this reality.

The drive to the facility blurred. My thoughts swirled, a storm of faith and fear colliding with every mile. I gripped the steering wheel, pleading, "Father God, You are the resurrection and the life. You've done it before; do it again. Don't let this be the end."

My faith unwavering. God is going to give me a miracle.

As I entered her room, a stillness filled the air. It was the kind of stillness that seemed to stretch time, making every step feel like an eternity. Her face looked peaceful—too peaceful.

I felt her presence in the room so strongly. It was tangible as if her spirit had stayed behind, lingering to comfort me. I could almost feel her eyes on me, watching me as I moved toward her lifeless body with tears streaming down my face.

My heart pounded in my chest as I approached her bed, every fiber of my being hoping for a miracle.

"Mother," I called softly, then louder, "Mother!" There was no response, still, I wasn't ready to give up—God, not yet.

"COME BACK, MOTHER": MY LAZARUS CRY

Evangelist Mays, who had joined me, prayed with me. I sang, declared life, commanded her spirit to return. I cried, my voice breaking, "Mother, don't leave me! You're my best friend, my only friend. We were supposed to walk this journey out together. Please, come back."

I grabbed the nasal cannula connected to the oxygen tank, my hands trembling as if trying to steady the weight of my hopes. Gently, I placed the two prongs into her nostrils, willing her - begging her - to take a breath. My whispered prayers hung in the air, pleading for a miracle to defy the stillness that clung to the room like a heavy fog. Yet, the silence remained, unbroken.

She didn't breathe.

Desperation makes us do things we'd never imagine when life feels unsteady.

My mind was racing, clinging to any hope or possibility this wasn't the end. I whispered, "God, please... please..." Yet, deep down, a quiet knowing began to settle in my spirit. Her body was still, her hands starting to cool. I left the room, the weight of disbelief and grief pressing down on me like a tidal wave. The tears came uncontrollably as I walked the halls, feeling lost and alone.

"God, am I really supposed to walk through this life without her?"

It was a sobering realization—confronting the limits of my humanity and surrendering to God's sovereignty. A quiet voice reminded me: "My

Grace is sufficient for you. My plans are perfect, even when they don't align with your desires."

Tears streamed down my face as I sat with this truth. I had prayed, fasted, and believed. And now, all I could do was trust God had seen the entire picture—the beginning, the middle, and the end—and somehow, even in this loss, His hands still guided me.

After a moment of gathering myself, I began calling and texting family and friends, my trembling fingers struggling to type the words mother passed away. When I called my oldest brother, who had stood by my side throughout this journey, my voice shaken as I tried to speak. "It wasn't supposed to be this way," I said. "It wasn't supposed to end like this."

RELEASING MOTHER TO HEAVEN'S EMBRACE

After two hours, I gathered the strength to return to the room. I approached her bed slowly, my footsteps heavy with sorrow. I sat beside her and placed my hand over hers, feeling the coldness that confirmed what I didn't want to believe.

Through the tears, I spoke to her.

"Mother, I know you think you'll somehow hold me back if you come back. But I need you to know—you wouldn't be a hindrance."

Perhaps she thought that by letting go, she was setting me free—to finally move forward after 15 years of caring for her.

But what she didn't know was that I wanted her by my side—to witness and enjoy all the beauty God was about to unfold.

The room was peacefully still.

"Mother, you've been my greatest blessing and friend. You've shown me what it means to love unconditionally... and I don't know how to do life without you."

And then, a quiet knowing settled in my heart: she had a choice—and she chose heaven.

Then I said what I never thought I'd say.

"Mother... I can only begin to fathom what you must be experiencing now. You are being wrapped in a peace that silences all fear. A joy no sorrow can touch. Saturated with a love that doesn't wound or abandon. You're enveloped in God's perfect presence—healed, whole, radiant. You finally know—deep in your soul—just how much God loves you."

Looking at her face, so calm and at peace, I knew—she was free. Free from the needle pricks, the endless surgeries, the excruciating bone pain that often left her breathless. She was now clothed in glory, her perfected body held in the embrace of the One who had always loved her best.

The atmosphere in the room shifted. Her presence lingered, full and holy. It felt as if her spirit was still reaching for mine—watching, blessing, releasing.

Softly, I whispered,

"Mother, I release you to be with the—the Lover of your soul, the One who has waited patiently to welcome you Home. I'll see you again."

Then I leaned down and kissed her forehead—one kiss for each of her children, and one from her beloved cat, Royal Blue.

"I love you, Mother," I said. "And I'll carry you with me—always."

THE FINAL WALK OF LOVE

Soon after, the funeral home transport team arrived. I recorded them placing a fitted sheet over her lifeless body. It was sobering in a way I can't fully describe. They gently transferred her onto a special bed, covering her with a velvet blue pall. It was surreal, a moment suspended between heartbreak and closure.

Mother never liked being alone. As they wheeled her down the hallway, I walked beside her one last time. It was the journey home, a sacred farewell filled with love, and appreciation of the years we shared. Each step echoed our bond, battles, and the promise her legacy would live on. I watched as they opened the back door to the white hearse, still recording, capturing every moment. As they placed her body inside, I blew her a kiss and whispered, "I love you, Mother."

As I watched the hearse drive away, I realized her journey had come full circle. The legacy she had carried though marred by struggles and setbacks was now entrusted to me.

Her prophetic words, spoken just months earlier, rang in my heart: "You must carry this forward."

As I watched the hearse disappear into the distance, a profound peace settled over me. It wasn't the peace of understanding, but the peace of surrender knowing God's plans are higher than ours and He sees the full tapestry when we only see the pieces.

This wasn't the ending I envisioned, but it wasn't the end of our story. Her legacy lives on through me—through the dreams she planted in my heart and the lives we'll continue to touch through my ministry as I share our story of healing, forgiveness and redemption.

Her final chapter had been written. Mine was just beginning.

SURRENDERED: THE LORD GIVES AND TAKES AWAY

Driving home, tears poured as I grappled with the finality of her passing. Every waking moment of my life revolved around my mother's care, her needs, and her dreams. Now the sacred assignment was complete, and I was left wondering how to make sense of life without her.

At home, I fell to my knees and sang through my tears: *"Hallelujah, God, You give and You take away. Hallelujah. Thank You for allowing my mother to spend eternity with You."* It was my act of surrender, a declaration of trust during unimaginable loss.

As I settled into the stillness of my life, no longer having to wonder when the next medical emergency would arise, I heard the Lord say,

"You've been promoted in the realm of the Spirit because you were obedient to complete the assignment I gave you with your mother."

GRIEF, GIVING, AND LOVE REMAINS

The holidays came swiftly, yet I wasn't ready to celebrate. The overwhelming grief took away my appetite; for ten days, I couldn't eat a thing. The very thought of food made me nauseous. In the weeks that followed, I could only manage a few bites of beets, olives, tuna, and avocado—enough to keep my strength, but nothing more.

I chose solitude, immersing myself in prayer and reflection, seeking God's direction for what lie ahead.

The next day, amid my grief, the Lord spoke gently: "Gather all her clothing and shoes and give them away". It felt overwhelming, but I obeyed. Within a day, I had filled twenty bags with her clothes and shoes, many with tags still attached, some shoes never worn.

I donated everything to a homeless giveaway. Watching people find joy in her belongings brought healing. I took photos, cherishing how her life still touched others.

This act of giving reminded me of her legacy – how she had always poured into others, through her work with the LaMaster Foundation, which she founded many years ago.

Even in death, love remains. My mother's love now fills the spaces she left behind – a life that was truly a testament to God's grace, goodness, and faithfulness.

CHAPTER 35:

HONORING MOTHER: A CELEBRATION OF LIFE

"Her children arise and call her blessed; her husband also, and he praises her. 'Many women do noble things, but you surpass them all."
(Proverbs 31:28-29, *NIV*)

THE FILLED SANCTUARY: A HOLY FAREWELL

Rain fell softly that morning, not as a storm but as Heaven's tears—gentle and reverent. On January 6, 2024, under that sacred sky, family and friends gathered at Christian Embassy International Church to celebrate the life of my mother. It was more than a homegoing—it was a radiant honoring of a woman once broken, now whole. The very walls of the church that had welcomed her, loved her, and embraced her return to faith now bore witness to her final exodus.

Honoring my mother was about celebrating the profound transformation of her heart, and how she prayed the salvation prayer just 28 days before she took her final breath. Her life became a testament to God's redeeming Grace, and this service needed to reflect that redemption.

God directed every detail, from designing the obituary program with white and gold roses, to enlarging the most glamorous photographs my father had taken of her in her youth into breathtaking 24-by-36-inch posters. These adorned the entrance and were displayed on both sides of her white and gold casket that was draped in custom fabrics from my company, Elegant Casket Drapes. The shimmering gold and pearl overlay mirrored the unique elegance she brought into our lives.

She wore the sequined gold gown I had once worn to my niece's wedding. It sparkled not just with fabric, but with redemption. A delicate bow rested atop her hands, holding a single white rose. I stood nearby in a champagne-colored gown, a silent echo of her glory. We were still bound—even in this farewell.

Over a hundred guests arrived, some from Memphis, Fort Wayne, and Ohio. Family I had never met embraced me as if we'd always known each other. Her obituary, which I had written, unveiled a side of her they'd never known—a woman marked not only by hardship, but by grace.

THE TESTAMENT AND THE TRIBUTE

During the service, I shared our story—fifteen years of caregiving and reconciliation under the theme "Walking with the Broken." I told of the raw beauty and redemptive hope embedded in every chapter of our journey. My brothers offered heartfelt tributes. Nedra, my college friend, sang, "His Eye Is on the Sparrow," and we all wept—some silently, others aloud—because that song had become her anthem.

Then Pastor Tim Lambert took the pulpit, his voice steady, filled with holy fire. "This body," he said, gesturing toward the casket, "is just a vehicle she no longer needs. Mama Bobbie will be more famous in death than in life." I believed him. Not because of the applause in the room, but because of the applause I could almost hear from Heaven.

THE PAINTING: A PORTRAIT OF REDEMPTION

God had placed something sacred on my heart: commission a painting—not of the woman the world saw, but of who she had become. In the portrait, she stood youthful, radiant, clothed in a white wedding dress, a bride prepared for her eternal groom. Jesus stood beside her, arms open, welcoming her home.

When Pastor Tim unveiled the painting, the room went still, reverent. For a breathless moment, Heaven touched Earth. This was no longer just a funeral. It was a divine unveiling. People saw her glorified. No longer broken or bitter—but whole. Beautiful. Redeemed.

Though the rain that day prevented us from following her to the cemetery, I knew she was going exactly where she wanted to be. "Don't you dare put me in the ground!" she had often said. I honored her wish—placing her in a marble mausoleum, a queen escorted to her eternal resting place.

IT IS WELL, IT IS WELL WITH MY SOUL

The repast overflowed with food, laughter, and reflection. My newly discovered Uncle Joe captured the day with his lens, while family reunited—Uncle Billy, Aunt Ruby, Aunt Gatha, and her daughter, Aunjella. They shared stories that filled in the blanks of a life none of us had known fully until now.

Sandra, who officiated parts of the ceremony, wept as she spoke. "Michelle's journey with her mother inspired me to forgive my own," highlighting the ripple effect of obedience and grace.

I had created a video montage—a collection of memories that blended laughter with reverence. One scene drew waves of laughter: the story of Mother using my anointing oil to fry fish. Another showed her smiling in her hospital bed. The video ended with my voice singing "It Is Well With My Soul," recorded beside her in a quiet hospital room. As the final notes played, the room filled with harmony. And then, my mother's voice—recorded weeks before her passing—echoed through the room:

"Be good to each other. Love one another. Forgive each other. I love you now."

These simple yet profound sentiments encapsulate her legacy—a call to cherish, love, and forgive.

MOTHER'S FINAL CHOICE: HEAVEN'S GLORY REVEALED

"No eye has seen, no ear has heard, no mind has conceived what God has prepared for those who love Him"
(I Corinthians 2:9, *NIV*)

After my mother's passing, I was engulfed in grief and questioned, "God, why couldn't we have fifteen more years together?" Gently, He reminded me, "I gave you fifteen years." Reflecting, I realized that from 2008 to 2023, He had indeed granted us a decade and a half of reconciliation and love—a gift not everyone receives.

One day, as I was reflecting on my mother, God gently whispered,

'She's with Me now.'

A week later, while watching Christian television, I heard the same comforting words. This reaffirmed God was intimately guiding me through this journey.

Still, the lingering question remained: What about our dreams and plans? In my spirit, I believe my mother was given a choice. Maybe God showed her both realms: the one where she'd return to fulfill the dreams we had, and the one where she could remain with Him—no more pain, no more waiting. I believe she chose eternal joy.

I remembered the stories I had once produced Crystal McVea McVea and Dawn Cypret, both women who glimpsed Heaven and described its indescribable peace. Both had been given the choice to return. Crystal chose Earth; Dawn came back because of her grandson's prayers. Yet some don't. Some, like my mother, look into the eyes of Jesus and stay.

These stories painted a vivid picture of Heaven's glory and helped me imagine what my mother must have seen in her final moments. She was no longer in pain or bound by the struggles of her earthly life. I imagined as she took her first breath in heaven, she was filled with the awe of seeing God's glory and the joy of being welcomed into His arms.

I realized my mother wanted it this way. I pictured her whispering, "Let my children live for You. Take care of my baby daughter. Let her fulfill her dreams," as she surrendered to Heaven's eternal embrace.

God also gently reminded me of something profound: "She was not alone." He was there with her. Angels and loved ones welcomed her into eternal peace through the gates of Heaven.

Revelation 21:4 reminds me of this truth: "He will wipe every tear from their eyes. There will be no more death or mourning or crying or pain……"

Through tears, I found peace knowing she was in perfect love and joy. Although I missed her deeply, I held onto the promise we'll reunite in that glorious place where all things are made new.

THE GLORY THAT SURPASSES EARTHLY RICHES

In the months following my mother's passing, life felt like a blur. Grief came in waves, and the weight of her absence was profound.

I had always dreamed of blessing my mother with earthly riches—lavish gifts and grand experiences. Yet, God gently reminded me, "No blessing or riches you could have given her on this earth can compare to the riches of glory she is experiencing now."

And yet, in hindsight, it seems God gave her a small glimpse of that glory one Sunday morning—long before the diagnosis, long before the hospitals and surgeries. I was leading worship at our church, Christian Embassy, singing "Fill my life till all they see is You, Lord—glorify Your name," when I noticed her.

My mother, moved by the Spirit, walked slowly but deliberately to the altar, lifted her hands toward heaven, and stood there in quiet surrender with others. We didn't know it then, but that moment was a foreshadowing—her spirit responding to a deeper call. She looked at me, her baby girl now grown, now a minister, a prophetic worshiper leading others into God's presence. And now—now she does in heaven what she once glimpsed on earth: worships freely, sings unrestrained, surrounded by angels and immersed in the glory of the One who loves her best.

Through my obedience, my mother experienced a life richer than she may have otherwise known—traveling to beautiful places, dining in fine restaurants, and enjoying rich fellowship among saints. Yet the richest part of her life was her surrender, and it is that surrender that ushered her into glory.

"GOD, DOES MY MOTHER NOW SEE
WHAT IT WAS ALL ABOUT?"

Yet, in the quiet aftermath, questions still surfaced in my heart.

Does my mother now see the full tapestry of our intertwined lives? Does she understand the divine purpose of our shared journey? Does she see now what was once hidden?

I truly believe she does.

With a heavenly perspective, she perceives the love, sacrifices, and obedience defined our relationship. She recognizes our time together was divinely orchestrated—a sacred assignment leading her to the ultimate reward which is eternity with God through her savior Jesus Christ.

The beauty of heaven is that there is no more regret, sorrow, or guilt—as Revelation 21:4 declares:

"He will wipe every tear from their eyes. There will be no more death or mourning or crying or pain, for the old order of things has passed away."

While she may have grieved her choices on earth, in heaven, she is fully restored—wrapped in joy, gratitude, and peace. She knows God's plan for her redemption worked through our journey, through my unwavering care and the prayers of many who interceded for her salvation.

She sees me as God does—a faithful daughter, a vessel of healing, and a warrior of intercession. And most importantly, she knows she is in heaven because of God's grace.

I know she is standing in eternal victory, free from earthly pain and embraced by cherished loved ones who preceded her and her savior in divine love.

CHAPTER 36:

EMBRACING MY MINISTRY CALL: HEALING FOUND IN OBEDIENCE

"In the crushing blows of pain and rejection, what once scarred us becomes the very oil God uses to transform us into instruments of His glory. The same pain that broke us becomes the refining force that allows the richness of His love to overflow from our surrendered vessels, allowing others—even those who caused the pain—to glean from the beauty of His eternal work in us. The light of Jesus shining so brightly through the cracks it not only illuminates the world but proves every tear, every scar, and every crushing moment was worth it, creating a masterpiece for His purpose and glory."

- Michelle B. Wilson, author, *In Search of a Mother's Love.*

GOD HAD NEED OF ME IN HER FINAL HOUR

Three months before my mother's transition to Heaven, the Holy Spirit whispered urgently,

"I have need of you. I have need of you. I have need of you."

As the words echoed in my spirit, I would silently shake my head, whispering, "I know." I believed this calling pertained to the plans my mother and I had envisioned. traveling the world to share our powerful story. Unbeknownst to me, God had a plan beyond my imagination.

One day, a woman approached me gently and said, "God wants me to tell you He's about to do amazing things in your life." Her words struck the same chord as a moment a year before—when my mother lay in the hospital, and I was sent to cover a story nearby. After my interviews, while I sat at a table finishing paperwork, a pastor approached with tears in his eyes. "You're not dreaming big enough," he said. "What you're envisioning is far smaller than what God has planned."

I had no idea that in the sacred wake of my mother's passing, purpose would be born—not in grand arenas, but in quiet corners filled with weathered hands, tear-stained faces, and souls longing to be seen.

A SACRED ASSIGNMENT:
DON'T DESPISE HUMBLE BEGINNINGS

The Lord led me into a community that many forget: senior citizens. Souls brimming with wisdom but aching with loneliness. It wasn't a flashy stage or global spotlight—it was a fellowship room with hungry hearts in a circle of wheelchairs – where Heaven bent low, and glory met the humble.

God gently whispered, "They need love too. Minister to them like you would anyone else. I can still bring great healing into their lives."

My first day, I was nervous. I wasn't sure if anyone would show up. And they came. In fact, more than expected. God anointed me to minister in ways I never imagined: singing treasured hymns like "Amazing Grace," "Rock of Ages," "We've Come This Far by Faith," and others that lit up their hearts I also shared scriptures and created moments of interaction that reminded them they were still seen and deeply valued.

The life enrichment director told me, "You're popular around here. Everyone loves you. This is one of the largest Bible studies we've ever had." Those words touched me deeply. I had stepped into unfamiliar territory, using my gifts freely under the leadership of the Holy Spirit – frightened and refreshed all at once. Without knowing it, I was being healed even as God used me to help heal others.

God's amazing grace began turning my pain into purpose and surrounding me with a community that looked at me with the love of Jesus, not through the lens of judgement. My heart was warmed by their attentiveness, their eyes fixed on me as if soaking in every word. One senior told me they love to come because they like the way I share God's word with them. I would pray boldly over them, declaring revival for their lives and their facility. I would tell them, "Revival is going to hit here and spread to the nations. The world will know there is a people here who are hungry for God and love God."

Sharing my mother's story brought moments of connection I didn't expect. One woman filled with tears, told me, "Your story was my story." She mentioned how she wanted to get up and run out before she burst into tears. We prayed together, commanding healing to come and declaring God's peace.

After each gathering, I gave small gifts - crosses with scriptures, blankets, back scratchers, blankets and other items they appreciated. They often said, "You are the gift." And God whispered to my heart, "When you give out of your pain, even when you are in need, the greatest blessings come."

What they didn't realize was they were the gift to me. Their smiles, hugs, and gratitude became a healing balm for my soul. In their eyes, I saw God's love reflected to me.

DR. VERNON FALLS: A PROPHETIC CONFIRMATION

One night, I sat quietly in CBN's Shaw Chapel in a service led by Dr. Vernon Falls. With gentle authority, he shared how his international healing ministry was birthed... in a senior home. He described how God moved powerfully among the residents, restoring some to the point of returning to independent living. My heart swelled. God was confirming my quiet obedience.

God was whispering, "When you trust Me and are faithful in the small things, I will open great doors for you."

Soon, I had a dream: God was building something within me beyond what I could see. I wasn't being "used" for ministry – I was being formed by it.

God was training me in compassion and calling me to love without an agenda. It was pure ministry – to simply be His arms of love in a forgotten place.

RISE AND WALK: GOD MOVES AMONG THE FORGOTTEN

One day, after ministering, a man who always used a wheelchair stood up and began pushing it. My heart overflowed with joy as I asked him what had happened. He said the Word of God I shared gave him the strength to get up and walk. I responded, "All Glory to God." God was moving, and He was giving me glimpses of what was to come in my future ministry. I was in awe.

Each hug, each word of thanks, and each smile became a testament to the healing power of love. One senior even showed me his planner, where he had written, "Ministry with Michelle." It was humbling to know my small acts of obedience were making an eternal impact in this precious community.

During each visit, I was shedding the old skin of rejection, peeling away years of pain, and stepping into the life God had always planned for me. The love cultivated in my heart through the trials and hardships of life was finally poured out. I could feel it – I was becoming the woman God created me to be – no longer who life shaped, but who Heaven ordained.

For the first time, I experienced the joy of a community that embraced me without judgment, or rejection - only with the pure acceptance of God's love. It was healing the broken places in my life. And it was here, in this simple act of ministering, I realized everything I had endured was worth it. The fires of life that had tried me were not wasted; they had refined me into a vessel God could now use to pour forth His love and glory through.

MOTHER AND ANGEL MOTHER CHEERING
ME ON FROM HEAVEN

Through this journey, I felt my mother's presence cheering me on. Her voice echoed in my heart: "Come on, baby daughter. Keep going for Jesus. Let Him use you. It will all be worth it."

I could picture her smiling from Heaven, proud of the legacy we were building together - a legacy of love, healing, and faith. Her journey laid the foundation for mine, and now, I was walking in the purpose God had always intended.

Angel Mother was also in Heaven, smiling with pride as she saw the spiritual legacy she had cultivated in my heart manifest. I could hear her voice saying, "Missy, I'm proud of you."

In every step I take, I carry the imprint of two mothers – one who birthed me, and one who birthed my faith. Now they watch together, arms linked, as the baton passes from their lives into mine.

HEAVEN IS ALWAYS BETTER: THE GREATEST GIFT

Though this journey began years ago, the over 6,000 hours poured into this book—equaling 8 months, stretched across seasons – from the first seeds of calling to the final pages written as my mother fought for her life.

I envisioned a different ending - my mother at my wedding, holding my children, launching her biscuit business with joy, and standing beside me in ministry as we recounted our journey together. I dreamed of her finally experiencing places and spaces she had never known.

God had a sovereign plan. And His plans are always best.

And though the ending I dreamed of didn't come to pass, the one He orchestrated was far greater. The ultimate victory wasn't in fulfilling earthly dreams but in her eternal salvation. She repented, surrendered to God, and gained the greatest gift of all: eternity with Christ.

As I move forward, I can hear her boldly petitioning Jesus:

"Lord, bless my baby daughter. She was a good daughter to me. Send her a husband, let her dreams come true."

Her final prayers for me were heartfelt and though these dreams weren't fulfilled during her earthly life, I entrust them to God, who perfects all things in His time (Psalm 138:8, *KJV*).

Through this journey, I've learned God truly sees us – El Roi. He walks with us in every season, comforting us beyond our understanding. And the greatest gift He offers is not here – but in eternity with Him.

One day, I'll enjoy my mother again. Until then, I hear her voice in my spirit:

"Come on, baby daughter Keep walking. Keep praying. Keep giving God the glory with that sweet voice. Trust in His unfailing hand. Stay humble and sweet. Your labor of love was not in vain. Thank you for loving me into salvation. I am at peace now. I'll see you again."

CHAPTER 37:

TRANSFORMING PAIN INTO PURPOSE

"I will betroth you to me forever; I will betroth you in righteousness and justice, in love and compassion. I will betroth you in faithfulness, and you will acknowledge the Lord."
(Hosea 2:19-20, *NIV*)

There's a certain kind of love that doesn't let go.

It doesn't turn away when shamed. It doesn't give up when promises are broken. It doesn't abandon when it's no longer reciprocated. It waits. It woos. It weeps. And then it pursues again.

That's the kind of love God revealed to us in the story of Hosea and Gomer.

In the pages of Hosea, we witness an almost unthinkable command: God tells His prophet to marry a woman known for unfaithfulness—a woman whose brokenness mirrors a nation's rebellion. And through Hosea's pain, God paints the portrait of His own heart—a heart that chases, redeems, and restores what others deem unworthy.

Gomer leaves. Hosea redeems her. She wanders again. Hosea welcomes her home. It is not weakness. It is divine love in human form—sacrificial, stubborn, sacred.

SEEING MY MOTHER THROUGH THE HOSEA AND GOMER BIBLICAL STORY

When I reflect on Hosea and Gomer, I see echoes of my journey with my mother. Like Gomer, my mother wrestled to receive the fullness of God's love. Her choices, shaped by pain, often pulled her away from the life He intended.

God chose me, like Hosea, to be a vessel of His pursuit. Not to fix her. Not to force change. But to love her as God did—consistently, faithfully, even when change seemed impossible.

In the end, I saw what I longed for—I watched my mother repent, surrender, and say yes to the One who never stopped knocking.

WHY THIS STORY MATTERS

The story of Hosea and Gomer reminds us: God's love isn't earned by performance—it's freely given, steadfast, and transformative. This truth is hope for anyone who feels too far gone or too broken. God's love doesn't just meet us in our brokenness, it transforms and redeems us, calling us into a new identity.

For my mother, this story became her testimony. God's Grace pursued her through the years, despite her struggles and pain which caused her to walk away from Him. It reminds us God's love doesn't stop where our brokenness begins; instead, it flows into the deepest wounds, offering restoration and hope, drawing us back to Him.

God's love is greater than any wound, any sin, or any regret. It is a love that heals, forgives, and redeems.

WALKING WITH THE BROKEN

As I cared for my mother and endeavored to love her in obedience to God's calling, I came to understand I was attempting to love someone who struggled to love herself and receive the love of God.

Loving someone who's broken is hard. It often feels like pouring water into a vessel with cracks—no matter how much you give, it leaks through. Yet, God doesn't call us to measure the results. He calls us to be faithful.

How do you love someone who struggles with self-worth or resists God's love? By guarding your heart and surrendering the outcome to God. You may not receive the relationship you hoped for, but your obedience still matters. It requires surrendering your expectations to Him and remembering that only God can heal a heart

WHEN PRAYERS REMAIN UNANSWERED

What if they never embrace God's healing? What if your parent, spouse, or child never becomes who you prayed for? These are painful questions. Yet in those moments, you must find peace knowing God sees, and He will surround you with the people you need to walk with you.

Loving the broken requires trusting God's purpose even when we cannot see the results of our labor. It is about planting seeds of love and forgiveness, trusting God to water them in His time. Everyone has a choice. Even God won't force healing or love—yet He does call us to reflect His heart and trust Him with the results.

GOD'S PURSUIT NEVER FAILS

Even when someone resists God's love, His pursuit of their heart doesn't stop. Psalm 139:8 reminds us, "If I go up to the heavens, You are there, and if I make my bed in the depths, You are there." God's love follows us wherever we go, patiently calling us back to Him. It is this unrelenting love that gave me hope for my mother and enabled me to love her even when it was hard

I surrendered my mother to God, trusting His love was stronger than mine. And in the end, she said yes. She repented. She was made whole in Christ. I'll see her again. That assurance brings me tremendous peace.

Loving the broken is a journey of faith, trust, and surrender. It is one of the most profound ways we reflect God's Heart.

THE BLESSING OF A DIAMOND

A diamond is forged through intense pressure and heat—the same conditions life often brings. Yet, every trial produces something radiant. My mother embodied that transformation. I wrote this poem for her, included in her obituary:

"MY DIAMOND"

By Michelle B. Wilson

In the tapestry of existence, my mother, a gem so exquisite,
Embodied with talents, possibilities are infinite.
Crafted by God, with his choicest Grace,
You could have been President, an inspiring face.
No bounds to your genius; you are truly amazed,
But life's crossroads led you through twists where purpose blazed.
Beneath the beauty, God breathed into your core,
A plan unfolded, revealing so much more.
God's intention to birth a vessel of love,
A child to shine forth, healing from above.
Resisting at first, yet over the years,
You opened your heart to God's plans, shedding fears.
Worshipping Him, longing to know His ways,
You embraced His fullness in a joyful daze.
Now, the scars of life's journey have faded away,
As you looked to Him, Lord and Savior each day.
Repenting and seeking God's forgiving Grace,
You smiled as He whispered, "Daughter, I embrace.
All your sins are forgiven, My love knows no end,
Enter Heaven's gates, my precious friend."
Though we thought there'd be more time to share,
You walked through Heaven's gates in celestial air.
Gazing upon your Savior in a boundless embrace,
No more pain or fears, just eternal Grace.
In the arms of Jesus, you're safe and sound,
Experiencing a love, once lost, now found.

More alive than ever, in Heaven's embrace,
Where the riches of eternity surpass time and space.
Through the years we spent together, a training ground,
The best preparation and ordination, where love abounds.
For my life's mission to help the broken find God's saving Grace,
An eternal purpose is born in your embrace.
My assignment with you on Earth is complete,
But I'll see you again where heavenly joys meet.
Eternally, I love you, dear Mom, so divine,
In the celestial realm, where you forever shine, my diamond.

CHAPTER 38:

THE PURSUIT OF LOVE AND REDEMPTION

There is a road less traveled, one paved not with ease, but with eternal purpose—a road called, "The Pursuit of Love." I didn't choose this road at first. It chose me. Or rather, God asked me to walk it for someone who, at one point in my life, I blamed for everything that went wrong. Then God asked me a life-changing question.

"What if I asked you to pray for your mother and stand in the gap for her—would you do it for Me?"

Without knowing the weight of that request, I said, "Yes."

I didn't yet know that saying yes would mean laying down the right to anger, to answers, to apology. All I knew was—she was a soul. A soul God loved as much as He loved me. And He was asking me to love her with His heart, not mine.

That yes placed me on a holy path called the pursuit of love and redemption. Not the kind of love that demands. The kind that dies to itself. The kind that doesn't wait for someone to be worthy before extending mercy.

"The Pursuit Of Love" is not about how much someone deserves it. It's about how much God wants to pour it through you. It's about shifting motivations - from revenge to obedience, from proving a point to glorifying God.

Forgiveness doesn't mean reconciliation in every case, and love doesn't mean access. However, it does mean release. The kind of release that Joseph experienced when he faced the very brothers who once tried to kill him. Scripture tells us to overcome evil with good (Romans 12:21, *KJV*), and Joseph did exactly that. He preserved the very people who tried to destroy him. But first, he allowed God to transform his heart—perhaps even using prison to purge the pain.

Sometimes God allows us to walk through our own "prisons" of disappointment, betrayal, and silence—not to punish us, but to prepare us. And when He finally brings us face to face with those who hurt us, He wants to know: "Will you be like Me? Will you love them like I loved you?"

This is the pursuit of love and redemption. Not a fairytale. Not always a reunion. Nevertheless, always a choice. A higher road. A holy road. A road that requires us to forgive, even if the person is no longer alive. A road that asks, "Will you let Me set you free by setting them free in your heart?"

You don't have to wait for their apology to be healed. You don't need their understanding to walk in wholeness. You just need to say yes to love. Not the world's version of love—but God's.

He is the One who sees the full tapestry of every life, every wound, and every wrong. And He invites us to become co-laborers in the ministry of reconciliation—not just between people, but between generations.

My search for a mother's love began with pain. Yet, it ended in the pursuit of something deeper. I was no longer just looking for my Mother's love. I was learning how to give God's love. And in doing so, I found the love I didn't even know I needed. I also became the instrument God used to lead her to repentance before entering her new, glorious life in heaven with Jesus.

This is the pursuit of love and redemption.

Not the love we demand, but the love we become.

Not the love that fixes everything, but the love that frees everyone.

And in the end, that kind of love—His love—is always worth the pursuit.

And if – despite your pursuit – you never find the love of an earthly parent, know this: there is a God who has been waiting all along to be your parent, your best friend, your everything. He is ready to fill every void, heal every wound, and right every wrong. He is not the author of your pain, but the redeemer of your story. What was meant for harm, He will use for your good. Open your heart and let Jesus in – and you will find a love beyond anything you've ever imagined. A love that restores, redefines, and never let's go.

EPILOGUE

*"And we know that in all things God works for the good of those who
love Him, who have been called according to His purpose."*
(Romans 8:28, *NIV*)

As I reflect, *"In Search of a Mother's Love"* reads like chapters of my heart—
each page filled with the ache of absence, the surrender of service, and the
rediscovery of love. The years of waiting, the call to care for a mother who had
stayed away—each moment was woven together by a hand greater than mine.

Every chapter was a step deeper into the heart of God. Every act of
caregiving, an altar. Every tear shed, a prayer.

I once thought this was about searching for my mother's love. Now I
know—this was always God's search for us.

When she left, I lost something I didn't know I needed. When she returned,
I found something I didn't know I had: grace that chooses love when it hurts.

My mother's death was unexpected, and no one can truly prepare you for
the final goodbye. Yet in her final days, God did something extraordinary. She
repented. She surrendered. She came home—not just to me, but to Jesus.

Her repentance became the bridge between us, finally uniting our hearts.

Her redemption became my healing.

Her salvation became my greatest reward.

She may be gone, but her legacy is not. It lives in every word written, every reader reached, every heart restored. She left this world wrapped in mercy, and now I carry the flame of her story—not as a wound, but as a witness.

If you've walked this far with me, I pray you leave not only with tears in your eyes but hope in your heart. There is no wound too deep for Jesus. No relationship too broken. No story beyond redemption.

The Holy Spirit walked with me through every trial, and He will walk with you, too. Trust Him. Invite Him in. Let Him rewrite your story.

This is not just the end of a book—it is the beginning of your breakthrough.

AN INVITATION TO SALVATION

Reflecting on this journey, I know now: a personal relationship with God is the true source of healing and hope. If you long to begin or renew that relationship, here's a simple prayer to guide you.

Invite Him in. Trust Him with your wounds. Seek Him through prayer, worship, and His Word. He is faithful to complete what He begins.

This is the God who pursued my mother, who didn't let her die in her sins, who writes love stories of redemption. The same God who gave her a second chance is calling you now.

If you're ready to give your life to Jesus, say this prayer:

THE MIRACLE OF SALVATION – ARE YOU READY TO BEGIN YOUR JOURNEY?

Lord, I come to You as a sinner needing Your mercy and grace.

I ask for Your forgiveness for fashioning a god that justifies my sins and ignoring the call to live as You intended rather than allowing Your truth to change me.

Instead of humbly seeking to be transformed into Your image, I have reshaped You to fit my desires—creating a version of You that aligns with a life I know does not honor You.

I repent of all my sins—those I know of and those I do not know of.

With your help, I desire to turn away from sin and toward the righteousness of Jesus Christ.

I ask that You remove everything in my life not pleasing to You and fill me with everything that comes only from You.

I believe Jesus Christ died for my sins, becoming a curse for me to pay a debt I could not pay. Jesus rose again and is now seated at the right hand of Father God in heaven.

I acknowledge Jesus is the only way, truth, and life to God, and I accept Jesus as my Lord and Savior in every area of my life.

Thank You, Lord, for redeeming me, for loving me, and for the gift of eternal salvation.

I surrender my heart and my life to You completely.

Lead, guide, and transform me into the person You created me to be.

Lead me to a Bible-believing church that teaches the full gospel with leaders who will love me through my journey and help me become all You created me to be.

Surround me with leaders who won't define me by my past mistakes and faults but will see me as a brand-new creation, Your beloved child with purpose and destiny—redeemed by Your blood.

Thank you for removing all distractions and leading me to a community of believers with wisdom to guide me into the fullness of Your calling on my life.

Thank You for equipping me to be a bright light in this dark world, pointing people to Jesus as the hope and redeemer of this world.

Thank You, Lord, for making me new in Christ and giving me hope, peace, and purpose.

Help me to glorify You in all that I do, say, and think. Thank you for receiving me.

In Jesus' name, Amen.

If you prayed this prayer, we rejoice with you! Please send us a message at **MichelleWilsonMinistries@yahoo.com** stating, "I prayed the prayer of salvation after reading your book, In Search of a Mother's Love."

We would love to celebrate with you and encourage you as you begin your journey with God.

PRAYERS FOR YOUR HEALING JOURNEY

"Be joyful in hope, patient in affliction, faithful in prayer."
Romans 12:12, (*NIV*)

As you step into this sacred moment of prayer, may your heart open to the One who heals and restores. These prayers are not just words—they are an invitation. A space for God to meet you in the quiet places of your soul and breathe life into what has felt broken or forgotten.

You don't need to rush. Let these words settle over you. Let the Holy Spirit speak between the lines and guide your heart toward deeper healing. He knows where you are—and He knows how to lead you home.

So, take a breath. Invite Him in. Let the healing begin.

PRAYER FOR PARENTS SEEKING
RECONCILIATION WITH THEIR CHILDREN

Dear Merciful Heavenly Father,

We come before You, broken and in need of Your grace. We acknowledge the years we have lived apart from our children, physically and or emotionally, and the choices we made that took us down a path far from them. We confess our sins and the strongholds in our lives — whether addiction, pride, shame, or fear — that separated us from those You entrusted to our care. Today, we repent with all our hearts, laying down every burden, every sin, and every wayward decision at Your feet, seeking Your mercy.

Lord, we ask for Your strength to humble ourselves and reach out with true repentance. As Your Word says in 2 Chronicles 7:14, "If my people, who are called by my name, will humble themselves and pray and seek my face and turn from their wicked ways, then I will hear from heaven, and I will forgive their sin and will heal their land." Father, we ask that You heal the land of our broken relationships.

We know we cannot redeem the lost years, but we can be present now with Your grace. Restore us, O God, and give us the courage to enter our children's lives again. Just as the prodigal son was welcomed back with open arms, we pray our children might find it in their hearts to forgive us. We ask for their hearts to be softened, that any walls of resentment or pain would be torn down, and that Your love and complete healing would cover the wounds we caused. Ephesians 4:32 reminds us to "be kind and compassionate to one another, forgiving each other, just as in Christ God forgave you." May this forgiveness flow freely, as only You can do.

Father, we pray for all chains to be broken. John 8:36 says, "So if the Son sets you free, you will be free indeed." Free us all from past mistakes, fear, rejection, and shame. Let Your Holy Spirit guide every step, every Word, and every moment of reconciliation. May Your grace cover us, and may You give us a new beginning with our children.

In Jesus' mighty name, we pray, Amen.

PRAYER FOR HEALING FROM CHILDHOOD WOUNDS

Dear Loving, Heavenly Father,

I come to You with a heart burdened by the wounds I carry from my past. You know every hurt, every scar, and every moment of feeling unloved, unstable, and abandoned. I lay these burdens at Your feet, trusting in Your promise to heal the broken-hearted and bind up their wounds (Psalms 147:3). You are the One who truly sees and understands my pain. I ask for Your grace to heal these wounds and the strength to let go of the burdens I've carried for so long.

Lord, You know the voids left by the absence of love, stability, and care I longed for. Yet Your Word says, "When my father and my mother forsake me, then the Lord will take me up" (Psalm 27:10). I hold on to this promise, knowing You are my perfect and eternal Parent, who never leaves or forsakes me.

Father, I ask for the grace to forgive those who hurt me. You know the depths of my pain, still You have called me to forgive as You have forgiven me. Help me to release the anger, bitterness, and resentment that weigh on my heart. Replace it with Your love, peace, and compassion so I may see myself and others through Your eyes.

Lord, restore what has been broken in my life. Fill every void with Your love and peace. Help me walk in freedom from the lies of the past, believing in the truth of who I am in You; worthy, cherished, and deeply loved. Renew my mind and heal the memories that still bring pain. I declare freedom from generational patterns that have bound my family, and I ask that future generations walk in Your ways and not repeat past mistakes. I trust You to make everything right in my life, for You alone can turn ashes into beauty. I pray for a new beginning, a life filled with joy and purpose beyond my past. Give me the strength to forgive fully and the courage to trust You for a greater outcome, even if it includes reconciliation. Fill me with selflessness and love so I might even bless my parents by giving gifts, praying for them, and taking care of them in their old age if You call me to partner with You in this way. Teach me to love with a heart like Yours, filled with compassion and grace.

Your word says, "For I know the plans I have for you, plans to prosper you and not to harm you, plans to give you hope and a future" (Jeremiah 29:11). I believe in Your promise and refuse to let fear dictate my future. Jesus, You came so we might have life and have it abundantly (John 10:10). Help me to live as a testimony of Your grace, healing, and redemption.

For those who have endured deep wounds — abuse, abandonment, or emotional harm — grant wisdom and peace. For those whose parents come with true repentance, guide them in forgiveness and, if possible, reconciliation. For those whose parents continue to reject them or have passed away, bring comfort and healing, reminding them You are the perfect parent who fills every void.

Father, I surrender my past to You. Teach me to love with a heart like Yours, filled with compassion and grace. Help me to bless and do good to those who have hurt me, trusting in Your promise that, "if you forgive others their trespasses, your heavenly Father will also forgive you" (Matthew 6:14). I surrender my heart to You, knowing You are my healer, hope, and peace.

Thank You, Lord, for walking with me through this journey of healing. Thank You for Your unending love and faithfulness. I trust You to bring me into a season of restoration, peace, and abundant life as you have promised in Your word. I love You.

In Jesus' name, I pray. Amen.

MOTHER IN ETERNITY'S EMBRACE

To Explore More of Our Story:

Note: The QR codes below are included in all versions of this book—hardback, paperback, and e-book.

The videos can also be found on the YouTube channel, "In Search of a Mother's Love."

■ Video Tribute: A Journey with My Mother

Scan the QR code below to watch the personal video tribute, featuring over 70 cherished photographs of my mother and our life together—capturing the beauty, and memories from beginning to end.

Please note: The earlier images you'll see of my mother were personally photographed by my late father, James D. Wilson, and are shared here for the first time. These few images represent just a small sampling of the thousands of photographs he lovingly captured of her throughout her life.

■ 700 Club Testimonies & Story Links

Scan the QR code below to access a collection of the 700 Club testimonial stories referenced throughout this book. This page includes clickable video links, Facebook posts, and additional stories that share this journey of healing, faith, and hope.

More resources and personal reflections can be found on the companion YouTube channel: YouTube.com/InSearchofaMothersLove, where Michelle shares behind-the-scenes stories, devotionals, and encouragement for healing and restoration.

These videos and stories bring our journey to life—capturing its depth through both visual and narrative storytelling. Enjoy.

AUTHOR'S NOTE TO THE READER

This book is not written with ink alone, but with tears, worship, and the fingerprints of God. These are not just memories—they are altars. These pages carry fragments of a girl who was once silenced, pieced back together by the voice of the One who never stopped calling her by name.

It was written from the deepest places of memory, healing, and obedience. It is not just a story—it is a surrender. Each word carries the weight of pain transformed, confusion clarified and love redefined. I did not write this for applause, nor for the approval of man.

This book is for every soul who has lived in the shadow of someone else's pain. This book became my offering to the world, a bridge between generations, a balm for the aching heart.

I wrote this for the daughters who wondered why.

For the sons who never got answers.

For the mothers and fathers who disappeared not out of indifference, but out of despair.

And for the God who redeems it all.

If even one life is changed, one soul healed, one family restored, then every hour spent in prayer and writing has been worth it. My hope is that this book won't just sit on shelves—but live in hearts, ignite conversations, and stir the kind of healing so deep, so divine, it echoes through time – transforming a thousand generations for the glory of God.

If this book helped you begin your own journey of healing, consider sharing it with someone walking a similar story. There's someone out there desperate for hope, someone yearning to know that they are not alone and that the same God who met you in your pain is waiting to meet them too. Your gift of this book could be the beginning of their breakthrough

ABOUT THE AUTHOR

Michelle Wilson has spent over two decades as a reporter and producer for *The 700 Club*, where she has shared powerful stories of redemption, healing, and transformation across the globe. A gifted storyteller and compassionate voice for the voiceless, Michelle carries a deep call to refresh others in the very areas where she herself was once broken.

She is the founder of Michelle Wilson Ministries, a 501(c)(3) nonprofit dedicated to meeting practical and spiritual needs—from helping single mothers with groceries and children with school supplies to delivering Christmas gifts to the homeless. Her passion for ministry flows from a life yielded to God's heart for the hurting and the overlooked.

Michelle is also an inventor, serial entrepreneur, prophetic minister, Bible teacher, singer, and songwriter. Her worship carries a prophetic anointing that brings freedom and healing. She is currently preparing to launch faith-based inspirational programming through her own media platform and is pursuing future global outreach initiatives that will impact lives across nations.

Whether through media, ministry, music, or mentorship, Michelle's mission remains the same: to bring hope, healing, and restoration to those who need it most—one story at a time.